Popular Culture: Shades and Shadows

Editors

Sarita Jain **Sarita Chanwaria**

Pustak Bharati
Toronto Canada

Book Title: Popular Culture: Shades and Shadows

Editors: Sarita Jain and Sarita Chanwaria

Published by:
Pustak Bharati (Books-India)
180 Torresdale Ave, Toronto Canada M2R 3E4
email : pustak.bharati.canada@gmail.com

Copyright ©2025

ISBN : 978-1-998027-27-9

ISBN 978-1-998027-27-9

© All rights reserved. No part of this book may be copied, reproduced or utilised in any manner or by any means, computerised, e-mail, scanning, photocopying or by recording in any information storage and retrieval system, without the permission in writing from the editors.

Concerned authors are solely responsible for their views, opinions, policies, copyright infringement, legal action, penalty/loss of any kind regarding their articles. Neither the publisher nor the editors will be responsible for any penalty or loss of any kind if claimed in future.

Contents

	Foreword	i
	Preface	iv
1.	The River and the Screen: Representations of *Mahakumbh* in Popular Culture Dr. Ashish Kumar Gupta	1
2.	Culture of Gender Discrimination in Traditional Society: A Rereading of Girish Karnad's Nagamandala Dr. Poonam Rani Gupta	17
3.	Decoding the Influence of Pop Culture Dr. Anoopama Yadav	25
4.	Reel to Real: The Cinematic Construction of Political Culture in India Dr. Deepshikha Parashar	39
5.	Unveiling the Meta-Narrative Paradigm: A Critical Exploration of Vijay Tendulkar's *Silence! The Court is in Session* Mr. L G More	58
6.	Manoeuvring the Dynamics of Youth, Afterlife, and Ecological Symbolism through the Supernatural Aesthetics of Indian Popular Fiction, focusing on the works of Nidhi Upadhyay and Vikrant Khanna Roshani Bhootra	75
7.	Youth Culture and Globalization Ms. Sangita S. Aher	88
8.	Recurrentmotifs of Casteism and Societal Discrimination in Indian Popular Culture: Insights from Omprakash Valmiki's Joothan Dr. Yasir Ahmad Khanday	99

9. Everyday Ironies: Satire and Pop Culture in Contemporary Indian Poetry with Reference to Nissim Ezekiel, Eunice de Souza, and Meena Kandasamy
   Dr. Supriya Mandloi 107

10. Popular Culture and Indian Society: Reflections of Social Change
    Dr. Vijay Kumar Banshiwal 119

11. The Kaleidoscope of Culture: Popular Culture's Reflection and Reflection of Indian Culture
    Dr. Shruti Srivastava
    Ms. Srishti 135

12. Fermented Flavors: Exploring Food Culture and Resistance in Axone
    Devika. S. Raj 145

13. Indian Eco-Fiction and Popular Culture: A Study of Environmental Narratives in Literature and Media
    Dr. Ashwini Ashok Kadam 160

14. The Undercover Over Screen: A Study of Real Life Espionage Narratives in Indian Cinema
    Dr. Shruti Dubey 176

15. Modernistic Unveiling of Myth in Popular Culture in Salman Rushdie's *The Ground Beneath Her Feet*
    Dr. Dimple Dubey 189

16. Scintillating contours of Ecocinema: Addressing Environmental Concerns through Popular Culture in *WALL-E*
    Dr. Siddhi Tripathi 207

17. The Interplay of Popular Culture and Indian English Literature 221
    Dr. Pranali Milind kunar Jadhav

18. Indian Poetry Slams: A Popular Youth Revolutionary Movement 236
    Heena Bindal

19. Mahesh Elkunchwar's *The Old Stone Mansion*: A Critical Response through Cultural Perspective 247
    Ayodhya Kalyan Jadhav

List of Contributors 256

Foreword

Popular culture has become an important area of study in English literature. It not only reflects the values, beliefs, and emotions of a society but also influences how people think, behave, and relate to one another. Literature today engages closely with films, social media, music, digital platforms, mythology, and other cultural forms. This book, *Popular Culture: Shades and Shadows*, brings together thoughtful essays that explore the close relationship between literature and popular culture in the Indian and global context.

The topics covered in this volume are wide-ranging and timely. Several essays explore how stories in books and films are used to raise awareness about climate change and environmental concerns. For example, the animated movie *WALL-E* and Indian eco-fiction are discussed as powerful tools to encourage audiences—especially young people—to think about sustainability. Similarly, Indian popular novels that blend supernatural themes with ecological warnings demonstrate how profound issues can be explored through popular formats.

The book also explores the intersection of gender and society. Some essays examine how women's voices are being retold in powerful ways, such as in Koral Dasgupta's modern take on the mythological figure Ahalya or in Girish Karnad's play *Nagamandala*. These readings highlight how literature can challenge patriarchal thinking and bring hidden stories to light.

Youth culture and digital media are also big concerns. The chapters on slam poetry and youth identity show how new generations are expressing themselves through performance, music, and online platforms. These essays explore how digital trends influence the ideas, lifestyles, and creative expressions of young people in urban India.

Cinema's influence on society is another key theme. Essays examine patriotic films like *Raazi* and *Mission*

Majnu, as well as political narratives in mainstream Indian movies. These discussions demonstrate how films contribute to shaping national identity, memory, and emotion. Religious gatherings, such as the Mahakumbh, are also examined to illustrate how spiritual events are presented through media and technology.

Myth and storytelling remain central to our cultural understanding. Authors like Salman Rushdie and Vijay Tendulkar are studied for their ability to bring new meaning to old stories, using modern language and structure to reflect contemporary society. These essays demonstrate how the blending of past and present enables literature to remain relevant.

Caste, identity, and discrimination are also explored through influential works, such as *Joothan* by Omprakash Valmiki and poems by Meena Kandasamy and others. These voices offer essential insights into India's ongoing struggles with social inequality.

The final chapters explore how Indian English literature itself is influenced by popular culture. From Bollywood to cricket and digital platforms, literature often draws on popular themes to connect with broader audiences. Writers such as Chetan Bhagat and Arundhati Roy utilise these references to reflect modern Indian life and its inherent contradictions.

Together, the essays in *Popular Culture: Shades and Shadows* offer a meaningful and timely reflection on the intersection of literature and culture in our contemporary era. The volume encompasses both serious concerns and creative possibilities, providing fresh perspectives on the meaning of popular culture today.

The contributors to this volume represent a diverse range of academic voices—emerging scholars, seasoned critics, and practitioners—whose research is grounded in cultural sensitivity, analytical clarity, and literary imagination. It is hoped that the anthology will serve not only as a repository of scholarship but also as a springboard for further inquiry in classrooms, conferences, and cultural discourse.

Amrendra K. Sharma, Dr.
Assoc. Prof. of English (Retd),
PG Dept of English, C. M. College, Darbhanga 846004, India,
MA in English (Patna Univ.),
MA in Linguistics for ELT (Lancaster Univ, England),
PGDTE (CIEFL, Hyderabad),
PhD in Applied Linguistics (Bhagalpur Univ, Bhagalpur)

Preface

Popular culture no longer craves archangels and new dawns. Pop culture traffics in vampires and deads of night.
James Wolcott

Popular culture refers to the set of ideas, practices, images, and phenomena that are prevalent and widely accepted within a society at a given point in time. It encompasses various aspects of daily life, including entertainment, fashion, music, sports, and technology, reflecting the shared interests and preferences of the general public. Popular culture is dynamic and evolves over time, influenced by social, political, and technological developments, making it a key area of study within the realm of social science. In the context of social science, studying popular culture provides valuable insights into the shared interests, preferences, and dynamics that shape societies. The 19th century witnessed a seismic shift in the nature of popular culture with the advent of industrialization and urbanization. The Industrial Revolution brought about mass production, making cultural products more accessible to a broader audience. preferences of the general public.
"Popular culture is the new Babylon, into which so much art and intellect now flow. "Camille Paglia

Urbanization further accelerated the transformation, creating spaces where diverse cultural practices converged. The city became a melting pot of traditions, fostering the exchange of ideas and influencing the emergence of new cultural expressions. The dynamic interplay of diverse cultural elements laid the foundation for the vibrant tapestry of popular culture seen today.

Dr. Ashish Kumar Gupta in his paper *The River and the Screen: Representations of Mahakumbh in Popular Culture*, aims to explore how popular media represent, reinterpret, and sometimes commercialize the Mahakumbh. **Dr. Poonam Rani Gupta's** paper Culture *of Gender*

Discrimination in Traditional Society: A Rereading of Girish Karnad's Nagamandala shows how women experience a survival of subjugation and compliance in a patriarchal society. Decoding the influence of Pop Culture, a paper by **Dr. Anoopama Yadav** adopts Ferdinand de Saussure's semiotic structuralism framework to analyze how signs—both linguistic and cultural—mediate the relationship between signifier and signified in the construction and dissemination of pop culture.

Reel to Real: The Cinematic Construction of Political Culture in India by **Dr. Deepshikha Parashar** investigates both historical and contemporary films, highlighting their role in constructing cultural legitimacy and influencing mass perceptions of leadership, nationalism, social justice, and dissent. **Mr .L. G. More** in his paper *Unveiling the Meta-Narrative Paradigm: A Critical Exploration of Vijay Tendulkar's Silence! The Court is in Session* aims to unravel meta-narrative storytelling, a postmodern concept utilised as a masterful element and builds a conversational discourse around the usage of this technique to provoke audience interaction through a surreal sub-textual narrative. **Roshini Bhootra's** paper *Manoeuvring the Dynamics of Youth, Afterlife, and Ecological Symbolism through the Supernatural Aesthetics of Indian Popular Fiction, focusing on the works of Nidhi Upadhyay and Vikrant Khanna* concerns itself with the authors attempts at bringing the supernatural as not merely an aesthetic for entertainment but also a phenomenon for critical scrutiny where cultural norms and environmental apathy come out as decisive factors.

Ms. Sangeeta s. Aher's paper *Youth Culture and Globalization* analyses the diversifying and homogenizing effects of globalization on youth culture as well as discuss the role of, media, fashion, technology, music, and social movements on youth culture. *Recurrent motifs of Casteism and Societal Discrimination in Indian Popular Culture: Insights from Omprakash Valmiki's Joothan* by **Dr. Yasir Ahmad Khanday** explore casteism and societal discrimination, the two dominant strands of Indian Popular Culture with reference to Omprakash Valmiki's autobiographical memoir, Joothan. **Dr. Supriya Mandloi** in *Everyday Ironies: Satire and Pop Culture in Contemporary Indian Poetry with Reference to Nissim Ezekiel, Eunice de Souza, and Meena Kandasamy* show how popular culture can serve as both a mirror, reflecting who we think we are, and a mask, hiding deeper social tensions.

Popular Culture and Indian Society: Reflections of Social Change by **Dr. Vijay Kumar Banshiwal** asserts how popular culture functions as both a mirror and a driver of social change in India, offering insights into the complexities of identity, modernity, and tradition in an increasingly globalized world. *The Kaleidoscope of Culture: Popular Culture's Reflection and Reflection of Indian Culture* by **Dr. Shruti Srivastava and Ms. Srishti** deals with the rich cultural heritage of India and echoes that while the nations embrace and acknowledge one another's cultural practices, the cultural legacy should remain intact and be not at stake. *Fermented Flavors: Exploring Food Culture and Resistance in Axone* a paper by **Devika. S. Raj** explores the broader implications of culinary practices as acts of resistance and the role of food in negotiating cultural boundaries.

Dr. Ashwini Ashok Kadam in the paper *Indian Eco-Fiction and Popular Culture: A Study of Environmental Narratives in Literature and Media* explores the evolution of Indian eco-fiction, from mythological storytelling to contemporary climate fiction, to examine how literature and media portray ecological crises, anthropocentrism, and sustainability challenges. **Dr. Shruti Dubey** in her paper *The Undercover Over Screen: A Study of Real Life Espionage Narratives in Indian* Cinema focuses on the Indian movies based on real life incidents loosely adapted from the legends of Indian spies and attempts to study the movies as popular on-screen delineations of the real-life covert operatives. **Dr. Dimple Dubey's** paper *Modernistic Unveiling of Myth in Popular Culture in Salman Rushdie's The Ground Beneath*

Her Feet has repurposed a classical myth and reimagined it in the light of pop culture and global relevance.

Dr. Siddhi Tripathi's paper *Scintillating contours of Ecocinema: Addressing Environmental Concerns through Popular Culture in WALL-E* intends to investigate into the intersections of ecocinema and popular culture so as to understand how mass appeal reflects on environmental dilapidation. **Dr Pranali Milind kunar Jadhav's** paper *The Interplay of Popular Culture and Indian English Literature* explores the intricate relationship between popular culture and Indian English literature, emphasizing how the latter reflects, critiques, and reshapes cultural narratives. *Indian Poetry Slams: A Popular Youth Revolutionary Movement* by **Heena Bindal** brings in light the study the co-construction of this sub culture of poetic slams among the youth which is seemingly turning into a popular one in the urban India; giving rise to the new poetic communities, literature, culture and identities. **Mahesh Elkunchwar's** *'The Old Stone Mansion': A Critical Response through Cultural Perspective* by **Ayodhya Kalyan Jadhav** explores the cultural elements through Elkunchwar's most celebrated play 'Old Stone Mansion' that is included into 'The Wada Trilogy'.

Our sincere thanks to Prof. Amrendra Sharma for writing the Foreword of the book and to the Publisher, Pustak Bharti for efficient typing.

Dr. Sarita Jain
Dr. Sarita Chanwaria

Chapter-1
The River and the Screen: Representations of *Mahakumbh* in Popular Culture

Dr. Ashish Kumar Gupta

1. Introduction

The *Mahakumbh*, one of the largest religious gatherings in the world, serves as a compelling intersection of the sacred and the spectacular. Held every twelve years at four different riverine locations—Prayagraj, Haridwar, Ujjain, and Nashik—it draws millions of pilgrims who converge to take a ritual bath in the holy rivers, believing it will cleanse them of sins and grant liberation. Though its spiritual essence is deeply rooted in Hindu cosmology and mythology, particularly the narrative of *SamudraManthan*—the churning of the ocean that led to the spilling of *amrit* (nectar of immortality)—the *Mahakumbh* has undergone significant transformations in how it is experienced, understood, and represented today.

In contemporary times, the *Mahakumbh* is not only a religious event but also a vibrant site of cultural production. It has transcended its ritualistic framework to become a spectacle—filtered, repackaged, and circulated through various modes of popular culture such as films, television series, advertisements, documentaries, and social media content. As Arvind Rajagopal notes in his study of religion and media in India, "mass media has increasingly become the lens through which modern publics encounter the sacred" (Rajagopal 68). The *Mahakumbh*, therefore, functions both as a lived religious reality and as a mediated cultural phenomenon.

This chapter, titled *"The River and the Screen: Representations of Mahakumbh in Popular Culture"*, aims to explore how popular media represent, reinterpret, and sometimes commercialize the *Mahakumbh*. The metaphor of the "river" signifies the timeless spiritual current of the Kumbh tradition, while the "screen" denotes the multiplicity of visual and digital platforms that frame this tradition for contemporary audiences. As Guy Debord articulates in *The Society of the Spectacle*, the spectacle "is not a collection of images, but a social relation among people, mediated by images" (Debord 4). The *Mahakumbh*, through the lens of popular culture, becomes such a spectacle—a site where faith and visuality converge.The chapter is structured to first contextualize the historical and mythological dimensions of the *Mahakumbh*, followed by an analysis of its depiction in Indian cinema and television. It then moves to digital and social media representations and ends with a critique of the commodification of spirituality in advertising and political discourse. Through this multidisciplinary lens, the study hopes to uncover how the sacred is reimagined in the contemporary media landscape, and what these reimagining reveals about the shifting nature of public religiosity in India.

2. *Mahakumbh* in Historical and Cultural Context

The *Mahakumbh* is not merely a religious gathering but a civilizational spectacle deeply embedded in the mythological, historical, and cultural consciousness of India. Its mythological origin is traced to the story of *SamudraManthan*—the churning of the cosmic ocean by the Devas and Asuras in pursuit of *amrit*, the nectar of immortality. According to Hindu belief, during this celestial event, drops of *amrit* fell at four locations—Prayagraj, Haridwar, Ujjain, and Nashik—thus sanctifying them as the sites of the KumbhMela (Darian 47). The belief that bathing in the sacred rivers at these locations during the Kumbh grants *moksha* (liberation) continues to draw tens of millions of devotees.Though often framed as timeless, the *Mahakumbh* has a rich historical evolution. The earliest written reference to a mass religious bathing festival at Prayag appears in the accounts of Chinese travelerXuanzang

Popular Culture: Shades and Shadows

(Hiuen Tsang) in the 7th century CE, who witnessed a month-long gathering of ascetics and pilgrims on the banks of the Ganga and Yamuna (Thapar 102). Over time, the event acquired its periodic rhythm, with a 12-year cycle corresponding to the movement of Jupiter (*Brihaspati*) through the zodiac, further ritualized by astrological calculations and texts such as the *SkandaPurana* and *MatsyaPurana* (Bhardwaj 56).

Culturally, the *Mahakumbh* is a complex tapestry woven from various strands of Hindu religiosity, ascetic traditions, folk beliefs, and regional practices. The event is not monolithic; it draws participation from a wide array of sects—Shaivites, Vaishnavites, Shaktas, and especially the Akharas, or monastic orders, who command considerable attention during the *ShahiSnan* (royal bath). The Naga Sadhus—naked ascetics smeared in ash—have become iconic figures within the visual economy of the Kumbh, symbolizing renunciation, mysticism, and militant devotion (Pinney 91).However, beyond its religious grandeur, the *Mahakumbh* also acts as a democratic cultural space. Devotees from across caste, class, linguistic, and regional lines assemble to perform collective rituals, listen to discourses, and participate in Kalpvas—a period of prolonged religious abstention and riverside dwelling. As Diana Eck observes, "The Kumbh is both the river's story and the people's story—of myths that shape geography and rituals that shape community" (Eck 215).

The *Mahakumbh* also plays a socio-political role. In colonial India, it was a site of resistance and identity formation. British authorities often viewed it as a site of potential disorder, while Hindu reformers used it to promote cultural unity (Jones 88). In the postcolonial period, it has continued to serve as a stage for religious mobilization, political symbolism, and state patronage, especially through infrastructural projects, security arrangements, and digital connectivity in recent editions. Thus, the *Mahakumbh* is a palimpsest of ancient cosmology, historical practice, and modern religio-cultural negotiation. Its enduring appeal lies not just in its sacredness, but also in its capacity to continually evolve while retaining its core spiritual significance.

3. *Mahakumbh* in Indian Cinema and Television

The *Mahakumbh*, with its visual grandeur and mystical ethos, has long captured the imagination of filmmakers and television producers in India. Its rich symbolism—ritual baths in the sacred river, saffron-clad sadhus, colossal crowds, and the interplay of devotion and spectacle—makes it a powerful cinematic and televisual trope. While early Indian cinema largely engaged with religious themes and mythological narratives, direct representations of the Kumbh were rare, often relegated to background motifs in films with broader religious or social themes.One of the earliest notable instances of the Kumbh in Hindi cinema can be found in *SeetaAurGeeta* (1972), where the protagonists, twin sisters separated at birth, are accidentally split during the Kumbh Mela—a direct nod to the earlier trope in *Kumbh Ka Melā* (1948), a film that popularized the now-clichéd image of siblings separated during the fair. This motif was so prevalent that it became a satirical shorthand in Indian pop culture for the trope of accidental separation (Dwyer 110). Such depictions reduced the Kumbh to a chaotic site of loss and reunion, sidelining its religious and philosophical depth in favor of melodrama.

More recently, the *Mahakumbh* was reimagined in the Life OK television series *Mahakumbh: Ek Rahasya, Ek Kahani* (2014–15), directed by Arvind Babbal. This series represented a major shift in how the Kumbh was used narratively. It blended mythology with science fiction and thriller genres, casting the protagonist as a divine warrior, one of the *Garuda*, who must protect the Amrit hidden beneath the *Mahakumbh*. The series framed the Mela not as a religious event but as a battleground between good and evil, drawing from esoteric Hindu symbolism and combining it with global themes of immortality and apocalypse (Sundar 68). This fusion of sacred myth with mass entertainment illustrates how the *Mahakumbh* has been adapted into narrative frameworks that appeal to contemporary sensibilities.Television's treatment of the *Mahakumbh* often draws on heightened visual stylization. Wide-angle shots of the riverbanks teeming with saffron flags, the rhythmic chants of mantras, and the ethereal portrayal of sunrise baths are all crafted to evoke both awe and authenticity. As TejaswiniGanti observes, "The televisual form lends itself to ritual dramatization, creating a grammar of sacredness through editing, music, and framing" (Ganti 145). In this grammar, the *Mahakumbh* becomes not just a setting, but a character—infused with mystery, sanctity, and cinematic power.

In films like *Water* (2005), directed by Deepa Mehta, the Ganges and its rituals play a symbolic role, although the Kumbh itself remains peripheral. The depiction of asceticism, widowhood, and social exclusion, however, echoes many of the real-life dilemmas visible during the Kumbh. Similarly, documentaries such as *KumbhMela: The Greatest Show on Earth* (BBC, 2013) and *Faith Connections* (2013) by Pan Nalin offer a more grounded, humanist view of the Mela. They highlight the logistical scale of the event, its religious diversity, and the individual spiritual journeys that converge at the confluence (*TriveniSangam*).While fiction often mythologizes the *Mahakumbh*, documentary forms tend to demystify it, focusing on infrastructure, human stories, and socio-economic dimensions. Pan Nalin's*Faith Connections*, for instance, interweaves stories of a runaway child, a wandering sadhu, and a woman in search of her missing son—all set against the backdrop of the 2013 KumbhMela. These narratives foreground the emotional and spiritual stakes of pilgrimage, while also capturing the chaos and contradictions of the modern-day Kumbh (Nalin). However, critical voices argue that such media representations often aestheticize poverty and exoticize faith for global consumption. As Anand Pandian notes, "the camera's gaze is not innocent; it frames religiosity as a performance for the other, especially in the age of cultural tourism" (Pandian 54). The *Mahakumbh* thus becomes a consumable image, tailored to the tastes of both domestic audiences and international spectators seeking spiritual exotica.Despite this critique, the presence of the *Mahakumbh* in Indian cinema and television serves a dual purpose. On one hand, it introduces global and urban audiences to a tradition that might otherwise remain abstract or inaccessible. On the other hand, it risks flattening a complex ritual landscape into a visual cliché. The challenge, therefore, lies in balancing reverence with representation, devotion with drama.Ultimately, the *Mahakumbh*'s cinematic and televisual incarnations reflect the broader dynamics of how faith is visualized in popular culture. As religion migrates from the ghats to the screen, it encounters the logics of spectacle, entertainment, and narrative closure. What emerges is a hybridized version of the sacred—filtered through lenses, edited for emotion, and broadcast for belief.

4. *Mahakumbh* in Contemporary Media and Digital Culture

The digital revolution has transformed how the *Mahakumbh* is experienced, represented, and disseminated. From livestreamed rituals on YouTube to Instagram reels capturing the flamboyance of Naga Sadhus, the *Mahakumbh* today exists as much on screens as it does on the riverbanks. Digital technologies have extended the spatial and sensory reach of the Kumbh, allowing global audiences to virtually partake in what was once an intensely localized, physical pilgrimage.The 2013 and 2019 editions of the Prayagraj

Popular Culture: Shades and Shadows

Kumbh saw unprecedented use of digital infrastructure. The government of Uttar Pradesh in collaboration with tech firms like Google and NIC developed real-time mapping apps, facial recognition services for lost persons, and drone coverage of events to enhance crowd management and security. The official Kumbh website, promotional YouTube channels, and multilingual social media accounts served not only as informational portals but as branding platforms, portraying the Mela as a fusion of ancient spirituality and smart-city innovation. As Ravi Sundaram notes, "the sacred has entered a technocratic mode of visibility" (Sundaram 122). Rituals are no longer just performed; they are performed for the camera.

Social media platforms, especially Instagram, Facebook, and Twitter (now X), have become central to the Mela's evolving image. Influencers, spiritual leaders, tourists, and even bureaucrats post content with hashtags like #KumbhMela, #DivineIndia, or #NamamiGange. These platforms have created a parallel devotional ecosystem, where the image of the *Mahakumbh* is curated in real time—featuring drone shots of the Sangam, slow-motion videos of the ShahiSnan, and selfies with ascetics. In this sense, the event aligns with what MircaMadianou and Daniel Miller term "polymedia"—a communicative environment where users move fluidly across platforms to build hybrid narratives (Madianou and Miller 169).The 2019 Kumbh, in particular, marked a turning point. Declared by the government as a "DivyaKumbh, BhavyaKumbh" (Divine and Grand), it was not only a religious but also a political and digital mega-event. High-definition livestreams of Ganga Aarti, a VR experience at the Kumbh pavilion, and mobile apps in multiple Indian languages illustrated the state's use of digital tools to brand India's spiritual heritage as globally consumable. Prime Minister Narendra Modi's visit to the Kumbh and widely shared images of him washing the feet of sanitation workers were amplified across state-controlled and independent media platforms to project an image of humility and service, deeply entwining religion with digital governance (Jaffrelot and Kalaiyarasan 56).

However, this digitization of devotion is not without critique. Scholars such as Anja Kovacs caution against the corporatization and surveillance embedded in these digital infrastructures. The use of facial recognition, for instance, raises questions of privacy and consent, especially when deployed on a largely rural and under-informed population (Kovacs 98). Moreover, the digital divide means that while the Kumbh is celebrated as a technological marvel, many of its most faithful participants remain disconnected from the digital narratives shaping its global image.Beyond state-led initiatives, independent content creators and digital media platforms also play a crucial role in shaping how the *Mahakumbh* is visualized. YouTube channels like "Spiritual India,""India in Pixels," and "The Lallantop" have produced mini-documentaries, cultural commentaries, and vlogs that blend anthropological curiosity with aesthetic stylization. These pieces often highlight the paradoxes of the Mela—the tension between faith and commerce, austerity and spectacle, tradition and modernity.

Memes, too, have entered the Kumbh's digital ecosystem. Images of ash-smeared sadhus juxtaposed with pop culture references often go viral, making the Mela a subject of irony, humor, and sometimes ridicule. While some argue this trivializes the sacred, others see it as a form of participatory culture where the sacred and the secular coexist playfully. As Henry Jenkins observes, "in a participatory culture, every cultural artifact becomes a text open to revision, remixing, and circulation" (Jenkins 133). The *Mahakumbh*, by entering meme culture, becomes a living text, constantly rewritten in pixels. A specimen of commercialization of *Mahakumbh* in the form of virtual devotion for modern man can be seen here in this advertisement, which I came across in Prayagraj in 2025.

Popular Culture: Shades and Shadows

Ah, the wonders of modern devotion— where enlightenment comes with a photocopy and salvation is just a WhatsApp away! Why bother with faith, penance, or personal presence when ₹500 and a passport-sized photo can fast track your blessings?

These kinds of "holy shortcuts" turn centuries-old spiritual traditions into a bizarre blend of superstition and customer service. Divine dip? Nah, just dip a Xerox in the river and call it a day. One wonders if the gods are also accepting Paytm now — maybe there's a cashback offer on karma too!

Spirituality has truly entered the digital age — just without the logic or dignity.

In short, contemporary media and digital culture have redefined the *Mahakumbh*. No longer confined to physical space or sacred time, it now circulates globally as data, image, and algorithm. While this brings new forms of visibility and accessibility, it also invites ethical, political, and aesthetic questions. Who controls the narrative? Whose gaze shapes the representation? And how does digital mediation alter the very nature of religious experience?

5. Commodification, Spiritual Branding, and Political Appropriation of the *Mahakumbh*

The *Mahakumbh* has always been a site of religious confluence, where spirituality, ritual, and community converge. In recent decades, however, the Mela has also become a site of economic opportunity, branding, and ideological performance. From the aggressive promotion of religious tourism to the appropriation of the event by political parties, the *Mahakumbh* today reflects the intermingling of faith, capital, and statecraft.The transformation of the *Mahakumbh* into a brand began in earnest with the 2013 and 2019 editions, where large-scale state investment and global promotion marked a shift toward spiritual tourism. In 2019, the Uttar Pradesh government allocated over ₹4,200 crores for infrastructure development, not only to accommodate pilgrims but also to promote the Kumbh as a 'world-class event' (Mishra 214). The Mela grounds were redesigned with art installations, smart lighting, digital displays, and pavilions sponsored by corporations, NGOs, and religious organizations.

Luxury tents marketed as "glamping" options, spiritual wellness camps for foreign tourists, and Kumbh-specific packages by travel agencies commodified the sacred space. These offerings often catered to upper-middle-class Indians and international tourists, thus stratifying the pilgrimage experience. Scholars like VrindaDalmiya argue that this turns the Kumbh into "a consumer event of performative piety, where spiritual authenticity is often overshadowed by curated experiences" (Dalmiya 51).The spiritual branding of the *Mahakumbh* has made it a symbol of India's cultural and civilizational heritage. Promotional videos created by the Ministry of Tourism use phrases like "Divine India,""Eternal Ganga," and "Pilgrimage of the Millennium," drawing on the language of timelessness and purity. This aligns with what Arjun Appadurai calls the "production of locality" (Appadurai 178), wherein religious spaces are packaged for both domestic nationalist sentiment and global spiritual consumption.

This image production is further facilitated by

Popular Culture: Shades and Shadows

Bollywood endorsements, celebrity visits, and collaborations with yoga gurus like Baba Ramdev and Sri Sri Ravi Shankar. Their presence at the Mela—and the media coverage surrounding it—contribute to an aura of sacred modernity, where yoga mats, herbal products, and devotional books coexist with drones and 5G networks.Moreover, Kumbh souvenirs—such as miniature TriveniSangam statues, saffron flags, incense sticks, and Ayurvedic items—extend the event's economy into global diaspora markets. E-commerce platforms list "Kumbh Packages" and spiritual subscription boxes. These commercial extensions indicate the transformation of the Kumbh from a ritual event into a lifestyle product.The Kumbh has also become a key site of political symbolism, especially for Hindutva ideologues and the Bharatiya Janata Party (BJP). The 2019 Kumbh was instrumental in projecting Prime Minister Narendra Modi's image as a devout Hindu leader. His publicized dip in the Sangam and visit to sanitation workers was widely broadcast, signaling a blend of humility and Hindutva nationalism. As Christophe Jaffrelot and A. Kalaiyarasan observe, "The state reconfigures religious spaces into political stages, where cultural majoritarianism is enacted with visual and symbolic force" (Jaffrelot and Kalaiyarasan 57).

The use of government funds, official slogans, and public infrastructure to promote the Kumbh reflects a politicization of religious practices. Political leaders invoke the Mela not just for spiritual legitimacy, but to reinforce cultural hegemony. The repeated emphasis on "Sanatan Dharma," Vedic heritage, and Hindu civilizational glory marginalizes the syncretic and pluralistic traditions historically associated with pilgrimage centers like Prayagraj.Moreover, the *Mahakumbh* is often used to project India's "soft power" on the global stage. The 2019 Mela saw participation from diplomats of over 70 countries, invited to witness "the world's largest peaceful gathering." Cultural diplomacy and spiritual spectacle intersected, presenting the Kumbh as both a domestic rallying point and an international exhibit of India's religio-cultural prowess (Rajagopal 87).

Despite these triumphalist narratives, several contradictions underpin the Kumbh's commodification and political appropriation. Dalit and Bahujan thinkers have critiqued the dominance of upper-caste imagery and rituals at the Mela. Activist KanchaIlaiahnotes"the Kumbh glorifies caste hierarchies through the visual prominence of sadhus and gurus from dominant traditions, while erasing non-Brahminical expressions of faith" (Ilaiah 109). Similarly, feminist scholars highlight the marginalization of women's voices and roles in organizing or interpreting the Mela, except as passive participants or symbols of purity.Ecological concerns also emerge. Despite government campaigns like "NamamiGange," the temporary infrastructure—tents, plastic waste, toilets, and crowd control mechanisms—places immense strain on the river and surrounding land. Media images of devout pilgrims bathing in a heavily polluted river clash with the "clean and green" narratives promoted by state PR machines.

Furthermore, the increasing presence of surveillance technologies—from facial recognition to drones—raises concerns about freedom, privacy, and the policing of bodies in a space traditionally marked by spiritual openness. Anja Kovacs warns"in the new digital Kumbh, every pilgrim becomes a data point, every act of devotion potentially monitored" (Kovacs 100).The *Mahakumbh* today is a confluence not only of rivers and religions but also of market forces, political agendas, and media logics. As it is branded, commodified, and instrumentalized, the challenge remains to preserve the spiritual core of the pilgrimage. What is at stake is not just the authenticity of faith, but also the very meaning of public religiosity in an age where spectacle often overtakes substance.

6. Conclusion

The *Mahakumbh*Mela, once understood primarily as a site of spiritual purification and sacred congregation, has in recent decades transformed into a complex cultural phenomenon shaped by media saturation, political symbolism, and economic interest. This shift reflects broader changes in how religiosity and public rituals are conceived in contemporary India, where tradition is increasingly mediated through technology and spectacle.As we have seen, the *Mahakumbh* is no longer confined to the ephemeral geography of the Sangam or to the intimate rhythms of ascetic devotion and ritual. It now circulates globally via digital platforms, embedded in visual economies that frame it as both cultural heritage and tourist attraction. With high-definition cameras capturing every sacred dip and social media influencing perceptions, the event becomes a curated experience—edited, filtered, and commodified. In such an environment, the authenticity of spiritual experience becomes intertwined with its reproducibility and share ability.

This shift raises pressing questions. What happens to the sanctity of the *Mahakumbh* when it is re-scripted for digital audiences and global tourists? How do commercial logics and political performances influence the meanings that pilgrims attach to the space? Moreover, can devotion retain its transformative power when enmeshed in what Guy Debord famously termed "the society of the spectacle," where appearances and representations often displace lived experience (Debord 13)? The answer may lie not in rejecting the new but in critically engaging with it. As scholars like Diana Eck have long pointed out, pilgrimage sites like the Kumbh have historically adapted to shifting social and political realities (Eck 74). The *Mahakumbh* has endured for millennia precisely because of its ability to encompass contradiction—ritual and politics, austerity and excess, the divine and the profane. Its current digital incarnation is thus not an aberration but part of a long continuum of reinvention.

However, what distinguishes the present moment is the scale and speed of transformation. The digital spectacle not only reshapes how the Kumbh is seen but also who gets to represent it. While the state, corporations, and dominant religious sects enjoy wide visibility, the voices of marginalized castes, women, and ecologically conscious stakeholders are often drowned out. To rethink the sacred in this context is to ask who controls the narrative, whose beliefs are platformed, and whose are rendered invisible.At the same time, the *Mahakumbh* also offers possibilities for new solidarities. The digital space, while commodified, is also porous. Alternative media, critical documentaries, and counter-narratives on platforms like YouTube, podcasts, and independent journalism provide space for dissent, reinterpretation, and grassroots representation. These emerging practices suggest that even in an age of spectacle, the sacred can remain a site of inquiry, resistance, and reimagination.

In conclusion, the *Mahakumbh* today is not merely a festival or a pilgrimage—it is a palimpsest of tradition and modernity, devotion and data, spectacle and sincerity. To study its representations in popular culture is not only to understand the evolving face of Hindu religiosity, but also to confront larger questions about faith, media, power, and identity in 21st-century India. As we navigate this terrain, the challenge remains to ensure that the river, the ritual, and the reverence do not drown in the flood of pixels and propaganda.

Works Cited:
Appadurai, Arjun. *Modernity at Large: Cultural Dimensions of Globalization*. University of Minnesota Press, 1996.

Bhardwaj, Surinder Mohan. *Hindu Places of Pilgrimage in India: A Study in Cultural Geography*. University of California Press, 1973.

Dalmiya, Vrinda. "Spiritual Tourism and the Marketed Sacred." *Journal of Indian Philosophy and Religion*, vol. 25, 2019, pp. 45–56.

Darian, Steven G. *The Ganges in Myth and History*. University of Hawai'i Press, 2001.

Debord, Guy. *The Society of the Spectacle*. Translated by Donald Nicholson-Smith, Zone Books, 1994.

Debord, Guy. *The Society of the Spectacle*. Translated by Donald Nicholson-Smith, Zone Books, 1994.

Dwyer, Rachel. *Bollywood's India: Hindi Cinema as a Guide to Contemporary India*. Reaktion Books, 2014.

Eck, Diana L. *India: A Sacred Geography*. Harmony Books, 2012.

Eck, Diana L. *India: A Sacred Geography*. Harmony Books, 2012.

Ganti, Tejaswini. *Producing Bollywood: Inside the Contemporary Hindi Film Industry*. Duke UP, 2012.

Ilaiah, Kancha. *Post-Hindu India: A Discourse in Dalit-Bahujan, Socio-Spiritual and Scientific Revolution*. Sage, 2009.

Jaffrelot, Christophe, and Kalaiyarasan A. "Performing Hindu Nationalism: The KumbhMela in the Era of Modi." *Contemporary South Asia*, vol. 28, no. 1, 2020, pp. 45–60.

Jaffrelot, Christophe, and Kalaiyarasan A. "Performing Hindu Nationalism: The KumbhMela in the Era of Modi." *Contemporary South Asia*, vol. 28, no. 1, 2020, pp. 45–60.

Jenkins, Henry. *Convergence Culture: Where Old and New Media Collide*. NYU Press, 2006.

Jones, Kenneth W. *Religious Controversy in British India: Dialogues in South Asian Languages*. State University of New York Press, 1992.

Kovacs, Anja. "Digital India and the Politics of Surveillance." *Economic and Political Weekly*, vol. 53, no. 5, 2018, pp. 96–101.

Kovacs, Anja. "Digital India and the Politics of Surveillance." *Economic and Political Weekly*, vol. 53, no. 5, 2018, pp. 96–101.

Madianou, Mirca, and Daniel Miller. *Migration and New Media: Transnational Families and Polymedia*. Routledge, 2012.

Mishra, Pankaj. "Sacred Infrastructure: The Kumbh and the Making of the Hindu Nation." *South Asian History and Culture*, vol. 10, no. 2, 2019, pp. 209–220.

Nalin, Pan, director. *Faith Connections*. Monsoon Films, 2013.

Pandian, Anand. *Reel World: An Anthropology of Creation*. Duke UP, 2015.

Pinney, Christopher. *Photos of the Gods: The Printed Image and Political Struggle in India*. Reaktion Books, 2004.

Rajagopal, Arvind. *Politics after Television: Hindu Nationalism and the Reshaping of the Public in India*. Cambridge UP, 2001.

Rajagopal, Arvind. *Politics After Television: Hindu Nationalism and the Reshaping of the Public in India*. Cambridge UP, 2001.

Sundar, Nandini. "The Sacred and the Supernatural on Prime Time: Reading *Mahakumbh*." *Economic and Political Weekly*, vol. 50, no. 10, 2015, pp. 66–69.

Sundaram, Ravi. *Pirate Modernity: Delhi's Media Urbanism*. Routledge, 2009.

Thapar, Romila. *Cultural Pasts: Essays in Early Indian History*. Oxford UP, 2000.

Chapter-2
Culture of Gender Discrimination in Traditional Society: A Rereading of Girish Karnad's Nagamandala

Dr. Poonam Rani Gupta

Abstract

The creation of female protagonists in fundamental manner is the most significant feature of Girish Karnad's plays. 'Naga-Mandala' is no exception to it. In this play, Girish Karnad has created the character of Rani, unusual and eccentric. This character is the creation of the post-colonial, post-modern world who wishes to attain what she lacks, upheavals against the patriarchy and male dominance, endeavours for survival and ends traditional notions forestalling change in the stance of the male-dominated society. In other words, Girish Karnad shows how women experience a survival of subjugation and compliance in a patriarchal society. The men use domestic violence as an armament to control and discriminate against their wives and their female counterparts who docilely endure all the pain and anguish.

Keywords: Culture, tradition, female, dominance, subjugation, patriarchy.

Girish Karnad (1938) is celebrated as one of the most significant dramatists of post - colonial India. He is perhaps the most renowned media personality in the contemporary India and also an adept practitioner of performing arts. While his contemporaries viz. BadalSircar and Vijay Tendulkar focus their attention on the problems of the middle class, GirishKarnad takes refuge in Indian myths, legendsand folklores. He marks his plays with new vision denoting cultural diversity and also provides an urgent need of a change in certain oral traditions of India.Girish Karnad is one of the leading playwrights in India who inscribes in Kannada and yet has moved away from the regionalist tradition to make new searches on the inarticulate.

Nagamandala (1988) is one of the famous plays of Girish Karnad which fetched him the Karnataka Sahitya Academy Award for the year (1989) as a most creative work. Patriarchy defines men as the rulers, women are seen as inferior, less capable, and weaker. In this play 'Naga Mandala', Karnad interlaces two Kannada folk tales together, the first one remarks on the paradoxical nature of oral tales, and the other is the story of Rani whose dilemma reflects the human need to live by fiction and half-truths. Nagamandala presents a perfect blend of a folktale and a myth where male chauvinism attempts hard not only to degrade females in all possible ways but alsoto exploit and confine them in the four walls of the house.Thus,*Nagamandala* is a feminist play that not only attacks and exposes male bigotry, the repression of women, the discrimination done to them by men and the patriarchal culture, but also quietly deflates the concept of chastity that aims to supress the female folk in a traditional. Many interpretations of "Nagamandala" consider it a feminist play that critiques the patriarchal system and its impact on women. The play's exploration of gender roles, power dynamics, and the concept of chastity makes it a powerful critique of patriarchal structure

It is the play consistently reverberate the persistent dilemma of women in the traditional Indian society. Apart from documenting the women's predicament, the play very strongly presents the protesting voice against the suppressing culturaltraditions of patriarchal society. While presenting a protest against the common culture of the suppression of woman Karnad very strongly affirms the views of Simone de Beauvoir who while dealing with the secondary place given to women in the society writes, "thus humanity is male and man defines woman not in herself but as relative to him; she is not regarded as an autonomous being" (Beauvoir 25). In this way the play attempts to provide an insight on the liberation and empowerment of the women who have to play an essential role for the revival of a depreciated social order. The women's story expresses the female outlook about their needs, problems and experiences within the patriarchal institutions.

Girish Karnad while using cultural mythology has put forward a question mark to some of the most popular values of the so-called modern society. In this way *Nagamandala*can be labelled as a feminist play that not only attacks and exposes male racism, the subjugation of women, the discrimination done to them by men and the patriarchal culture, but also questions those traditional and mythological values that force the female folk to live under the umbrella of fake chastity. It is the play echoing the persistent quandaries of women in the traditional Indian society.

The play is about Rani, newly married to Appanna.She can be seen as a metaphor for the situation of a young girl in the bosom of a joint family where she sees her husband in two unconnected roles- as a stranger during the day and as a lover at night. The empty house Rani is locked in could be the family she is married into.Girish Karnad portrays the character of Rani from an unconventional approach to demonstrate that the society is terribly puritanical, patriarchal and prejudicial to women. Rani represents the common submissive Indian rural girl who becomes the victim of the unfair social order through the institution of Marriage. Her parents decide her marriage without even asking for her choice thinking that she is incapable of taking her own decision. She is asked to marry a person named Appanna, literally means 'any man'. So, it is a not just the story of Rani and Appanna but that of any man and woman united in a wed-lock. Marriage is the age-old institution that has always been unfair to women. Women are exploited physically, mentally, emotionally, socially and intellectually.

In fact, "to be a woman is something strange, so confused, so complicated, that no one predicate comes near expressing it and that the multiple predicates that one would like to use are so contradictory that only a woman could up with it" (Kierkegaard 175).

Appanna represents thatmale folk in a traditional society that enjoys all rights to thinkand decide about himself but a woman is not permitted to think and decide about herself without the permission of man whom she has to follow in the form of a father, brother or a husband. Appanna is viewed as a suitable groom for Rani by her father or rather the decider of her future from the perspective of economic criteria. He was rich and wealthy with a good reputation in the society. Therefore, Rani's father takes him as a suitable candidate for Rani! Ironically enough in the due course of the story the readers come to realise thatAppana is adulterous and not at all suitable for a simple girl like Rani. Rani mirrors the image of a common woman who comes to her husband's house with sweet dreams and desires of happy domestic life. But she has to face another side of reality. Appanna has a mistress withwhom he passes his good time and visits her every night.He does not pay any attention to Rani's emotional needs andcomes to her only at noon.

Appana's treatment with Rani is also monstrous and animalistic. He keeps her locked up inside the house so that she cannot express her grievance to anyone. Her sexual desires are neglected. She is frequently beaten for no apparent cause. He never cares for her emotions and crushes them pitilessly. He does not allow her to communicate with anyone outside the house. The house seems a slaughter house to Rani where all her dreams and desires are crushed mercilessly. She is turned voiceless and choice less by her husband. The institution of marriage is proving a big prison house to her as she does not find emotional, social or sexual satisfaction from the institution of marriage. Appanna's inhuman treatment is witnessed on the first day of their marriage when instead of being with Rani, Appanna goes to meet his mistress and locks Rani up in the house. He says, "...I'll be back tomorrow at noon. Keep my lunch ready. I shall eat and go" (6). He doesn't even tell her the reason. Neither does he tells her where he is going. Because of the patriarchy-conditioned mind, she even does not gather courage to question his night-visit. Her upbringing in patriarchal setup has made her timid, shy and submissive. She has lost her capacity to question. As a result, she fails to gather courage and confidence to question the exploitative and oppressive system. Women do not have freedom to question. However, they are questioned in case they deviate slightly from the prescribed path of patriarchal system. In this regard Jessica Benjamin said, "the male-ego and dominance is the key note in the analysis of man-woman relationship where the male attributes are associated with the mental thought and positive activity while the woman is regarded as a passive creature that is forced to respect the male sexual drive for the subsequent reproduction of the human species" (Figes 125). Women are continuously forced to face injustice, suppression, subjection, and exploitation in the world of patriarchy.

The hypocrisy of the patriarchal society is excavated in another common ideology which goes with the idea of chastity, i.e. having more than one relationship orsex as sin. The patriarchal society in different ways sometimes directly through moral teaching and at certain times indirectly preaches that chastity is more important than life. It also emphasises thatthe loss of chastity brings an unbearable social stigma which is worse than death. On the one hand, it relates to forms of sexual abstentionas morality and on the other it highlights the sanctity of marriage only for the method of procreation or giving birth to a child. The play deconstructs the concept of chastity, exposing it as a tool used to control and oppress women. Rani is forced to undergo a "chastity test" to prove her virtue, while

Appanna's infidelity goes unpunished, demonstrating the double standards prevalent in the patriarchal society.

Discussing with the same issue philosopher David Hume pointed out in his discursive and incessant idea about social mores, childbirth and fidelity in *A Treatise on Human Nature* that 'a man only wants to support a child that is related to him biologically'. In order to remain sure about the paternity of the child, he has to primarily ensure that his wife is dedicated and loyal to him. As a result, woman's liberty and sexual expression is curtailed to a large extent. The play vividly portrays how Rani is subjected to the whims of her husband, Appanna, who also maintains a mistress. This highlights the disparity in power dynamics, where women are often relegated to subservient roles within the patriarchal system.

In the traditional Indian society, what one constantly observes is that, the double standard of contemporary patriarchal society idolizes the porn-stars who serve the male chauvinism but condemns the rape victims who are made to suffer unbearable humiliation and disgrace for crimes committed by somebody else against them, this way this chastity convicts the innocent rape victim with double punishment for no fault at all. Committing adultery by the husband in the present play is not taken as a social inequity because even the village elders administer a positive response in relation to the male system of adultery. But the same is not allowed to the female protagonist i.e. Rani. The village court tries the case of Rani only and it ignores the same crime of Appanna, her husband. In this way the traditions Indian society seems to highlight very strongly the gender-bias and the optimum futility of justice. Nobody believes in the innocence of Rani. Rani sleeps with Naga in the disguise of Appanna who visits her every night in guise of her husband, whatever follows happens only because in the traditional social culture the females are not allowed to question to the demand of the males. Rani is never allowed to question her husband during the day and Naga during the night. This demand for submission without reasoning keeps Rani ignorant. Had she discovered the real identity of Naga, she would not have allowed him to enter her bedroom and touch her. As a typical Indian woman, she is not only frigid in her idea about sexbut alsodespisesit. What she craves for is love, affection and warmth which only Naga could give her. By Praising, caressing and arousing, Naga removes her frigidity. While Rani is initially presented as a submissive and vulnerable figure, she gradually begins to assert her agency and resist the oppressive social structures. The play explores the subtle ways in which women can negotiate with patriarchal structures and assert their own power.

It is concluded that although the ending of the play is not within the orthodoxy of Indian epic texts and Hindu philosophy, it can be seen in the cultural context of Indian woman of today who seeks to fulfil her needs and aspirations. It covers the theme of woman's destiny, her chastity and societal role and merges it with an unpredicted ending latent on double crossing and reviving of old customs. Through the character of Rani, Girish Karnad shows how women experience an existence of subjection and obedience in patriarchal society. The men use domestic violence as a weapon to dominate and discriminate their wives and their female counterparts meekly tolerate all the pains and sufferings. Therefore, Karnad has been successful in portraying the cultural tradition of gender discrimination in the Indian society. The author portrays male domination in the society by presenting how shamefully Appannacarries relationship with a concubine and at the same time marries a young girl named Rani. He never cares for the happiness of his wife. As others in the society, he suppresses her both physically and mentally. He also does not care for social customs and culture. Even society never questions him when he locks his wife and spends time with Chelvi, his beloved, but the same people raise questions when Appanna stood against her and doubted. *Nagamandala* has both magic and religious effects where the snake is worshipped as God of Fertility. Naga has magical powers it is folk drama but if Naga is her lover, then it creates a critical image and questions on both man and woman equality also. Karnad brings out directly or indirectly that all three characters Naga, Appanna, and Rani have lost their chastity. It also brings out the female narrative story in the patriarchal society.

Thus, In Girish Karnad's *Nagamandala,* gender discrimination is a central theme, highlighting the societal subjugation of women and the hypocrisy of patriarchal norms. The play exposes how women are often treated as possessions and judged by their chastity while men are free from similar scrutiny. Through the character of Rani, Karnad critiques the double standards of patriarchal society, where women are expected to be virtuous and loyal, while men are allowed to indulge in infidelity. *Nagamandala* challenges the traditional patriarchal norms that dictate women's roles and responsibilities. By portraying Rani's struggle against these norms, Karnad raises questions about the legitimacy of the existing social order.

References:
Beauvoir Simone de. The Second Sex. New Delhi: Penguin Books, 1972.

Figes Eva. Patriarchal Attitudes: women in Society. London: Macmillan, 1986

Karnad Girish. Naga-Mandla: A Play with a Cobra. New Delhi: Oxford UP, 2004.

Kierkegaard. Quoted from Beauvoir, Simone de. The Second Sex. New Delhi: Penguin books, 1976.

Chapter-3
Decoding the Influence of Pop Culture

Dr. Anoopama Yadav

Abstract

Pop culture has become an inescapable part of contemporary life—shaping our experiences through music, movies, fashion, social media, and more. Yet, how often do we pause to consider its profound influence on society? Popular culture not only entertains; it informs values, challenges societal norms, and offers new modes of self-expression. As a mirror to the collective consciousness, pop culture reflects societal dynamics, including its aspirations, anxieties, and transformations.Defined broadly as the culture of the people, pop culture encompasses a range of social phenomena, including belief systems, communication styles, consumer behaviors, and lifestyle choices. In India, the past decade has witnessed a remarkable evolution of pop culture, expanding beyond its traditional associations with Bollywood, cricket, and political discourse. Today, India's cultural landscape is shaped by a dynamic interplay of global and local influences—fueled by the proliferation of social media platforms such as Instagram, Twitter, and TikTok; the rise of OTT content; international music festivals; online gaming communities; and the integration of AI and digital technologies.These platforms have become incubators of cultural trends, memes, and viral phenomena, driving participatory culture and democratizing content creation. Music, in particular, continues to demonstrate pop culture's unifying and transformative power. Moreover, pop culture holds the ability to normalize behaviors, attitudes, and ideologies, rendering them socially acceptable or even desirable. This paper adopts Ferdinand de Saussure's semiotic structuralism framework to analyze how signs—

both linguistic and cultural—mediate the relationship between signifier and signified in the construction and dissemination of pop culture's influence.

Keywords: Pop culture, social media, fashion, food, music, Saussure, semiotics

The term "popular culture" was coined in the mid-19th century to describe the cultural traditions of the general populace. Scholars often trace the rise of popular culture to the emergence of the middle class, a direct consequence of the Industrial Revolution. As individuals were increasingly categorized into working classes and relocated to urban environments, far removed from their agrarian roots, they began to forge their own distinct cultural identities, which they shared with fellow workers.

Following the end of World War II, rapid innovations in mass media sparked significant cultural and social transformations, particularly in the Western world. Concurrently, capitalism—especially the drive for profit—played a pivotal role in shaping these changes. Newly invented consumer goods were marketed to various social classes, leading to the commodification of culture. Over time, the concept of popular culture increasingly merged with terms such as "mass culture," "consumer culture," "image culture," "media culture," and "culture created for mass consumption by manufacturers."

American popular culture has a lasting global influence, particularly in the realms of fashion, literature, and politics. The American way of life resonates deeply with youth around the world, shaping pop culture behaviors and trends that are observed globally. The U.S. has also led in technological innovation and communication, with companies such as Apple, Microsoft, and Google serving as prime examples of American dominance in these fields.

However, the widespread dissemination of American cultural elements has also led to the erosion of local traditions and customs in various parts of the world. Television sitcoms like *Friends* and others had a profound impact, bringing together diverse audiences across different cultures, ethnicities, and races. These shows fostered a sense of belonging to American popular culture, and non-native English speakers gradually adopted American slang and expressions as part of their daily vocabulary.

In his book *Cultural Theory and Popular Culture*, British media scholar John Storey offers six distinct definitions of popular culture:

1. Popular culture is culture that is widely favored or well-liked by many people, without any negative connotations.
2. Popular culture is whatever remains after high culture has been identified. In this view, pop culture is considered inferior, functioning as a marker of status and class.
3. Popular culture consists of commercial objects produced for mass consumption by non-discriminating consumers. In this definition, it is seen as a tool used by elites to control or exploit the masses.
4. Popular culture is folk culture, something that arises organically from the people rather than being imposed upon them. Pop culture is considered authentic (created by the people), as opposed to being commercial (imposed by enterprises).
5. Popular culture is negotiated: partly imposed by the dominant classes and partly resisted or altered by subordinate groups. While dominant groups may create culture, subordinate groups decide what to keep or discard.
6. In the postmodern world, the distinction between authentic and commercial culture is blurred. Today's pop culture allows users the freedom to embrace manufactured content, alter it for personal use, or completely reject it and create their own.

All six of Storey's definitions remain relevant today,

though they shift depending on the context in which pop culture is analyzed (Storey, 2019). Ultimately, pop culture is more than a series of trends—it is an emotional experience expressed through the clothes we wear, the food we eat, the movies we watch, and the homes we decorate.

Today, people increasingly use references to TV series and movies as a way to connect and communicate with one another. This has become a unique form of social interaction. With the proliferation of television channels, social networking sites, blogs, music, film genres, video games, and other media, today's youth live in a world dominated by technology and pop culture. The pressure to fit in and be part of the crowd is so overwhelming that many young people structure their lives around what they see in movies, TV shows, and fashion advice from popular magazines.

Popular culture is also closely tied to the economy, as it drives the sales of various mainstream merchandise products associated with well-known TV shows, films, comic books, and more. These products can range from clothing and accessories to mugs, notebooks, posters, and any other item adorned with recognizable logos or characters. Many well-known clothing brands have even become integrated into global pop culture, further blurring the lines between commercial products and cultural symbols.

Pop culture has become an integral part of popular media and is used strategically to spread messages, promote products, and influence public opinion. It plays a pivotal role in shaping societal attitudes, creating social change, and influencing political decisions. Furthermore, it has significantly contributed to the realization of a global society by providing people around the world with common topics to discuss. Often seen as a reflection of societal values and norms, pop culture has the power to shape young people's thoughts, behaviors, and beliefs. For instance, it can influence how young people perceive body image, relationships, and gender roles. Popular media plays a key role in shaping how young people view themselves and their place in the world.

With the increasing number of internet users, India has emerged as a major player in digital media, facilitating a cross-pollination of global and local cultures. Platforms such as YouTube, Instagram, Netflix, and Spotify have enabled Indian audiences to engage with Western pop culture firsthand, creating a two-way exchange that infuses Indian creativity with international trends. Indian brands have adopted similar techniques, incorporating animation and CGI in advertisements and music videos, which have become crucial elements of the pop music industry.

Popular movies and TV shows often portray specific lifestyles or ideologies as aspirational. For instance, the depiction of successful, glamorous characters in films can shape our perceptions of what success looks like. Similarly, the representation of social issues in popular media can raise awareness and contribute to social change. The advertising and music industries have embraced this shift, blending artistic storytelling with advanced technology to enhance the global perception of brands and artists.

Artists such as Talha Anjum, Talha Yunus, and Seedhe Maut frequently address themes of pain, struggle, and hardship in their songs, often drawing from the realities of life in Southeast Asia. Their lyrics touch on issues like addiction and the difficulties faced by marginalized communities. These artists often present a mix of personas—at times friendly and professional, at other times intense and aggressive—reflecting the complex emotions and experiences they seek to convey through their music.

Musicians have long been seen as trendsetters in popular culture, with their unique style and fashion choices influencing their followers. They are often the first to experiment with new fashion trends, expressing their individuality through collaborations with global brands like Coca-Cola, Versace, Adidas, and Gucci. Fashion and music are closely intertwined, as both serve as forms of self-expression. Musicians convey their emotions and personalities through their music, while fashion allows them to showcase their identity through style. Their fashion choices often reflect their inner spirit and personal narrative.

India's hip-hop, pop, and indie music scenes have gained significant momentum, driven by an audience eager to explore beyond conventional boundaries and engage with both global and local cultural expressions.The impact of global fashion is increasingly evident in India, with major brands like Gucci and Louis Vuitton establishing a strong presence and influencing local designers. A notable milestone in India's integration into global pop culture was a recent Dior event held in Mumbai, which showcased international fashion and celebrated India's growing influence in the luxury sector. Similarly, global music festivals like Lollapalooza have made their mark in India, highlighting how the country's music scene is evolving beyond traditional Bollywood.

We often take our own perspectives for granted, as they are shaped by our unique life experiences and the surrounding world. However, we seldom consider the complex relationship we each have with media and how this shapes our perception of reality. As individuals, we have always sought to contextualize our human experience within the larger world. Media provides us with a tool to do so, but the ways in which we engage with it are influenced by factors beyond our control—our age, race, ethnicity, class, gender, and more. These factors expose us to different types of media and, as a result, each of us develops a unique relationship with it.

Our perceptions of the world can diverge significantly even when we are exposed to the same facts, images, or content. For example, we might all be looking at the same Facebook post or watching the same news clip, yet each person may see and feel something entirely different. As digital platforms become ever more pervasive, they function as filters for how we perceive society and reality. In today's world, where many of us are constantly connected to our devices, it's crucial to recognize that we each inhabit distinct digital worlds. Our unique filters manifest on platforms like Facebook and Instagram, where the content we consume is tailored to our individual preferences, emotional needs, and biases.

While these divergent filters may have little impact in trivial areas like memes or the public figures we follow, they become more problematic when it comes to serious issues that require thoughtful discussion, empathy, and understanding. In these areas, our digital eco-chambers reinforce our pre-existing beliefs, often leading to self-indulgence and the consumption of clickbait that affirms our emotional drives and insecurities. The internet, social media, and news platforms ideally should bring us together, breaking down the barriers of physical distance. Yet, in reality, they often pull us apart, deepening societal divides.

In the current economic, social, and political climate, it seems unlikely that the role of media will fundamentally change. Media has become a zero-sum game, with platforms vying for our attention in an ever-competitive market. This phenomenon has led scholars to label the current era as an "attention economy." Media is no longer merely a tool for disseminating information; it has become a source of entertainment and emotion. Magazine covers, advertisements, and social media posts are carefully designed to evoke specific emotions, spark outrage, and encourage sharing- all driven by profit motives.

As we reflect on these dynamics in the context of today's theme of "ignorance," it's important to acknowledge

Popular Culture: Shades and Shadows

that media is a double-edged sword. On one hand, it has allowed us to transcend our immediate realities, exposing us to ideas, cultures, and events we might not otherwise encounter. This has empowered people in places like India to stay informed about issues happening in different parts of the country and around the world. On the other hand, media—particularly through our digital filters—limits our worldview, feeding us only the content we already agree with, reinforcing existing biases.

These tensions are ongoing, and unfortunately, media companies and platforms are not obligated to resolve them. In fact, they are more likely to exploit these dynamics to maintain user engagement. By curating content tailored to our passions, insecurities, and egos, they ensure that we remain hooked to their platforms. As a result, we feel comfortable in our echo chambers, avoiding perspectives that challenge our worldview.

The question then becomes: How do we navigate these divergent digital worlds? How can we respect our differences while also striving for unity? How can we engage with the unknown—other people, ideas, and cultures—in a meaningful, authentic, and lasting way? Media, as a tool for connection, often inhibits our self-awareness and motivates us to project our insecurities outward rather than introspect. To build unity in an age of digital divergence, we must curb our dependence on filtered experiences and instead immerse ourselves in direct, unmediated encounters with the world around us.

With the creation of music videos, the connection between music and fashion has become more significant than ever. Music videos not only capture the cultural essence of the time they were created but also reflect the prevailing fashion trends. The rise of social media has amplified this impact, granting artists an unprecedented reach and making their fashion choices more accessible to a global audience.

Popular Culture: Shades and Shadows

The influence of global fashion is particularly evident in India, where major brands like Prada, Zara, and Louis Vuitton have established strong presences, influencing local designers. A notable example of India's growing integration into global pop culture was the recent Dior event in Mumbai, which showcased international fashion and celebrated India's increasing influence in the luxury sector. Similarly, global music festivals like Lollapalooza have made a significant impact, highlighting how India's music scene is evolving beyond traditional Bollywood. As the popularity of international genres grows, India's Hip Hop, Pop, and Indie scenes have gained momentum, fueled by an audience eager to explore new musical boundaries.

Social media has also provided a platform for sharing and celebrating food and drink. Platforms like *Delhi Diaries* and *Zaike ka Safar* have popularized food culture in India, with countless blogs, articles, and videos dedicated to culinary trends. This obsession with food and drink has even led to entire TV shows and magazines focused on media, people can connect with others who share their passion for food, while also gaining the subject through social access to new trends and products. Food and drink in popular culture are now tools for advertising, demographic targeting, and identity creation. For instance, food can symbolize wealth and status, with its portrayal in films, TV shows, and other media shaping our perceptions. If characters are frequently depicted eating unhealthy foods, viewers may come to see such behaviors as normal or desirable. Similarly, if characters engage in risky behaviors like excessive drinking, audiences may begin to accept these actions as part of everyday life.

Ferdinand Saussure, a foundational figure in linguistics, introduced the concept of the 'sign,' which is composed of two parts: the signifier and the signified. The signifier refers to the physical form of a word or symbol—the sound or image we perceive. For example, the word "coffee" is the signifier, the combination of letters or sounds we encounter. The key idea is that the signifier has no inherent meaning by itself. The signified, on the other hand, is the mental concept or the idea associated with that word. When we hear or see the word "coffee," we conjure an image of coffee in our minds. The signified is abstract and varies from person to person, influenced by individual experiences and context. Together, the signifier and the signified form a sign, the fundamental unit of meaning in language. According to Saussure, the relationship between the signifier and the signified is stable, grounded in a social agreement about the meaning of words (Saussure).

Coffee, as a symbol, has been featured prominently in popular culture. Coffee houses have become iconic social spaces, often depicted as gathering spots for friends, intellectuals, and creatives. Numerous films and TV shows, such as *The Breakfast Club*, *Seinfeld*, and *Koffee with Karan*, highlight characters discussing their lives over coffee. Similarly, pizza has transcended cultural boundaries and genres in popular media. The portrayal of pizza in shows like *Friends*, *The Simpsons*, and *Spider-Man: The Animated Series* emphasizes its connection to comfort, socialization, and shared experiences. Pizza is more than just food; it has become a symbol of connection, creativity, and community, reflecting its integral role in our collective social life.

Social media has become a powerful platform where visual and social cues, coupled with the food choices of those around us, influence individual decisions about what to eat. People are increasingly influenced by what their favorite celebrities post, often gravitating toward the diets of public figures who embrace vegetarianism, veganism, or plant-based eating. Foods that are visually appealing are often perceived as healthier and lower in calories compared to their less aesthetically pleasing counterparts. This visual appeal not only shapes how we judge the healthiness of food but also how we connect with food on a deeper emotional level. In some cases, individuals have overcome eating disorders by finding inspiration and support on platforms like Instagram.

Pop culture's impact on food choices is neither a recent phenomenon nor one that is fading. Food continues to be a central element in various aspects of popular culture, from movies and songs to everyday conversations. Mentioning iconic foods, such as *batata vada*, *bhel puri*, *Cadbury*, *dosa*, and *Coca-Cola*, further solidifies the link between food and culture. However, the responsibility ultimately lies with us to distinguish between healthy and unhealthy choices, authentic recommendations and product placements. By doing so, we can curate a healthier social media feed that fosters better choices and promotes well-being.

In today's rapidly evolving global landscape, popular culture serves as a dynamic force that shapes identities, behaviors, and societal norms. From fashion and food to music and media, pop culture offers both a mirror and a mold for our values, aspirations, and realities. The role of social media in amplifying these influences cannot be overstated, as it has democratized access to global trends while allowing individuals to curate their own cultural narratives. India's growing impact on global pop culture, fueled by technological advances and cross-cultural exchanges, underscores the country's potential to shape the future of entertainment, fashion, and social discourse on a global scale. By blending international trends with local expressions, India has created a unique space within the global pop culture landscape.

However, the power of popular culture comes with a dual-edge. While it promotes innovation and self-expression, it also contributes to the commercialization of culture, creating pressures to conform and fostering the attention economy. Understanding this complexity allows individuals to critically engage with media, fashion, and food culture, enabling them to make more informed choices and navigate the pervasive influence of pop culture in a balanced way.

As we look ahead, the future of popular culture seems intertwined with technological advancements, especially in the realms of virtual reality, artificial intelligence, and immersive media experiences. These technologies will likely continue to shape the way pop culture is consumed, offering new forms of interaction, creativity, and cultural exchange. Social media platforms, with their evolving algorithms and capabilities, will play a central role in these developments, further transforming the way global and local cultures merge and influence one another.

Moreover, the increasing emphasis on sustainability and inclusivity within global pop culture suggests that future trends will prioritize ethical production, diversity, and environmental responsibility. As the younger generation, particularly Gen Z, gains more influence, we can expect these values to become even more pronounced in the cultural products they create, consume, and advocate for. The fusion of technology, sustainability, and inclusivity will likely define the trajectory of pop culture, making it more reflective of a global society that is more connected, diverse, and socially conscious.

In this evolving landscape, India will continue to be an important player, both in terms of consumption and production of cultural content. As India's digital media landscape grows, we may see new forms of storytelling, innovative music genres, and fashion movements emerging from this rich cultural intersection. The future of global pop culture will be increasingly collaborative, inclusive, and dynamic, with individuals, communities, and nations influencing and reshaping its course.

References:

"American Popular Culture and Globalization."*Los Angeles Times*, highschool.latimes.com/arts-andentertainment/americanpopularcultureandglobalization/#:~:text=American%20Movies%2C%20music%2C%20and%20television,obsered%20anywher%20in%20the%20world.

"Are Young People of a Society More Influenced by Pop Culture?" *Times of India*, timesofindia.indiatimes.com/readersblog/areyoung-people-of-a-society-more-influenced-by-pop-culture-50519/.

"Decoding the Pop in Popcorn: Popular Culture and Its Influence on How We Eat." *MonkPrayogshala*, monkprayogshala.in/blog/2024/2/26/decoding-the-pop-in-popcorn-popularculture-and-itsinfluence-on-how-we-eat.

"Globalization and Popular Culture." *International Journal of Cultural Studies*, vol. 14, no. 3, 2011, pp. 335-353. DOI:10.1177/1367877911406167

"How Global Pop Culture Has Influenced India: Evolution in Entertainment." *Your Story*, yourstory.com/ys-life/how-global-pop-culture-has-influenced-india-evolution-in-entertainment.

"Pizza in Pop Culture: 5 Iconic Pizza Moments in Films and TV." *Rosey Pizza*, roseypizza.com /insights/ pizza-in-pop-culture-5-iconic-pizza-moments-in-films-and-tv#:~:text=Pizza%20occupies%20a%20unique%20spot,that%20transcends%20mere%20food%20preference.

"Pop Culture's Influence on the Global Youth Market." *The Conversation*, 4 May 2023, theconversation.com/pop-cultures-influence-on-the-global-youth-market-168195.

"Popular Culture: Definition and Meaning." *ThoughtCo*, thoughtco.com/popular-culture-definition3026453#:~:text=In%20the%20modern%20West%2C%20pop,majority%20of%20a%20society's%20population.

Popular Culture: Shades and Shadows

"The Role Played by Food and Drink in Popular Culture." *That's Pop Culture*, thatspopculture.com/the-role-played-by-food-and-drink-in-popular-culture#:~:text=From%20the%20earliest%20days%20of,create%20a%20sense%20of%20id entity.

"YouTube Video: ZpjWioF6iMosi=z5GzOHZq_19yPX49." *YouTube*, youtube.com/watch?v= Z pjWio F6i Mosi =z5GzOHZq_19yPX49.

Bourdieu, Pierre. *Distinction: A Social Critique of the Judgement of Taste*. Harvard University Press, 1984.

Derrida, Jacques. "The Sign, Signifier, and Signified." *Philosophy Institute*, philosophy.institute/research-methodology/derrida-language-sign-signifier-signified/.

Gans, Herbert J. *Popular Culture and High Culture: An Analysis and Evaluation of Taste*. Basic Books, 1999.

Lury, Celia. *Branding: A Very Short Introduction*. Oxford University Press, 2011.

McRobbie, Angela, editor. *Postmodernism and Popular Culture*. Routledge, 1994.

Miller, Toby, et al. *A Companion to Media Studies*. Wiley-Blackwell, 2008.

Saussure, Ferdinand de. *Course in General Linguistics*. Edited by Charles Bally and Albert Sechehaye, translated by Wade Baskin, McGraw-Hill, 1959.

Storey, John. *Cultural Theory and Popular Culture*. 8th ed., Routledge, 2019.

Chapter-4
Reel to Real: The Cinematic Construction of Political Culture in India

Dr. Deepshikha Parashar

Abstract

This study explores how Indian cinema, particularly mainstream films, has contributed to the construction of political culture. By examining the portrayal of political figures, state institutions, and social movements, the research analyzes how cinema mirrors political narratives. The paper investigates both historical and contemporary films, highlighting their role in constructing cultural legitimacy and influencing mass perceptions of leadership, nationalism, social justice, and dissent. The cinematic medium serves not only as entertainment but as a potent tool for political communication and ideological dissemination in the Indian context.

Keywords: Indian cinema, nation building, social awareness, Political Culture

Introduction

The intersection of cinema and politics in India presents a compelling area of study, particularly in the way films shape and reflect the political consciousness of the masses. Indian cinema, especially mainstream Bollywood and regional films, has historically served not only as a medium of entertainment but also as a powerful cultural and political instrument (Gokulsing&Dissanayake, 2013). This research paper explores the transformative role of cinema in influencing political awareness, attitudes, and participation, a journey from "reel" portrayals to "real" political impact.

At the heart of this inquiry lies the concept of political culture, which refers to the collective attitudes, beliefs, and values that individuals hold towards political institutions, processes, and their own role within the political system (Almond &Verba, 1963).

In the Indian context, cinema has also emerged as a potent agent of political socialization. Films have the unique ability to present complex political realities in accessible narratives, thereby informing and influencing public opinion, political ideologies, and social movements (Rajadhyaksha, 2009). From highlighting issues of corruption, inequality, and governance to portraying revolutionary ideas and leaders, Indian cinema contributes actively to the formation and evolution of political culture. This paper seeks to analyze how cinematic representations contribute to political consciousness, thereby shaping the broader political culture in India.

Theoretical Lens

To understand the influence of Indian cinema on political consciousness, applying theoretical frameworks from political communication, cultural studies, and media theory provides a nuanced lens. Notably, Antonio Gramsci's concept of *cultural hegemony* and Benedict Anderson's idea of *imagined communities* offer foundational insights into how cinema operates as a political and cultural apparatus.

- **Gramsci's Hegemony and Indian Cinema**

Gramsci's theory of cultural hegemony argues that dominant ideologies are maintained not just through coercive state mechanisms but also through consent manufactured by cultural institutions (Gramsci, 1971). Indian cinema, particularly Bollywood, functions as a cultural apparatus that often reproduces dominant ideologies by embedding them in narratives, character arcs, and aesthetic choices. For example, films that glorify the state or promote a homogenized idea of nationalism contribute to the normalization of state-centric discourses, subtly shaping the political attitudes of viewers (Vasudevan, 2010).

Cinema's repeated portrayal of gender norms, caste hierarchies, and national identity can serve hegemonic functions by appearing "natural" or "entertaining," thereby reducing critical resistance. However, films can also challenge hegemonic structures — as seen in parallel cinema or politically charged films like *Haider* or *Article 15* offering counter-narratives that question mainstream political ideologies (Chakravarty, 1993).

- **Benedict Anderson's Imagined Communities**

Benedict Anderson's concept of "imagined communities" (1983) is pivotal in understanding how Indian cinema helps forge a collective national identity. According to Anderson, nations are socially constructed through shared symbols, language, and media. Cinema, with its mass appeal and narrative power, acts as a tool to "imagine" the Indian nation. Through emotionally resonant stories and symbolic representations (e.g., the tricolor, military heroes, rural-urban archetypes), films construct and reinforce the notion of a unified Indian identity, often glossing over regional, linguistic, and religious diversities (Rajadhyaksha, 2009).

This theoretical approach explains why cinema becomes particularly powerful in a multilingual, multiethnic country like India, where direct political communication might be fragmented. Film transcends these boundaries, forging a cohesive political consciousness among viewers.

- **Political Communication and Media Theory**

From the standpoint of political communication, cinema serves both as a direct and indirect mode of ideological dissemination. Unlike traditional news media, films engage audiences emotionally, making political messaging more palatable and impactful (McNair, 2011). Political leaders and parties in India have recognized this and frequently use cinema or cinematic techniques in campaign strategies. The rise of film stars as political figures— such as M.G. Ramachandran, N.T. Rama Rao, and more recently,

PawanKalyanexemplifies the convergence of cinematic charisma and political capital (Pandian, 1992).

Media theorists also suggest that audiences are not passive recipients but active interpreters of media texts (Hall, 1980). Thus, the political impact of cinema depends not only on content but also on audience reception, context, and interpretive frameworks. The encoding/decoding model allows scholars to analyze how different viewers might align with, negotiate, or resist the political meanings encoded in a film.

Methodology

The present study conducted is qualitative in nature. The source of data is secondary extracted from books, journals and newspapers. Moreover, the study has tried to analyse various Bollywood movies in trying to understand their influence on Political Culture.

Conceptualizing Political Culture

Political culture refers to the set of attitudes, beliefs, and sentiments that shape the behavior of citizens and their perceptions of the political system. It constitutes the psychological and emotional orientation of citizens toward the polity and significantly influences their political behavior.

The significance of political culture lies in its ability to influence how people perceive political authority, engage in political processes, and interpret the responsibilities of citizenship. It acts as both a mirror and a mold reflecting historical experiences and societal values while simultaneously guiding future political developments (Lane, 1992). Almond and Verba (1963) categorized political culture into three types:

- **Parochial Culture**: Citizens are mostly unaware or indifferent toward politics. They have little or no awareness of the political system and limited expectations from it.

- **Subject Culture**: Citizens are aware of the political system and its institutions but play a passive role, with little direct participation.
- **Participant Culture**: Citizens are actively involved in the political process, including voting, campaigning, and expressing political opinions.

These cultures can exist separately or in combination. A **civic culture**, as per Almond and Verba, is a balanced mix of all three, ideal for stable democracies.

Indian Political Culture

In democratic societies, political culture plays a vital role in shaping civic engagement, determining the legitimacy of governance, and fostering political stability (Pye&Verba, 1965). India's political culture is characterized by diversity, dynamism, and a strong presence of charismatic leadership. The diversity stems from caste, religion, region, and language, all of which influence political behavior.Despite formal democratic institutions, personality-driven politics is common, where leaders like Jawaharlal Nehru, Indira Gandhi, and Narendra Modi have shaped political discourse through personal appeal and mass media strategies.

Reel to Real: Indian Cinema's Influence on Political Consciousness

Indian cinema, since its inception, has played a significant role in not just entertainment but also in shaping political attitudes and public consciousness. Through narratives on nationhood, social justice, dissent, political iconography, and electoral engagement, cinema has influenced how citizens perceive and participate in politics. From promoting national unity to challenging injustice and mobilizing voters, Indian cinema serves as a vital force in shaping political consciousness. It is not merely a reflection of society but also a catalyst for political engagement, creating an informed and aware citizenry. Films act as agents of political socialization, transmitting political values, ideologies, and expectations to the public. Indian cinema, especially popular Bollywood and regional films, often reflects socio-political themes, inequality, corruption critique and commendation of governance.

1. Nation-Building and National Integration

Nation-building in post-independence India was a formidable challenge, marked by the trauma of Partition, communal violence, and widespread economic underdevelopment. Amidst this turmoil, cinema emerged as a powerful tool in shaping national identity and fostering unity. Films such as *Mother India* (1957) portrayed the ideal Indian citizen as resilient, self-sacrificing, and deeply patriotic, aligning personal struggles with the larger national narrative (Vasudevan, 2011). The iconic works of veteran actor Manoj Kumar including *Upkar*(1967), set against the backdrop of the 1965 war, as well as *Kranti* (1981) and *PurabAurPaschim*(1970)promoted themes of patriotism, national unity, social responsibility and also juxtaposed Indian values with western lifestyles and reinforced superiority of Indian moral traditions.

Films like *1942: A Love Story* (1994) brought the Quit India Movement to life, highlighting the sacrifices made by freedom fighters, while *Rang De Basanti* (2006) inspired the youth to confront corruption, embrace civic responsibility, and actively participate in democracy (Gokulsing & Dissanayake, 2009). Similarly, movies such as *Chittagong* (2012), *Viceroy's House* (2017), *Lagaan*(2001), and *Kesari* (2019) vividly depicted pivotal moments from the freedom struggle, instilling a sense of pride and historical consciousness.

War films, sports dramas, and biopics have also played a crucial role in evoking nationalistic sentiments. Films like *Uri: The Surgical Strike (2019)*, *Chak De! India (2007)*, *The Legend of Bhagat Singh (2002)*, and the *Chhava* (2025) have stirred patriotic emotions and reinforced a collective national identity. Through these narratives, cinema has significantly contributed to post-independence nation-building by promoting shared cultural values, unity, and a spirit of patriotism.

2. Social Justice and Class Consciousness

After achieving independence, India continued to grapple with deep-rooted issues such as caste and class struggles, religious violence, poverty, and inequality. In response to the escapist tendencies of mainstream cinema, the 1970s and 1980s saw the rise of parallel cinema—a movement that critically engaged with social realities, including class conflict, caste oppression, and rural injustice (Rajadhyaksha&Willemen, 1999). ShyamBenegal's*Manthan* (1976) depicted the transformative White Revolution, highlighting the role of dairy cooperatives in liberating villagers from exploitative middlemen. *Bandit Queen* (1994), based on the life of Phoolan Devi, portrayed the brutal realities of caste-based violence, abuse, and oppression that shaped her rise as a feared bandit.

Director Prakash Jha's*Satyagraha* (2013) and *Aarakshan* (2011) tackled contemporary socio-political issues such as corruption and the contentious debate around caste-based reservations. Regional cinema has also played a vital role in addressing social inequalities. The movie *Article 15* (2019) directly confronts casteism and structural inequality. The Marathi film *Fandry* (2013) presents caste discrimination through the perspective of a Dalit boy in rural Maharashtra. Kannada film *NaanuAvanalla. Avalu* (2015) highlights the struggles of the transgender community, while Tamil film *PariyerumPerumal* (2018) focuses on the resistance against caste-based oppression and the pursuit of social justice.

3. Political Movements and Dissent

Indian cinema has often been a mirror of political turmoil. The 1970s marked the advent of parallel cinema, driven by filmmakers like Satyajit Ray and ShyamBenegal. They offred a critique of societal inequalities and raised issues like poverty, corruption and communalism.

During the period of national emergency, the movie *Sholay's*(1975) climax was changed in the interest of the rule of law as depicting the former police officer as vigilante would be dangerous at the time of emergency. The movie *Aandhi*(1975) was banned as it was believed that it is based on the Indira Gandhi's life and her relationship with her estranged husband. *KissaKursiKa*(1978) was also a political satire was also banned. The film *Nasbandi* (1978) is a political spoof which portrayed excesses of emergency

Films like *HazaaronKhwaisheinAisi* (2003) reflect the disillusionment with post-Emergency politics. The movie acknowledges the the co – dependence of politics and social change and deals with political struggle and caste dynamics. WhileFiraaq (2008) is a tale of deep wounds left by Gujrat riots. *Haider* (2014). Political satire in films like *Peepli Live* (2010) and *Newton* (2017) challenges governance failures and electoral manipulation, contributing to a growing cinematic culture of dissent (Kumar, 2018).

4. Creation of Political Icons and Celebrities

Several actors of Indian Cinema have made the leap from the silver screen to political arena, **blurring** the boundaries between on-screen heroism and real-life politics. Recently actor Vijay has announced the launch of his political party and make his electoral debut in 2026. The political journey of veteran actor Kamal Haasan has been marked by his commitment to social justice and reforms. The stars like M.G. Ramachandran and Jayalalithaa used their cinematic image to cultivate mass political appeal (Pandian, 1992). Their films often reinforced populist narratives and constructed personalities that transcended the scene to dominate the political sphere. This phenomenon reflects cinema's power to manufacture political legitimacy

(Srinivas, 2009).
5. Catalyst for Social Awareness

Indian cinema has increasingly emerged as a powerful platform for addressing deep-rooted social issues, serving both as a mirror to society and a catalyst for reform. Films such as *Pad Man* (2018), directed by R. Balki and inspired by the real-life story of ArunachalamMuruganantham, bring to light critical yet often neglected topics like menstrual hygiene and women's health, challenging long-standing taboos. Similarly, *Chhapaak* (2019) narrates the harrowing journey of an acid attack survivor, shedding light on the trauma faced by victims and the systemic changes needed for their justice and rehabilitation.

Toilet: EkPrem Katha (2017) addresses the issue of sanitation through the lens of the Swachh Bharat Abhiyan, advocating for the construction of toilets and promoting dignity and safety for women, especially in rural India. Meanwhile, *TaareZameen Par* (2007) sensitively portrays the struggles of a young boy with dyslexia, raising awareness about learning disabilities and the need for inclusive education.

These films go beyond mere entertainment; they educate, inspire, and provoke meaningful discourse. By influencing public opinion and shaping political narratives, such cinema contributes to the evolution of political culture. It often spurs policy attention, stimulates public debate, and inspires grassroots movements. Reaching vast and diverse audiences, Indian cinema proves to be a potent tool for social change and political engagement.

Historical Overview of Politics in Indian Cinema

- **1950s–1970s: Nation-Building Themes and Nehruvian Socialism**

The early decades following India's independence saw cinema becoming a tool for promoting national unity and socio-economic development, mirroring the aspirations of a newly sovereign nation. Influenced heavily by Nehruvian socialism, films from this era often highlighted rural development, industrialization, and social justice. Directors like Mehboob Khan, in *Mother India* (1957), projected the ideal Indian woman and the agrarian struggles within a nationalist framework. Similarly, films such as *Do BighaZamin* (1953) by Bimal Roycritiqued economic disparity while aligning with Nehru's vision of a socialist state (Chatterjee, 2011).

Cinema served as a cultural force that attempted to construct a national identity. This era also saw the rise of parallel cinema, with filmmakers like Mrinal Senand ShyamBenegalproducing films that addressed caste, poverty, and the failures of governance, fostering political consciousness among urban intellectual audiences (Gokulsing&Dissanayake, 2004).

- **1980s–1990s: Rise of the Angry Young Man, Corruption, and Disillusionment**

The post-Emergency period witnessed a significant shift in the political tone of Indian cinema. With the disillusionment stemming from political corruption and growing unemployment, the "angry young man" archetype, personified by Amitabh Bachchan, became central. Films like *Zanjeer* (1973), *Deewar* (1975), and *Coolie* (1983) depicted protagonists fighting against systemic injustice and corrupt institutions (Mazumdar, 2007).

This cinematic trend resonated with the frustrations of the Indian middle class, reflecting the socio-political instability of the time. The 1980s and 90s also marked the decline of the Nehruvian consensus and the rise of identity politics and regionalism, themes that began to emerge more explicitly in films such as *Roja* (1992) and *Bombay* (1995) by Mani Ratnam, which dealt with insurgency, nationalism, and communal tensions (Vasudevan, 2010).

Popular Culture: Shades and Shadows

- **2000s Onward: Globalization, Identity Politics, Biopics, and Political Thrillers**

With the onset of economic liberalization in the 1990s and globalization in the 2000s, Indian cinema began to reflect a more cosmopolitan yet fragmented political discourse. Issues such as religious fundamentalism, terrorism, and national security became dominant themes. Films like *Rang De Basanti* (2006) questioned state accountability and youth apathy, sparking real-life protests, such as those surrounding the Jessica Lal murder case (Thomas, 2013).

Since 2014, Indian cinema has witnessed a significant surge in genres such as political biopics, sports dramas, historical epics, war films, and socially-driven narratives. Patriotic films like *Uri: The Surgical Strike* (2019) and *Shershaah* (2021) have stirred nationalistic fervor and shaped public perception of military valor and national security. Historical dramas such as *Manikarnika: The Queen of Jhansi* (2019), *Chhava* (upcoming), and *SamratPrithviraj* (2022) not only revive India's rich past but also reinforce cultural pride and identity.

Political biopics like *PM Narendra Modi* (2019) and *The Accidental Prime Minister* (2019) have blurred the lines between cinematic storytelling and political commentary, influencing viewers' understanding of leadership and governance (Punathambekar, 2015). Similarly, sports films like *Dangal* (2016), *MS Dhoni: The Untold Story* (2016), and *83* (2021) celebrate national heroes and promote narratives of perseverance, discipline, and collective pride.

Cinema has thus emerged as a powerful medium to shape public opinion, elevate political discourse, and foster a sense of collective consciousness. Through compelling storytelling, evocative imagery, and emotionally resonant themes, films often become catalysts for social and political awakening, impacting how audiences engage with issues of identity, patriotism, and historical memory.

Themes and Patterns

- **Idealism vs. Realpolitik**

This dichotomy is frequently depicted in Indian cinema, where characters are torn between idealistic visions of justice and the harsh pragmatism of political reality. For instance, *Sarkar*(2005) presents a Godfather-like figure who dispenses justice outside institutional mechanisms, challenging democratic idealism. Films like *Yuva* (2004) and *Rang De Basanti* (2006) showcase youth embracing politics with a sense of idealism, only to confront systemic corruption, leading to radical transformations (Kumar, 2013).

- **Corruption and Governance**

Corruption remains a dominant theme in Indian political cinema. Films like *Nayak: The Real Hero* (2001) and *Satyagraha* (2013) portray the inefficiency and moral bankruptcy of political leaders and institutions. These narratives often resonate with the public's disillusionment, serving both as critique and catharsis (Rajadhyaksha, 2009). The depiction of bureaucratic apathy and political manipulation reflects real-world frustrations and can influence voter behavior and political engagement.

- **Political Violence and Caste/Communalism**

Several films have tackled the grim reality of political violence rooted in caste and communal tensions. *Ankur* (1974) and *Aarakshan* (2011) delve into caste-based oppression and reservation politics, while *Haider* (2014) and *Parzania* (2005) address communal violence and insurgency. These films attempt to unravel the complexities of identity, marginalization, and state complicity, contributing to political discourse and awareness (Chakravarty, 1993).

- **Biopics and Cult of Personality**

Recent years have witnessed a surge in political biopics, contributing to the glorification of political figures. Films like *Thackeray* (2019), *PM Narendra Modi* (2019), and *Indu Sarkar* (2017) blur the line between cinema and propaganda, often released strategically around elections. These portrayals build a "cult of personality," shaping public perception through cinematic narrative and visual spectacle (Ghosh, 2020). Critics argue these films can reinforce political biases and sanitize controversial histories.

- **Youth and Political Awakening**

Films like *Rang De Basanti*(2006) and *Yuva*(2004) present youth as agents of political transformation. In *Rang De Basanti*, historical consciousness awakens political activism against state injustice, linking past sacrifices with present responsibilities. *Yuva* depicts youth entering the political sphere to challenge the status quo, suggesting cinema's potential to inspire civic engagement among younger demographics (Mazumdar, 2007).

- **Influence on Political Culture**

Indian cinema has long served as more than just entertainment; it has been a potent medium in shaping the country's political culture. From mythologizing political leaders to functioning as a platform for dissent, the Indian film industry especially regional cinema, has had a profound influence on the political consciousness of its audience.

- **Cultivation of Political Icons and Mythology**

Cinema has played a pivotal role in constructing the larger-than-life images of political figures, often blurring the lines between reel and real personas. Actors like M.G. Ramachandran (MGR) and N.T. Rama Rao (NTR) began their careers by portraying heroic, god-like characters on screen, which cultivated a mass following that translated into political capital. Their cinematic representations often drew from mythological or moral narratives, creating a quasi-divine aura that resonated deeply with the masses (Hardgrave, 1973; Pandian, 1992). The cinematic portrayal of such figures contributed to a political mythology that endowed them with near-sacrosanct status in public life.

- **Mobilization of Political Support**

The seamless transition of actors into political leaders in India underscores cinema's unique ability to mobilize public sentiment. Figures like MGR, NTR, and Jayalalithaa leveraged their cinematic fame to build strong emotional connections with voters, transforming fan clubs into political cadres (Dickey, 1993). Their films often embedded messages of social justice, anti-corruption, and regional pride, which were later carried into their political manifestos. These celebrities used their screen identities as a political tool to project themselves as protectors of the common man, thereby fostering mass mobilization.

- **Cinema as Protest or Resistance**

Beyond its instrumental use in electoral politics, Indian cinema has also functioned as a medium of resistance. Films like *Haider* (2014), *Court* (2014), and *Fandry* (2013) confront issues such as state violence, judicial apathy, and caste discrimination. *Haider*, for instance, critiques the Indian state's role in Kashmir through a Shakespearean lens, pushing boundaries of mainstream political discourse (Vasudevan, 2016). Similarly, *Court* exposes systemic injustices in the legal system, and *Fandry* offers a raw portrayal of caste-based oppression in rural Maharashtra. These films challenge dominant narratives and cultivate critical political awareness among viewers.

- **Shaping Attitudes Toward Democracy, Justice, and Nationalism**

Cinema has the power to shape popular attitudes toward democracy, justice, and nationalism by embedding political values within cultural narratives. Films such as *Rang De Basanti* (2006) and *Chak De! India* (2007) promote civic engagement and national pride, reflecting and reinforcing democratic ideals and collective identity (Gokulsing & Dissanayake, 2004). These narratives often appeal to youth and urban audiences, fostering a politically aware citizenry that questions authority and celebrates diversity.

Critiques and Limitations of Indian Cinema's Influence on Political Consciousness

While Indian cinema has undeniably played a significant role in shaping political consciousness, several **critiques and limitations** temper its effectiveness and authenticity as a political medium.

1. Romanticizing or Oversimplifying Politics

One of the primary criticisms is that mainstream Indian cinema often romanticizes or oversimplifies complex political realities. Filmmakers tend to present a binary narrative of goodversus evil, which reduces nuanced political issues into overly simplistic moral dilemmas (Ghosh, 2010). For instance, movies like *Nayak* (2001) and *Sarkar* (2005) depict a lone righteous hero fighting a corrupt political system, which can distort the multifaceted nature of political processes.

Such portrayals may lead to misinformed audiences, who may start to view politics through a lens of individual heroism rather than collective action and institutional dynamics (Mehta, 2012). As a result, this oversimplification contributes more to emotional gratification than to critical political engagement.

2. Propaganda Potential

Indian cinema has also served as a vehicle for political propaganda, especially during election seasons or times of political unrest. Films funded or supported by political parties often promote nationalist, populist, or ideological agendas, subtly influencing voter perceptions (Vasudevan, 2011). For instance, certain films have been released close to elections that glorify specific leaders or parties, blurring the line between entertainment and political marketing.

This manipulative potential undermines democratic

discourse and can polarize public opinion based on emotionally charged and dramatized portrayals rather than factual debate (Rajadhyaksha, 2009).

3. Limited Space for Alternative or Marginalized Voices

Mainstream Indian cinema has historically marginalized subaltern, Dalit, tribal, LGBTQ+, andminority perspectives. Even when such themes are addressed, they are often filtered through a dominant caste, class, or genderlens, leading to partial or stereotyped representation (Gopal, 2011). The control of production houses by elite groups further reinforces the underrepresentation of alternative political viewpoints.

Although independent and regional cinema has begun to challenge this trend, their limited reachand funding constraints restrict their impact on the broader political consciousness (Sarkar, 2020). Consequently, Indian cinema often reflects the concerns of the dominant classes while muting dissenting voices or radical alternatives.

Conclusion

Indian cinema, as both a cultural mirror and a political instrument, occupies a unique space in shaping and reflecting political consciousness. From early post-independence films that echoed nationalist sentiments to contemporary works that critique governance and mobilize public opinion, Indian cinema continues to influence how politics is perceived and performed in the public sphere. The medium transcends mere entertainment, engaging audiences in political discourse through symbolism, storytelling, and character arcs that resonate with real socio-political contexts.

At the same time, cinema does not just passively reflect political culture—it actively constructs it. The portrayal of political leaders, communal tensions, corruption, and civic activism often informs audience understanding and even voting behavior (Pendakur, 2003). Films like *Rang De Basanti* (2006) or *Article 15* (2019) have demonstrated the power of cinematic narratives in fostering political awareness and civic engagement among youth (Virdi, 2020). Thus, the reel becomes a potent force in the shaping of the real.

In the era of media convergence, where cinema merges with digital platforms and social media, the influence of filmic narratives multiplies. With the increasing accessibility of content, there is a pressing need for filmmakers to adopt a more responsible approach. Misrepresentation, sensetionalism, or the glorification of regressive ideologies can reinforce harmful stereotypes and polarize public opinion (Rajadhyaksha, 2009). Therefore, the onus lies on content creators to be mindful of their narrative choices and the political culture they propagate.

To ensure cinema continues to act as a progressive force in society, there must be greater accountability, media literacy, and critical engagement with film as a sociopolitical text. As Indian cinema moves from reel to real, its role in shaping democratic consciousness becomes not only evident but essential.

References:
Almond, Gabriel A., and Sidney Verba. *The Civic Culture: Political Attitudes and Democracy in Five Nations*. Princeton UP, 1963.
Anderson, Benedict. *Imagined Communities: Reflections on the Origin and Spread of Nationalism*. Verso, 1983.
Chakravarty, Sumita S. *National Identity in Indian Popular Cinema, 1947–1987*. U of Texas P, 1993.
Chatterjee, Shoma. *Cinema and the Indian Freedom Struggle: Covering the Movement through the Lens*. Harper Collins, 2011.
Dickey, Sara. *Cinema and the Urban Poor in South India*.

Cambridge UP, 1993.

Ghosh, Abhijit. "Political Cinema in the Age of Modi: Biopics and the Rewriting of History." *Economic and Political Weekly*, vol. 55, no. 15, 2020, pp. 43–48.

Ghosh, Abhijit. *Cinema and Politics in India: A Study in Popular Narratives*. Oxford UP, 2010.

Gokulsing, K. Moti, and Wimal Dissanayake. *Indian Popular Cinema: A Narrative of Cultural Change*. 2nd ed., Trentham Books, 2004.

Gopal, Priyamvada. *Conjugations: Marriage and Form in New Bollywood Cinema*. U of Chicago P, 2011.

Gramsci, Antonio. *Selections from the Prison Notebooks*. Edited and translated by Quintin Hoare and Geoffrey Nowell Smith, International Publishers, 1971.

Hall, Stuart. "Encoding/Decoding." *Culture, Media, Language*, edited by Stuart Hall et al., Hutchinson, 1980, pp. 128–38.

Hardgrave, Robert L. "Politics and the Film in Tamil Nadu: The Stars and the DMK." *Asian Survey*, vol. 13, no. 3, 1973, pp. 288–305. https://doi.org/10.2307/2643089

Kumar, S. *Cinema and Society: Film and Social Change in Pakistan*. Oxford UP, 2018.

Kumar, Sanjay. *Cinema, Politics and the Nation: Indian Cinema after Independence*. Routledge, 2013.

Lane, Robert E. "Political Culture: Residual Category or General Theory?" *Comparative Political Studies*, vol. 25, no. 3, 1992, pp. 362–87. https://doi.org/10.1177/0010414092025003004

Mazumdar, Ranjani. *Bombay Cinema: An Archive of the City*. U of Minnesota P, 2007.

McNair, Brian. *An Introduction to Political Communication*. 5th ed., Routledge, 2011.

Mehta, Nalin. *Bollywood and Globalization: Indian Popular Cinema, Nation, and Diaspora*. Anthem Press, 2012.

Pandian, M. S. S. *The Image Trap: M. G. Ramachandran in Film and Politics*. Sage Publications, 1992.

Pendakur, Manjunath. *Indian Popular Cinema: Industry, Ideology, and Consciousness*. Hampton Press, 2003.

Punathambekar, Aswin. *From Bombay to Bollywood: The Making of a Global Media Industry*. NYU Press, 2015.

Pye, Lucian W., and Sidney Verba, editors. *Political Culture and Political Development*. Princeton UP, 1965.

Rajadhyaksha, Ashish. *Indian Cinema in the Time of Celluloid: From Bollywood to the Emergency*. Indiana UP, 2009.

Rajadhyaksha, Ashish. "The 'Bollywoodization' of the Indian Cinema: Cultural Nationalism in a Global Arena." *Bollywood: Popular Indian Cinema through a Transnational Lens*, edited by Rajinder Kaur and Ajay Sinha, SAGE Publications, 2009, pp. 17–40.

Rajadhyaksha, Ashish, and Paul Willemen. *Encyclopaedia of Indian Cinema*. 2nd ed., British Film Institute, 1999.

Sarkar, Bhaskar. *Documentary Filmmaking in India: Ethics, Aesthetics and Politics*. Routledge India, 2020.

Srinivas, S. V. *Megastar: Chiranjeevi and Telugu Cinema after N. T. Rama Rao*. Oxford UP, 2009.

Thomas, Rosie. *Indian Cinema: Pleasures and Popularity*. Open UP, 2013.

Vasudevan, Ravi. *The Melodramatic Public: Film Form and Spectatorship in Indian Cinema*. Palgrave Macmillan, 2010.

Vasudevan, Ravi. *The Melodramatic Public: Film Form and Spectatorship in Indian Cinema*. Palgrave Macmillan, 2016.

Virdi, Jyotika. *The Cinematic Imagination: Indian Popular Films as Social History*. Permanent Black, 2020.

Chapter-5

Unveiling the Meta-Narrative Paradigm: A Critical Exploration of Vijay Tendulkar's *Silence! The Court is in Session*

Mr. L G More

Abstract

Vijay Tendulkar and his prolific writing in generational plays has been appreciated and critiqued worldwide and is influential in inspiring discourses based on feminist, socio-psychological and formalist critical approaches. His plays like *Sakharam Binder, Silence! The Court is in Session, etc.*, have proved to be effective in generating a discussion around themes like abuse, sexual desires, adultery, betrayal, cruelty and the social disparity between individuals and groups. His writing style is masterful as he integrates persuasive storytelling skills in his plays, giving them a more sub-textual narrative rather than a straightforward style. The themes of patriarchal dominance, adultery, abortion and infanticide are also placed in significance in this research as they're used to illustrate Tendulkar's archetypes throughout the play and how he explores these social issues through the lens and personal biases of the audience, a resultant phenomenon of the aforementioned meta-narrative storytelling.

This research aims to unravel meta-narrative storytelling, a postmodern concept utilised as a masterful element of *Silence! The Court is in Session* and builds a conversational discourse around the usage of this technique to provoke audience interaction through a surreal sub-textual narrative around one of his most renowned plays *Silence! The Court is in Session* while delving into other theories that help support the element of meta-narrative, thus exponentially enhancing the play and its themes.

Additionally, the paper aims to bring meta-narrative storytelling into the spotlight, as it allows for fresh perspectives on the same since it showcases the potential to translate into a sub-genre.

Keywords: Meta-Narrative Storytelling, Elements of Suspense, Conceived Truth, Perceived Truth, Metaphysical Connection, Patriarchal Dominance, Dramatic Irony.

Unveiling the Meta-Narrative Storytelling in the play

Tendulkar's *Silence! The Court is in Session* is a magnum opus which exemplifies his writing style and dealing with social issues through his trademark social realism. This play follows a troupe of experimental actors touring around villages and towns, performing plays for money and as a recreational hobby. The protagonist, LeelaBenare, a schoolteacher, is a jolly and happy-go-lucky woman who alludes to a dark past. When the troupe reaches their next destination, with a member absconding, they search for a new person to play the part. While doing so, they stage a mock play involving a courtroom drama, unbeknownst to Miss Benare, involving the allegation of infanticide. Ironically enough, unbeknownst to the troupe actors, Benare's past involved connecting the loose dots of the absconding cast member and infanticide, wherein she had an illegitimate affair with Prof. Damle, the absconder and aborted the child they had accidentally. This complex situation causes Benare to panic, and as the mock drama places her front and centre of the allegations, the lines between truth and lie become hazy, reinforced by the cast members ambiguously alleging real-life scenarios under the guise of a mock drama meant to familiariseSamant (The new cast member) with theatre and acting.

This research involves the complex notions of meta-narrative storytelling to analyse the various facets that make the play effective as a structuralist and formalist device, analysing the archetypes present in this play. Using devices such as dramatic irony, play within a play, breaking the fourth wall, establishing a metaphysical connection with the audience, Alfred Hitchcock's Bomb Theory, the underlying layers of suspense, the notions of conceived and perceived truth, the influence of patriarchal dominance and societal hegemony in the audience as well as the characters in the play to conclude the situations within the play; Tendulkar builds the element of meta-narrative storytelling within *Silence! The Court is in Session* as a literary device to engage the viewers and readers in a brilliant play, which without the usage of meta-narrative storytelling would have just been another social radicalism-laden play for the audience to see.

As observed in research titled "Structural Features and Stylistic Devices in Vijay Tendulkar's *Silence! The Court is in Session and Kamala*" by S. Suma, the stylistic devices utilised by Tendulkar in his plays, especially *Silence! The Court is in Session is*analysedtechnically, but reference to meta-narrative storytelling within similar research is scarce (Suma). Similarly, the mentions of meta-narrative storytelling in an Indian context, especially involving Tendulkar and the titular play in particular, have also seen rare references, with the focus being on Tendulkar's social radicalism and dissecting his plays via a sociological point of discussion, as evident in a research paper titled "Social Reality in Vijay Tendulkar's *Silence! The Court Is In Session*," which "tries to make an attempt to grasp the dramatist's view on the issue of exposing the hollowness of the middle class morality and dual standards of society" (Mandhan 356). Hence, this research goes into detail and aims to create a discourse and a discussion as well as set a formalist guideline of thought for future researchers to delve into the topic of meta-narrative storytelling by utilising these aspects of Tendulkar's play as a benchmark of meta-narrative storytelling.

Popular Culture: Shades and Shadows

The thrust of this research is to unravel meta-narrative storytelling. While there are numerous definitions for this concept, it can be termed as beyond the narrative. In the book, *The Postmodern Condition: A Report on Knowledge*, meta-narrative is debated heavily through the lens of postmodernism, with the author highlighting local narratives and nuances with the story rather than a global one (Lyotard xi). In another work titled *Retelling Stories, Framing Culture: Traditional Story and Metanarratives in Children's Literature*, the authors describe it as "...a global or totalizing cultural narrative schema which orders and explains knowledge and experience" (Stephens and McCallum 06). Simply put, meta-narrative storytelling entails any story, play, or other form of media that goes beyond its narrative and the conventions of narration, and it finds itself in interactions about worldviews, structures and theoretical idiosyncrasies with audiences, readers and critics alike. It utilizes various devices such as a metaphysical entity within the story or a metaphysical connection with the audience. The connections established with the audience through meta-narrative storytelling transcend a traditional piece of work, giving it its distinctive characteristic of being a story within a story.

As evident in *Silence! The Court is in Session*, Tendulkar utilises the element of meta-narrative storytelling by establishing a metaphysical connection with the audience. This connection gets established through the lens of play within a play supplemented by the characters showcasing ambiguity through their actions and the condemnation of the protagonist through a manipulative sense of ambiguity, invoking the audience's reaction like no other. The audience is drawn into the play as a fourth character. Tendulkar not only breaks the fourth wall but also invites the audience to interact with the elements of the play. The following characteristic points come to the fore through interaction:

1. The device, play within a play, utilising a mock trial of real allegations and the reality of which only the audience notices.
2. The line between reality and fiction is blurred as Ms.Benare's past catches up with her through the allegations made but have not yet been revealed.
3. The other cast members mistake Miss Benare's disposition to be a masterfully crafted act instead of perceiving her emotions as authentic.

Dramatic Irony: Dramatic Irony is "a literary device by which the audience's or reader's understanding of events or individuals in a work surpasses that of its characters" ("Dramatic Irony | Definition & Examples"). This interaction is an elaborate understanding of Dramatic Irony, where the characters don't seem to know what the audience knows. However, the factor that transcends it from being dramatic irony to meta-narrative storytelling is the way the audience is deliberately invited to react to Tendulkar's masterful execution of the play. Tendulkar's play will be simply termed a work of dramatic irony if he does not contemplate the execution. The main point of the play in this context is that Tendulkar utilizes the societal backdrop of patriarchal domination and societal hegemony to differentiate the allegations made from fiction to reality. Benare, and by extension, the audience, also feels that attacks are directed towards them instead of the characters being in their world, whereas the attacks are directed solely at the characters. This characterization of the audience as a part of the Grand Narrative, Lyotard explains, is instrumental in creating the element of meta-narrative storytelling.

The notion of dramatic irony is present throughout the play as the audience seems to know more than the characters. The playwright, however, masterfully maintains the ambiguity between the characters and audience by not exactly showcasing which characters are in control of which narrative, how many seem to know the truth and how many are just 'staging a mock play'. The characters of Dr.Ponkshe, BaluRokde, Samant and Karnik are all ambiguous; the audience does not know whether they are feigning innocence or they know Benare's secret. The audience is in a dilemma because they know Benare's secret but are still doubtful whether everyone else knows it. Similarly, Benare also exhibits her full range of emotions, which are real, as inferred by the audience, but are still perceived to be an excellent act put up by Benare in the mock trial by the other cast members. This, as a result, is the strongest example of meta-narrative storytelling, as it enables the audience to connect with and interact with the characters in the play metaphysically.

Play within a Play: One of the most important aspects of this play is its setting. It is set as a mock courtroom drama created for an impromptu cast member to understand the basics of theatre in the absence of an absconding cast member. This results in the device of 'play within a play' creating the most effective form of dramatic irony as the audience is pushed to bridge the gap between the actual play and the play staged within it. This leads to the characters having two very separate dispositions, one relegated to the surface level and the other one about the underlying intentions of the characters. This anomaly is the leading factor of ambiguity. Tendulkar creates the preface of a mock play, which is structurally and symbolically devised against Benare. The mock play is the chief perspective of the other characters. Although the dialogue exceptionally edges the fine line between truth and fiction, the end is seemingly set to ensure the audience that, for the other characters, it was a mock play from the beginning. Ms.Benare seems to show direct indifference towards the mock play simply because the audience understands that her disposition throughout the mock play is effectively genuine. The events that seemingly transpired impromptu by the cast members were the events that led to Benare's inevitable breakdown as a character.

The Bomb Theory: The sudden unearthing of Benare's dark past, her being labelled as an uncouth woman who's committing adultery and the shattering of her image in front of a hapless audience can be attributed to the inclusion of a brilliant concept by Alfred Hitchcock called the Bomb Theory. This concept is integral to understanding the argument about meta-narrative storytelling and is highly influential in the whole suspense around the play. The themes of betrayal, forced assumptions and connecting the dots are all supplements of The Bomb Theory, and this research aims to analyse this topic in detail to explicate its implications. Hitchcock says,

There is a distinct difference between 'suspense' and 'surprise,' and yet many pictures continually confuse the two. I'll explain what I mean. We are now having a very innocent little chat. Let's suppose that there is a bomb underneath this table between us. Nothing happens, and then all of a sudden, "Boom!" There is an explosion. The public is surprised, but prior to this surprise, it has seen an absolutely ordinary scene, of no special consequence. Now, let us take a suspense situation. The bomb is underneath the table and the public knows it, probably because they have seen the anarchist place it there. The public is aware the bomb is going to explode at one o'clock and there is a clock in the decor. The public can see that it is a quarter to one. In these conditions, the same innocuous conversation becomes fascinating because the public is participating in the scene. The audience is longing to warn the characters on the screen: "You shouldn't be talking about such trivial matters. There is a bomb beneath you and it is about to explode!" In the first case we have given the public fifteen seconds of surprise at the moment of the explosion. In the second we have provided them with fifteen minutes of suspense. The conclusion is that whenever possible the public must be informed. Except when the surprise is a twist, that is, when the unexpected ending is, in itself, the highlight of the story."("Quote by Alfred Hitchcock").

In his article, Matt Allegretti maintains, "according to Hitchcock, the second scenario is more captivating because the audience is actively participating in the scene and they dying to warn the characters" (Allegretti). This concept is essential in understanding the core element of suspense, which is anticipation. Suspense is anticipation with time or lack thereof. The more time an anticipation takes to build up, the more intense the payoff can be of the suspense element. The element of suspense depends on not 'if' the situation will escalate; it is about 'when' the situation will escalate. The 'bomb under the table' is also an extended version of dramatic irony itself, however, it is commonly relegated to suspense in plays, films, TV and other forms of media because of Alfred Hitchcock's influence over the media. The differentiating factor is The Bomb theory is applicable in situations about tension and anticipation of a more localised narrative.

Taking this element in the context of *Silence! The Court is in Session,* one understands that the same theory applies to the play entirely. The allusions made by Benare towards a dark past through her sing-song about betrayal and sadness mashed in with jolly songs that she uses to teach little kids is a sign of the ominous anticipation that is to follow. The suspense is brought as per the following:

1. **Background:** Prof. Damle is declared absconding, and the troupe searches for a new member to play the part assigned to him. Samant meets the cast in the village where they were scheduled to perform, and Benare immediately confides in him about her pleas via rhyme and sing-song. While the songs start as jolly and childlike, they take a dark and ominous turn, alluding to a past unknown about Benare. The audience is made to believe the happy-go-lucky

disposition that Benare exhibits is just a facade for a dark past that gets revealed later.

2. **The idea of a Mock Trial:** The background carries itself into a pivotal point of suspense, as the cast members, enthusiastic about Samant joining them, decide to stage a mock trial, which can show Samant how a real trial works in a court. This all happens unbeknownst to Benare, however, and the cast members take it in good spirits, believing that, being the good actor she is, she will catch on to the bit and follow along. However, the topic they chose for the allegation is infanticide, and they deem Benare as the accused. This marks a turning point in the play, as the events that transpire are full of suspense.

3. **The Bomb under the Table:** Benare is placed violently within the accusations, as the characters relentlessly target her for committing a heinous crime. Initially, Benare takes the mock trial in a light-hearted manner and does not exhibit seriousness about it until the accusation is revealed to her. After the cast members accuse Benare of infanticide and adultery, her disposition suddenly turns silent and defenceless, and the panic that ensues allows the audience to connect the dots about Benare's dark past. The audience connects that Benare actually did commit infanticide and did have an illegitimate relationship with Prof. Damle and that the mock trial, at least in Benare's eyes, is an elaborate plan to expose her truth. The audience is shown this 'bomb under the table,' and the anticipation builds up. As the mock play goes on, the audience automatically perceives the allegations as true in light of Benare's disposition and finds themselves at the centre of an important sociological debate between patriarchy and taboos. Benare visibly grows frustrated and defenceless and starts to panic because the 'bomb under the table' for her is the inability to differentiate between reality and fiction, as she fails to understand why the mock play is realistically targeted towards her. The audience is also forced to make assumptions about the entire situation, and a

metaphorical complacency in the plot occurs. The fact that the first dot is connected, i.e., Benare being visibly distressed from the first allegation and Karnik and Ponkshe being suspicious of Benare for a while, leads the audience to autonomously connect the other dots as well, unearthing that the allegations are incidents in the real life of Miss Benare.

Conceived Truth and Perceived Truth: As the play deals with themes of manipulation by some characters, it is important to understand how the audience is involuntarily expected to react to the same. The notions of conceived truth and perceived truth come into play numerous times throughout the performance, particularly when the characters display signs of ambiguity. The allegations levelled against Benare are real from her perspective, but they are chalked up as an elaborate act, a masterful performance, and a thrilling story for the other characters. The crime of infanticide is indeed disgusting and a social evil for the other characters, but in the context of the mock trial, it is just a fake allegation to make the trial sound serious. For LeelaBenare, however, it is an unfortunate reality. The characters remain ambiguous to this fact, only alluding to it once during the play when Ponkshe and Karnik make assumptions about Ms.Benare's illegitimate affair with Prof. Damle. Benare, unaware of the mock trial staged to show Samant the traits of good theatre, is trapped in the dilemma between reality and fiction, and she slowly undergoes a severe breakdown. Tendulkar forces the audience to choose the truths according to their biases, and this is where the entire notion of conceived truth and perceived truth comes into play.

The simplest way to explain conceived truth is by connecting the loose ends through biases formed in different situations as a result of a central understanding of the character's disposition. The audience is left to choose, within the facets of ambiguity, which of the various dispositions they want to place at the center for the consequent biases to influence their conception of the truth. Here are some

examples of how truth can be conceived in the play.
1. The first scenario is, given the situation is taken at face value, the truth is, Benare has actually committed all the acts that the cast members have identified, in the same manner, and in the same circumstances, and the characters getting all the situations right was merely a coincidence on their part. The characters on the other hand are simply unaware of Benare's past, only a hint of suspicion is aroused. But the mock trial is simply a mock trial that the characters take too seriously while in character, but fall out of it when its conducted fully, as a stylistic method acting job.
2. The second scenario can be analysed with Benare's disposition as genuine and connecting the dots, keeping her truth at the epicentre. We can analyse the mock play as an elaborate way of trapping Benare and unearthing her secret to the world, thus condemning her for having committed a heinous crime. This makes the characters aware of the situation at hand, especially the fact that they are not only suspicious but are fully confident about Benare's illegitimate affair and infanticide. This conception means characters stage a mock play to avoid accountability, with their allegations about Benare, manipulating her sense of reality but denying the truth in their intention.
3. The third scenario can be analysed with the cast members at the epicentre. In this, Benare is a suspicious character; however, the mock play is staged only to show Samant the characteristics of a courtroom drama and by extension, electing him as the perfect person to play the part of the missing Prof. Damle. The characters are unaware of the hurt caused to Benare; as a result, the entirety of her breakdown is simply a masterful act she put on to engage in the mock play.

These are but three scenarios out of the many through

which the truth can be conceived. Taking various apparent biases into account and leading to an epicentral discussion has its fallacies as well because the conceived truth is often rigid and does not explain the subtle nuances that emphasise the need to explore the situation in a tamer manner. It is also highly subjective because of factors like writing style, depth in ambiguity, layers to characterisation, and a salient characteristic of unreliable narrators. Tendulkar also blurs the line between truth and conceived truth by venturing perilously close to an interesting phenomenon known as 'The Rashomon Effect,' made popular in the eponymous film by Akira Kurosawa. In this, the presence of unreliable narrators, or different versions of the same story is presented in front of the audience, without anyone but the audience to properly adjudge them to be true, due to lack of any evidence but the witness/narrators' word (Deguzman).

This is where the notion of perceived truth comes into play, as it is not bound by the notions that are explored within the play but rely heavily on audience bias instead. Each audience member can perceive the truth in a biased manner relating to their choices, dispositions, internal biases and their mindsets. This also completes the factor of meta-narrative storytelling within any given piece of work, especially *Silence! The Court is in Session*, as the interpretation of the work in a supposed 'grand narrative' is more important than the narrative itself. This notion is not entirely meant to be a personal interpretation of the play, however, as the perspective of the audience is not imposed upon the play. The subtle nuances between the silent breakdown of Benare to the cast members being relentless with their male gaze and patriarchal ideologies can be instrumental in perceiving the situation differently with a wide range of audiences. This nuance in the audience is also characterised by the longevity of *Silence! The Court is in Session* as a play, performed in front of nearly five decades of people, ideas, mindsets, behavioural traits and ideologies.

Popular Culture: Shades and Shadows

What remains constant is the ideology of truth and ambiguity within the play but the change occurs when a particular type of thinking is introduced that critiques the issues from a different perspective. Abortion, infanticide, illegitimate relationships etc., have a more nuanced position in society now than in the 1970s. This has caused the perception of these conceptual truths to change over the years. This change remains instrumental in orchestrating a different version of the play each time as interpreted by various audiences, as discourses change flow and subject matter as per the perceptions of various social themes change over time.

The influence of patriarchy can be seen inadvertently throughout the play, with the characters being incessant with their allegations about LeelaBenare. Crucially, the very fact that they deem Benare's supposed mistakes as a heinous crime and abhor the fact that Benare committed it. It showcases the imbibed patriarchal mindsets that Tendulkar aims to attack through the play. The characters of Karnik and Ponkshe have been suspicious of Benare about the mock trial being a reality; although they do not showcase an innate drive to prove the suspicion right, the mention of the illegitimate affair is enough for audiences to grasp the mentality of both of the characters.

The male gaze is also predominantly showcased within the play, as the entire staging of the mock play is carried out by the characters unbeknownst to Benare, who becomes the defendant against her knowledge. It causes Benare to be initially unaware of the plan, which leads to a trial completely dominated by the men in the mock court. Even as a woman, Mrs. Kashikar is also susceptible to traditional beliefs about women, and instead of showing empathy, she decides to take a stand against what's wrong according to her own beliefs. Other characters like BaluRokde and Mr. Kashikar are placed in pivotal roles of Male Gaze as well, as the dismissive Mr. Kashikar displays feelings of a traditional patriarchal lawmaking figurehead, while BaluRokde vents out his frustration against Benare by labelling her as uncouth, and vilifying her vehemently, thus being a portrayal of male insecurity within the play.

The whole storyline of the mock play and the tonality of the allegations are set from the tone of a man accusing a woman. The general insensitivity towards Benare's feelings, the remarks made on the issues at hand, and viewing the issue of infanticide as a social evil through and through perfectly encapsulate the cornered feeling Benare gets during the mock play. Moreover, it is observed that the way the characters keep interrupting Benare, they exhibit insecurity that Benare will be able to defend herself soundly. The whole mock play is designed to ensure that the defendant, in this case Ms. Benare loses and accepts that what she did was a heinous crime. This is an excellent example of how the male gaze works. The subtle attacks, the shattering of dispositions, maintaining ambiguity, and brushing off as a rehearsal or a staged play are all aspects that Tendulkar masterfully shows as the process of how the accusations turn out in the end.

Tendulkar brilliantly amalgamates form and subject matter by virtually placing the issues of abortion, infanticide, male dominance, patriarchal insecurity as well as subtle but harsh attacks via the male gaze onto a representation of a woman denied her choices in the form of Ms.Benare front and centre. As it builds a Metanarrative, it forces the audience to relegate their biases to the front, as the perception changes over time. The audience can show the mindsets exhibited throughout the eras, from the 1970s to the modern day, as the subtle nuances are not only instrumental in creating a bias but also encouraging a bias. The victims of patriarchy face inherently unfavourable circumstances that completely shatter their worldview and way of living, and a lack of empathy towards any circumstance leading to the metaphorical guilt of punishment regardless of whether it is a mistake or not is put forth by Tendulkar in the last monologue. Not only is it a brilliant question to the audience, but it also mirrors the reality around us.

Tendulkar even uses the breakage of the fourth wall by Benare in the end, thus imparting a direct connection instead of the metaphysical one apparent until the climax, to create a discourse about the effects the patriarchal manipulation can have on you. In research titled "Patriarchal Domination and Inequal Power Structure in *Silence! The Court Is In the Session*," ArkaPramanick tackles the issue of patriarchal dominance and the oppression of women in detail within the play (Pramanick). The audience not only feels empathetic towards Benare, but they also begin to question the cruel punishment she has been put through in the form of the mock trial. What was a game for the other cast members was an instrument of breakdown for LeelaBenare.

Conclusion

The playwright demonstrated a masterclass of meta-narrative storytelling by exploring aspects like play within a play, dramatic irony, Hitchcock's Bomb Theory, and the notions of conceived and perceived truth. However, numerous critics have argued Tendulkar's plays are like problem plays; he refutes these charges by highlighting the fact that his plays involve formalist devices, but they are not limited to meta-narrative storytelling, thus creating plays that are as excellent in their written form and quality as they are illustrious for their subject matter. Not only is *Silence! The Court is in Session is* celebrated as one of the most refined plays of its generation, but Tendulkar is also hailed as a herald of social radicalism; he influenced other scholarly parallel writers to create plays and other forms of media with a cult following. The inception of meta-narrative storytelling begins with the transcendence of a metaphysical connection with the audience in this play. It is achieved by expediting the audience as a fourth character within the play, effectively building on their reactions to delve into meta-narrative storytelling. The dramatic irony of the characters not being privy to everything that the audience seems to know is also predisposed by a masterful element of suspense known as the Bomb Theory by Alfred Hitchcock. Hitchcock uses the creation of anticipation and time or lack thereof to create suspense, and throughout the play, Tendulkar uses a similar device to execute his play effectively. The research is built on a general parameter for the meta-narrative storytelling displayed within the play; instead of delving into the different forms of meta-narrative storytelling, it has chosen to use it as a salient feature of *Silence! The Court is in Session*. Research about Indian plays in the context of meta-narrative storytelling is limited. This research signifies the importance of such writing and its application to the numerous forms of media in the Indian context. It also helps researchers to explore Tendulkar's oeuvre with fresh perspectives.

This research broaches discussions about the formation of meta-narrative storytelling within a wide variety of media, not just limited to literature but also Film Studies, Television and other modern forms of media. This research affords a hermeneutics or a critical approach to understanding the various methods a particular work can utilise to create a narrative transcending its traditional narrative. Thus, the paper confirms the hypothesis that the play comprises characteristics of meta-narrative storytelling in a plausible manner.

Works Cited:
Allegretti, Matt. "What Advertisers Can Learn From Alfred Hitchcock - The Master of Suspense." *Dumbstruck Blog*, 31 Oct. 2017, blog.dumbstruck.com/what-advertisers-can-learn-from-alfred-hitchcock-the-master-of-suspense.

DeGuzman, Kyle. "The Rashomon Effect Explained — Who Do You Trust?" *Studio Binder*, 12 Sept. 2022, www.studiobinder.com/blog/what-is-the-rashomon-effect-definition/.Accessed May 2023.

"Dramatic Irony | Definition & Examples." *Encyclopedia Britannica*, 22 Apr. 1999, www.britannica.com/art/dramatic-irony.

Lyotard, Jean-François. *The Postmodern Condition: A Report on Knowledge*. U of Minnesota P, 1984.

Mandhan, Usha. "Social Reality in Vijay Tendulkar's Silence! The Court Is In Session." *Research Journal of English Language and Literature*, vol. 7, no. 3, Sept. 2019, pp. 355-358, doi.org/10.33329/rjelal.73.355. Accessed May 17, 2023

Pramanick, Arka. "Patriarchal Domination and Inequal Power Structure in Silence! The Court Is In the Session." *IOSR Journal of Humanities and Social Science*, vol. 19, no. 12, 2014, pp. 10-13.

"A Quote by Alfred Hitchcock." *Goodreads | Meet Your Next Favorite Book*, www.goodreads.com/quotes/728496-there-is-a-distinct-difference-between-suspense-and-surprise-and. Accessed 17 May 2023.

Stephens, John, and Robyn McCallum. *Retelling Stories, Framing Culture: Traditional Story and Metanarratives in Children's Literature*.Routledge, 2013.

Suma, S. "Structural Features and Stylistic Devices in Vijay Tendulkar's Silence! The Court Is in Session and Kamala." *Language in India*, vol. 19, no. 5, May 2019, pp. 320-23, www.languageinindia.com/may2019/sumacourtisinsessionstylisticfeatures.

Tendulkar, Vijay. *Silence! the Court is in Session*. Translated by PriyaAdarkar, Oxford University Press, 1978.

Chapter-6
Manoeuvring the Dynamics of Youth, Afterlife, and Ecological Symbolism through the Supernatural Aesthetics of Indian Popular Fiction, focusing on the works of Nidhi Upadhyay and Vikrant Khanna

Roshani Bhootra

Abstract

Haunting narratives reflecting deeper societal as well as personal concerns through the exploration in and around the supernatural and the mundane have seen a considerable surge in Indian popular fiction. This study aims at articulating the complexities of youth, the concept of afterlife, and the notion of ecological symbolism in Nidhi Upadhyay's *That Night* and Vikrant Khanna's *The Girl Who Knew Too Much*, both being remarkable amongst the Indian readers as part of the popular culture. Nidhi Upadhyay uses the paranormal as both a narrative device as well as a metaphor to explore the persisting trauma of youthful transgressions highlighted through uncanny encounters. The prologue with quotations such as "I had buried the demons. But on this sinister night, someone, somewhere, had unleashed another demon", setting the gloomy tone for the narrative. It carries some sort of moral weight from the past decisions that have found their way into the present, making the whole adulthood stigmatic, the souls heavier, and the spirits clutched in fear. Khanna's narrative in *The Girl Who Knew Too Much* plays on similar themes, but more from an optimistic outlook making these two works alike and distinct at the same time. Together these two not only make the fundamental questions of the afterlife and the existence of the supernatural more relatable but also come up with environmental degradation, suggesting an inherent connection between humanity's neglect of the earth and its spiritual consequences.

The study also concerns itself with the authors' attempts at bringing the supernatural as not merely an aesthetic for entertainment but also a phenomenon for critical scrutiny where cultural norms and environmental apathy come out as decisive factors. Collecting the direct excerpts of Upadhyaya and Khanna's works along with supplementary information from different sources, this paper examines the universality of fear, regret, trauma, and ecological imbalance through Indian mythos and Western horror motifs. By addressing this blend of cultural influences, the making their narrative significant to the current global discourses. To a more extended sense, the study tries to offer supernatural answers to the modern human dilemmas and to find the impact of Indian popular fiction in redefining societal concerns.

Keywords: Supernatural, Indian popular fiction, afterlife, youth, ecological symbolism.

Introduction

Indian popular fiction can be seen as having huge possibilities of portraying the complex cultural, ecological, and social issues, notably through the supernatural perspective, making this style of storytelling compelling as well as fascinating. Nidhi Upadhyay and Vikrant Khanna emerge as two of those writers who not only become prominent figures in this direction but, at the same time, address the moral and existential predicaments of youth, the concept of the afterlife, and the emblematic interplay between humanity and the supernatural world. While being deeply rooted in the Indian motifs, these works also seek to paint the global landscape of supernatural fiction, having universal themes catering to the nerves of the masses. The incorporation of literary theory and cultural studies to find the modern understanding as well as the relevance of such narratives while situating them within the larger discourse of popular fiction is what the paper goes behind.

The surreal realm, which sets the reality away from the metaphysical, has its framework of historical exploration into the desires, fears, human anxieties, and existential dilemmas through close examination of these narratives. The argument presented by Todorov in *The Fantastic: A Structural Approach to a Literary Genre* (1975) is striking here, where he positions the supernatural as a point of existence in the form of a tension between the real and the imagined, pressing the readers to confront the unknown. As far as the case of Indian literature is concerned, this tension is augmented by the interaction of primitive mythologies, indigenous traditions, folklore, and contemporary societal issues. Both these writers skilfully employ the mentioned elements in their narratives to create an everlasting impact that is not only about the mystical phantoms but also concerns itself with the moral, psychological, and ecological repercussions of human actions.

In Nidhi Upadhyay's *That Night*, the supernatural becomes a medium to explore the moral reckoning of youth. One of the opening lines casts a prognostic reflection of the novel: "That night wasn't just an incident; it was the beginning of the end for all of us." The core thematic concerns of inescapable guilt, secrets, and the inevitability of consequences are embedded in this line. The use of a Ouija board during their youth by a group of friends that started a chain of paranormal experiences makes the centre of the whole narrative, so much so that they turn out to be manifestations of the characters' unsettled guilt, suppressed fears, and the driving force behind their helplessness towards confronting the consequences of their actions. This fearsome exploration leads to the characters taking charge of their psychological states after being heavily burdened with the fragility of youth and the weight of the moral choices that have clutched their souls to a strange, unimaginable degree. This can be placed alongside Sigmund Freud's concept of the uncanny (Das Unheimliche), which postulates that the supernatural is unresolved precisely because it brings into light hidden, repressed truths about the self. Upadhyay's ghosts are not merely external entities but testimonies of internal guilt, constructing a dual layer of horror—one entrenched in the psychological and the other in the metaphysical.

The interweaving of supernatural elements with emotional depths gives it the grey colour that surpasses the physical realm, leaving behind a canvas painted with love, loss, and feelings of grief, preparing the ground of narrative building in Vikrant Khanna's *The Girl Who Knew Too Much*. Harry's unreciprocated love for Sahiba and his abysmal connection with Akshara are not merely narrative curvatures but symbolic representations of unsettled emotions, close to spectral residences that persist and shape lives. Making its trail through Mikhail Bakhtin's concept of the chronotope (the intersection of time and space in narratives), Khanna posits these emotional turmoils within specific moments—Harry's reiterating of his past and Akshara's present anguish, which eventually paves the path for both of them to realise their shared humanity through love and loss, whereas the supernatural lingers as a catalyst. When Harry says, "Some emotions never leave; they are like shadows, always with us," it accentuates the novel's thematic core on the permanence of emotional ties.

The narrative gets more profound by the integration of supernatural and ecological symbolism, enhancing the impact of the story on a wider scale. Much unlike his other works, Khanna's *The Girl Who Knew Too Much* does not explicitly deal with the issue of environmental degradation, yet the metaphorical traces of balance and natural order remain dominant. Harry's emotional equilibration is disrupted by his inability to liberate himself from Sahiba, much like the ecological losses disturb natural harmony. The same can be seen in the spiritual ecology reflected through Akshara's belief that her mother's spirit guides and protects her against all odds, signalling an interrelated system of emotional bonds that require love, care, and nurture. Here a strong alignment is evident with Timothy Morton's notion of "dark ecology," where human and non-human forces are inextricably linked (*Dark Ecology: For a Logic of Future Coexistence*, 2016). Akshara's proclamation, "My mom is still with me, protecting and guiding me," fortifies this perspective, presenting the supernatural as a force for resurrection and balance.

Retribution and retrospection finding their way through the realisation of the afterlife are also two of the key aspects in both Upadhyay and Khanna. In *That Night*, the ghosts are not merely premonitions of fear but are deeply roped to the characters' moral catastrophes. The shadowy presence acts as a mirror, forcing the protagonists to confront their unsolved guilt. This deploying of the afterlife shares proximity with Carl Jung's theory of the shadow self, where the suppressed aspects of the psyche become apparent as external entities. Similarly, Khanna's spectral apparitions often signify the natural world's resoluteness and memory, indicative of the afterlife's fundamental presence as an extension of ecological balance and not merely as an abstract concept.

When viewed through the lens of cultural studies, the works of Upadhyaya and Khanna exhibit Stuart Hall's concept of "cultural encoding and decoding," which suggests that popular culture is both a reflection of and a commentary on societal values and anxieties (*Encoding/Decoding*, 1980). The popularity and relatability of supernatural fiction can thus be taken as a response to the constant state of suspense in a swiftly modernising society. While rooted in Indian traditions, the paranormal elements in these works make room for themselves to breathe with global influences, such as Western horror facets of haunted houses and rancorous spirits. This blending gives birth to narratives that are accessible to a global audience while maintaining their cultural veracity.

There are moral implications also involved in the works of Upadhyaya and Khanna when previewed in the broader context of ethical criticism. Martha Nussbaum, in *Poetic Justice: The Literary Imagination and Public Life* (1996), comes up with the argument that literature fosters empathy and moral reconsideration by allowing readers to dwell in the perspectives of others. While in Upadhyay's *That Night* the journey through fear, guilt, and redemption is what strikes the readers to recollect their own moral choices, for Khanna it is the solace in Akshara's belief in her mother's spiritual presence around her and Harry's acceptance of the true essence of love echoing the order sustained by nature that plays the crucial role of making the story relatable for the readers across boundaries.

In the last resort, the transformative power of Indian popular literature deductively and the genre of supernatural inductively get themselves manifested in the works of Nidhi Upadhyay and Vikrant Khanna. By the evocative interweaving of youth, afterlife, and ecological symbolism, both the authors bring to us narratives that not merely serve the entertainment purpose but go as far as to provide in-depth insights into the human psyche and its complex equation with the vivid societal dynamics. The use of supernatural elements, both metaphorically as well as critically, makes it appealing for a larger audience inside the literary tradition, which eventually works as a bridge between the local and the global, the conventional and the contemporary. This paper will be an attempt to demonstrate the supernatural as an impactful medium of storytelling, retrospection, and critique instead of merely being a source of fear.

Youth and Moral Reconsideration

Youth is often portrayed as a decisive stage in life, a period dominated by transformative powers, impulsive behaviours, the quest for identity, and the purpose of existence. The ethical and phantasmal repercussions of the choices made when we are at the high point of our youth are further explored by the concerned writers through their works. The chilling declaration in one of the opening episodes of *That Night* goes as follows: It wasn't just a secret—it was a ticking time bomb, waiting to explode." It sets the tone for the whole narrative—how youthful indiscretions, shrouded in mystery, can resurface in petrifying and unexpected ways.

In Upadhyay's novel, the youthful transgression of experimenting with a Ouija board becomes a symbol for the frailty of decision-making during seminal years. The characters' inability to anticipate the long-term ramifications of their actions is highlighted by the frightful message: "Revenge. And I am here to get it". This act of experimentation done in the spirit of youth goes side by side with Judith Butler's theory of performativity, where identity is taken as a construction through repeated actions (*Gender Trouble*, 1990). The supernatural becomes a lens to ruminate about the aftermath of these performances, stressing the moral responsibilities inherent in even presumably harmless decisions.

Khanna's *The Girl Who Knew Too Much* probes youthful recklessness from the viewpoint of love, loss, and regret, explicitly in the love triangle of Harry, Sahiba, and Siddharth. Harry's incertitude in confessing his feelings for Sahiba and his resentfulness towards Siddharth highlight the impulsivity and moral complexity of youth. His emotional idleness, captured in the line, "Sometimes, the love you don't act on becomes the heaviest burden," is analogous to Akshara's distress over her mother's death, as both characters grapple with unresolved emotions.

Through these interwoven narratives, Khanna explores how youthful discretions, or the lack thereof, create lasting effects. Akshara's quest for meaning in her loss parallels Harry's persisting guilt, with the spectral acting as a catalyst for emotional recalling. The novel intrinsically shows how love and grief are driving forces that surpass time, providing opportunities for answerability and healing.

The Afterlife as Reflection and Answerability

In the works of Nidhi Upadhyay and Vikrant Khanna, the afterlife rises above the conventional spectral frightenings to become a dimension where unresolved conflicts ask for accountability of actions. Grounded in Indian mythological notions of karma and moksha, the afterlife is presented as an extension of ethical and emotional reckoning. In *That Night*, the line, "I want to talk. Can I come inside?" subsumes the unsettled tension between the living and the dead, indicating how guilt and moral failings linger beyond death. These paranormal presences are not merely plot devices but manifestations of the characters' inner scuffles, forcing them to denounce their repressed fears and failures.

This depiction aligns with Carl Jung's theory of the shadow self, where suppressed attributes of the psyche materialise as external entities (*The Archetypes and the Collective Unconscious*, 1959). Likewise, Khanna's spectral figures often act as ecological admonitions, presenting the afterlife as nature's response to human dilapidation. Cursed rivers and haunted lands in his works bring out environmental determination as a spiritual transgression, echoing Timothy Morton's concept of "hyperobjects"—vast entities like climate change that connect humanity to nature across time and space (The Ecological Thought, 2010).

Derrida's concept of hauntology further elucidates the narratives, describing how inconclusive pasts linger and affect the present (*Spectres of Marx*, 1994). For both authors, spectral omens and unfinished narratives come to blows with the characters to find closure through acceptance and atonement. By interconnecting these elements with Freudian and Jungian psychological theories, Upadhyay and Khanna enhance their stories, transmuting the afterlife from a determinant of fear into an insightful tool for retrospection and redemption. Their narratives foreground that moral accountability, whether personal or ecological, is inevitable, and true closure demands both reflection and action.

Ecological Symbolism in Supernatural Fiction

Ecological symbolism is pivotal to Vikrant Khanna's works, where the supernatural functions as an allegory for humanity's exploitation of nature. His cursed landscapes—be it forests teeming with revengeful spirits or rivers conveying the echoes of ecological devastation—underscore the innate connection between human actions and environmental consequences. These dynamics align with the expanding body of ecocriticism, which inspects the rendition of nature in literature and its reverberations for environmental ethics. As Timothy Clark argues, literature has the power to challenge anthropocentric standpoints, urging readers to consider the non-human as an integral part of the ecological web (*Ecocriticism on the Edge*, 2015).

Khanna's portrayal of haunted natural landscapes also reflects primordial Indian ecological philosophies, which often view nature as divine and animate. In his stories, forests are not plainly backdrops but active participants in the narrative, exhibiting nature's retort to human interference. This perspective pulsates with Arundhati Roy's *The God of Small Things* (1997), which similarly depicts nature as a repertory of memory and resistance. The amplification of this idea gets its fuller form in Khanna's supernatural narratives, which employ ghosts as embodiments of nature's resilience and the spiritual effects of environmental decadence.

The ways to put across this idea of ecological symbolism get subtler with Nidhi Upadhyay's *That Night*. The fogbound woods and morbid landscapes in her novel create an atmosphere of unrest, suggesting that nature itself becomes witness to human triviality. This representation aligns with the Romantic tradition, where natural backgrounds often reflect the psychological state of characters. Upadhyay's use of environmental imagery, while less definitive than Khanna's, contributes to the narrative's entire sense of tension and unavoidability.

Both authors substantiate that ecological themes and the supernatural are not mutually independent. By cementing the interrelation among these elements, they challenge readers to view environmental loss as not just a physical adversity but a moral and spiritual one. This ingenious approach situates their works within the larger discourse of environmental humanities, accentuating the exigency of ecological awareness in the Anthropocene.

Supernatural as a Cultural and Global Narrative

Though allying with the global literary trends, the cultural traditions continue staying as an ineradicable factor of Indian supernatural fiction, as delineated by Upadhyay and Khanna. The assimilation of pretas (restless spirits) and pishachas (malevolent entities) reflects the vibrancy of Indian mythology, grounding the narratives in local cultural pretexts. At the same time, both authors make use of Western horror tropes, such as bewitched houses and vengeful spirits, creating a hybrid perspective that intrigues global audiences.

This intermixing of cultural and global influences goes hand in hand with Homi Bhabha's concept of hybridity, which describes the creation of new cultural forms through the interaction of different traditions (*The Location of Culture,* 1994). In Upadhyay's and Khanna's works, hybridity claims its existence in the seamless fusion of Indian folklore with collective themes of fear, remorse, and redemption. This dualism enhances the approachability of their narratives, making them resonate with diversified readerships.

Furthermore, the supernatural elements in their stories serve as a disquisition of societal norms and concerns. As Raymond Williams argues in *Culture and Society* (1958), literature often serves as a site for arbitrating social values and exploring the conflicts between tradition and modernity. The works of Upadhyay and Khanna, with their supernatural tropes, delve into crucial issues such as morality, identity, and environmental sustainability, situating them as significant partakers in contemporary popular Indian literature.

Conclusion

The works of Nidhi Upadhyay and Vikrant Khanna hold the potential of transforming supernatural fiction and taking it beyond the debates of popular and classic. By addressing the themes of youth, the afterlife, ecological symbolism, and cultural hybridity, these authors leave behind the boundaries of entertainment, delivering deep preludes into human nature and societal equations. Supernatural in their work shines as a critique of human actions as well as interference, in the end leading to broader global literary understandings of this genre, becoming a bridge between the modern and the conventional. The surreal is not merely something awful, but it is the essence of the suppressed, the unsaid, and the hidden, which ultimately finds its way through the feelings of redemption, guilt, and acceptance.

References:
1. Todorov, T. (1973). The Fantastic: A Structural Approach to a Literary Genre. Cornell University Press.
2. Freud, S. (1919). The Uncanny. Penguin Classics.
3. Morton, T. (2016). Dark Ecology: For a Logic of Future Coexistence. Columbia University Press.
4. Jung, C. G. (1959). The Archetypes and the Collective Unconscious. Princeton University Press.
5. Derrida, J. (1994). Specters of Marx: The State of the Debt, the Work of Mourning, and the New International. Routledge.
6. Nussbaum, M. C. (1996). Poetic Justice: The Literary Imagination and Public Life. Beacon Press.
7. Clark, T. (2015). Ecocriticism on the Edge: The Anthropocene as a Threshold Concept. Bloomsbury Academic.
8. Hall, S. (1980). Encoding/Decoding. Routledge.
9. Butler, J. (1990). Gender Trouble: Feminism and the Subversion of Identity. Routledge.
10. Smith, A. (2010). The Ghost Story 1840–1920: A Cultural History. Manchester University Press.
11. Khanna, V. Selected Works. HarperCollins India.
12. Upadhyay, N. (2020). That Night. Penguin Random House India.
13. Bhabha, H. K. (1994). The Location of Culture. Routledge.
14. Morton, T. (2010). The Ecological Thought. Harvard University Press.
15. Hogle, J. E. (2002). The Cambridge Companion to Gothic Fiction. Cambridge University Press.
16. Chakrabarty, D. (2009). The Climate of History in a Planetary Age. University of Chicago Press.
17. Mukherjee, M. (2000). The Perishable Empire: Essays on Indian Writing in English. Oxford University Press.

18. Bhattacharya, N. (2012). "The Ecology of Fear in Indian Gothic Fiction." Postcolonial Text, 7(3).
19. Aravamudan, S. (2006). Tropicopolitans: Colonialism and Agency, 1688–1804. Duke University Press.
20. Easthope, A. (1983). Literary into Cultural Studies. Routledge.

Chapter-7
Youth Culture and Globalization

Ms. Sangita S. Aher

Abstract

The term 'Youth Culture' refers to the social norms of adolescents and young adults and comprises the symbolic systems and processes showed by the youth. They are different from the symbolic systems and processes of the adults in the society. Youth culture is visible in several forms such as fashion, lifestyle choices, music and language. Although youth culture is extremely localized and formed by national circumstances, it is gradually influenced by global trends too particularly because communication technologies have broken down terrestrial barriers.The connection between globalization and youth culture is both dynamic and complex. The forces of globalization have greatly influenced young people's way of interacting with the world and in determining their attitudes,values, identities and behaviors over the last few decades. There is great need to explore the impact of globalization on youth culture in the contemporary age because the youth is the pillar of society.The researcher intends to explore the connection of youth culture and globalization through this research paper. This study also highlights the intricacies of global interconnectedness in relation to youth. It will analyze the diversifying and homogenizing effects of globalization on youth culture as well as discuss the role of, media, fashion, technology, music, and social movements on youth culture.

Keywords: Youth Culture, Globalization, Cultural Homogenization, Cultural Diversification

Introduction

The term 'Youth Culture' refers to the social norms of adolescents and young adults and comprises the symbolic systems and processes showed by the youth. They are different from the symbolic systems and processes of the adults in the society.

The existence, presence and origin of youth culture is a much debated fact as some researchers think that youth culture is not separate from the adult culture because the morals and values of the youth are not different from that of their parents. According to Merten and Schwartz, youth culture is different from the other people in the society. For Schwartz, the vocabulary used by the high school students for creating meanings is different from that of the adolescent students. There is a difference in social structures and the social reality is experienced differently by the teens and the adults. Therefore, there are cultural differences between the adults and the adolescents which points to the presence of a separate culture of the youth.

1) The researcher intends to explore the connection of youth culture and globalization through this research paper.
2) This study also highlights the intricacies of global interconnectedness in relation to youth.
3) It will analyze the diversifying and homogenizing effects of globalization on youth culture as well as discuss the role of, media, fashion, technology music, and social movements on youth culture.

Youth culture is a recent historical phenomenon and there are various theories which refer to the emergence of culture in the 20th century. These theories include hypotheses regarding the psychological, economic and historical influences on the presence of youth culture. The emergence of youth culture is credited to the beginning of compulsory schooling by one historical theory .For James Coleman, the root cause of separate youth culture is age segregation. Many children and adolescents used to interact with adults before education was mandatory. Contrary to this, modern children tend to associate with others of their age. Due to this, the adolescents are able to develop shared experiences which are the cause of youth culture.

Another theory posits that while some cultures facilitated the growth of youth culture others do not do so. This happens due to two types of norms present in the society-particularistic and universalistic. Universalistic norms are applicable to all people in the society while particularistic norms are the guidelines for the behavior of people which change from one person to another. Industrialized societies have universalistic norms. These norms are encouraged by the process of modernization in the last century as everyone needs to learn same norms for interacting in modern society. Universalistic norms and modernization have together caused the development of youth culture.

Age grouping is used by many societies for educating their children on the norms of societies and for preparing them for adulthood and youth culture is produced through this process. Children develop their own different culture because they spend much time together and learn similar things as the other children of their age. The youth culture also plays an important role in the development of identity as noted by the psychological theorists.

Youth culture is fluid and it is discernible by resistance to adult authority, and established social norms reflecting a period of social and personal experimentation. Youth culture is visible in several forms such as fashion, lifestyle choices, music and language. Although youth culture is extremely localized and formed by national circumstances, it is gradually influenced by global trends too particularlybecause communication technologies have broken down terrestrial barriers.

Features of Youth Culture
1) Relationship of youth lifestyles with class, gender and ethnicity: Youth cultures often express resistance

whichstems fromone's class, gender and ethnicity. In the 19th century in Australia there was youth culture based on class called Larrikinism. Larrikanism refers to the culture of the working class who attacked the citizens in different forms such as assaults,insults, loitering, and riots. They rejected the capitalist work ethic. Gender based roles and values are also expressed by Youth cultures. For instance,motorcycle gangs are an example of the use of motorbikes for expressing a particular form of manliness. A very few females are present in political-cultural youth groups.Hip-Hopis an example of ayouth culture based onethnicity whichis amusical movement of the African diaspora and African youth against discrimination and racism.

2) **Generational consciousness**: A sense of generational consciousness is another feature of Youth culture. It denotes a particularconsciousness of having lived through particular sociopolitical happenings. For illustration, the generation of Indian children who were born soon after the economic reforms of liberalization in 1991 are called'The children of liberalization'.It was a period in India which witnessed rapid technological, social and economic changes as a result of opening up of its market to the whole world. The 'Liberalization Children' are unlike thosechildren who were born before them since they have not experienced the philosophy of self-restraint and the policies of protection of socialism.They had also not experienced the political oppression of Emergency and the violence of partition. They are living in the age of a growing, vibrant and free economy and experiencing a global culture of innovation. As well as they have seen Indians writing success stories all over the world. Through these opportunities they have got a sense of generation.

3) **Lifestyle**: The particular objects like leather jackets or denim jeans or motorbikes are the dominant features of the life style of the youth culture. These features express a

variety of meanings and values of a specific youth culture. For instance, motorbike symbolizes male centered pragmatic sensibilities like quest for freedom, rashness which are pursued by the members of the motorbike bands. The automated features of the motorbike also relate to the features of the motorbike gangs.

4) Impact of mass media, technology and consumerism: The ideas spread by the cultural activities like music, fashion and media affect youth culture. Youth cultures are becoming more diverse and less stagnant due to the dispersal of cultural images such asmusic, fashion, language and cultural practices through technology. The youth have adapted different styles, and different types of cultural practices are coexisting. Today's youth do not usually identify with only one style but they get influences from different styles andthey create their ownstyle. There is productive receptionof mass media images among the youth and they are not just passive receivers of ideas of mass media. Theycreate a different identity by taking the ideas, concepts and images from media and using themas they wish.

5) **Counter culture**: Youth culture is usually described as a resistance against the dominant culture. It is perceived as counter "establishment" and anti-parental culture. The ways of youth are in conflict with the adult world. Therefore, the young members of a particular subculture constantly strive for the mechanisms for creating their own space.

6) **Help in developing the dominant culture**: The fashion and the life style of the general culture is influenced by thelanguage, practicesand fads of the youth culture as it inevitably mixes into the other culture. According to Steve Mizrach (2006) new identities are created for people in the cyber age such as themutant and mediant, cyborg, virtual and slacke. Most of the subcultures of today like cyberpunks, zippies, modern primitivesand ravers, are experimenting with these new types of identities and it has become a sort of

practice.Thus, the youth culture is leading the society into new spaces of development.

Globalization and Its Effect on Youth Culture

Globalization denotes thepractices by which the world becomes increasingly interconnected through economic, political, cultural, and technological exchanges. This interconnectedness has restructurednumerous aspects of life, from personal relationships to economies. The influence of globalization on youth culture is indubitable, and it exhibits in numerous ways as follows:

1. Technological Developments and Digital Connectivity

The most noteworthycharacteristic of the impact of globalization on youth culture is the growth of digital technology. The way of interacting with each other and with the world on the part of the young people is extremely changed by the advent of thesocial media platforms, internet and mobile communication. Young people from all over the world can create, share, and consume cultural content through social media platforms like, TikTok, Instagram, YouTube and Twitter. These platforms have contributed a lot for nurturing a sense of global youth culture due to thequicktransmission of fashion, cultural trends, language, and music. Due to the spread of technology all over the world, virtual communities are created by which youth can find similar peers irrespective of their geographicallocality. Therefore, a new form of identity is created which is free from physical boundaries and is influenced by global ideas and trends

2. The Role of Media and Pop Culture

The youth culture is largely shaped by global media which includes film, television and music.Media has multiple forms such as print media, electronic media and digital media. Print media includes newspaper, pamphlets, magazines, books and comics. Electronic media comprises radio, television, laptops, cell phones, films, CD ROMS,

Popular Culture: Shades and Shadows

DVD,mp3 players, game systems and tablets. While digital media includes internet, mobile apps and social media, etc. Theseforms have infused the lives of human beingsbroadly, affecting specifically the youth in substantial way, in their, studies, daily activities, social relationships, their worldviews and their work. Thepresentage group is frequently referred to as the "Net generation", the "millennium generation", and "digital natives". These young people are, to a great extent, engagedin using cell phones and connecting with their friends,computers, playing online games, constantly communicating by using other electronic devices, from their earlylife. They use more and more media devices, as they grow up and they have become a part of their leisure, entertainment as well as learning.They are described as having created a different culture that helps their use of media without parental control.

Media offers opportunity to youth to produce content on social media. On social media content is generated by users.Young people are able to create their identities and socialize with other people by writing blogs .They share their personal feelings, thoughts and views through social media. They can also post news and analysis of news, filmsand music.Young musicians present their music and upload their videos on social media platform. Some new photographersalso post their photos on social media.Now youth are not the pawns in the hands of commercial companies which have controlon media .The youth are using digital spaces to empower themselves by producing content on social networking sights. In this way they are reaching out to huge and global audience.

Involvement in the media culture impacts the interests and skills of teens significantly. Today's youth think differently and process information in a different way from previous cohorts. They take the help of media technologies for getting information as well as for learning and interacting with other people.. In this way theirknowledge and social preferences are shaped by media. Theyouth are also keen to acquire the skills which are needed to build their creative multimedia presentations. Youth have to be multitasking because it has become the need of the time. Youth are continuously switching between posting on Facebook, Instagram, what's app, checking email, sending messages to peers on their cell phones and browsing the netfor getting required information While being in contact with friends through social media and experimenting with social media sites out of curiosity, the young people are also at risk of exposing to harmful websites and getting contacted by strangers. There is also a significant dangerof being addicted to Internet for this Net generation.

The global pop culture, particularly from the United States, was dominant historically in the Western media,which has influenced the youth all over the globe. Pop music, Hollywood films and fashion trends were considered more desirable. A global youth culture is fostered by the spread of music genressuch as pop, K-pop, and hip-hop.At the same time, globalization has caused the upsurge of regional and local youth cultures which intermingle with global trendsexceptionally. Thus, a hybridized form of youth cultureis produced that is both global and local because local culturesinstantaneously embrace and challenge global tendencies.

3. Fashion, Trends and Consumerism

There is also the influence of fashion on youth culture whichis another important area in which globalization has shown its impact. Today's youth express themselves through accessories, clothing, and footwear and there is the influence of the global brands like Apple, Adidas and Nike on them. A more homogenized youth culture noticeable by shared styles and consumption patterns has emerged due to the growth of fast fashion. Theavailability of online shopping has made it easier for young people to access global fashions. Nevertheless, it is vital to know that globalization has also led to the rise of otheryouth cultures which resist conventional styles. Certain subcultures like punk, goth, skateboarding, and street wear have challenged global fashion standards and highlighteddistinctpersonality. Though these subcultures embrace global influences, they holddistinctivefeatures which replicatesocial contexts, local experiences, and values.

4. Youth Activism and Social Movements

Globalization has also led to new methods of youth activism and political movements. The young people can organize, mobilize, and raise their voices on global concerns such as racial inequality,climate change, gender rights, and LGBTQ rights due to internet. Young people have used digital platforms to create awareness and bring change by driving the movements likeBlack Lives Matter, Fridays for Future and Me Too. Simultaneously, youth activism frequently takes on local forms.The young people in different parts of the globe addresssuch problems that replicate their exclusive economic, political and cultural contexts.

One chief debate which arises in the study of youth culture and globalization is to what extent globalization causes cultural homogenization versus cultural variation.On the one hand, globalization causes cultural homogenization, where the global things such as McDonald's, Hollywood, and Coca-Cola have spread all over the world, which leads to a standardization of youth culture .Due to this, Western cultural goods are exported throughout the globe and they are consumed by the youth. This process is called as "Westernization" or "Americanization". Western fashion trends as well as films and music have become popular among the global youth. The tastes, lifestyles and behaviour of the youth from different parts of the world are almost similar. On the other hand, globalization enables cultural variation and hybridization by mixing local and global cultural forms rather than deleting local cultures.Instead of

Popular Culture: Shades and Shadows

passively consuming global trends, young people vigorously reinterpret, remix,and localize these trends to suit their cultural backgrounds. In various parts of the world, the Western hip-hop music is fused with indigenous music which is an example of how the youth adapt global cultural goods to their inimitable cultural identities.

It means that globalizationnot only leads to a uniform international youth culture, but also causes the creation of various, hybrid identities whichreplicate the connection of global and localimpacts. Suchhybridization manifests in the growth of new musical types like reggae ton, which is a blend of Latin rhythms and global pop impacts. Similarly, Bhangra pop is an example of the fusion of folk and western elements which is very popular amongthe north Indian youth. In terms of fashion it can be said that the popularity of Indo-western dresses is increasing amongIndian women and men day by day.It is not surprising that even the international restaurant chains such as McDonalds, Pizza Hut, Dominos and Kentucky Fried Chicken (KFC) have Indianized their food stuffs to suit the tastes of Indian people. Similarly, there is hybridization in the fashion trends where global styles are merged with traditional fashion styles.

The effect of Globalization is different on different segments of society and they use different strategies while dealing with globalization. Some people in society adopt western things easily while others oppose certain western ideas because they think that the western concepts are a threat to the Indian culture. For example, Bajrang Dal is the youth wing of a Hindu Nationalist party called Vishwa Hindu Parishad. It opposed the celebration of Valentine's Day in the Hindu locality because according to them it is a western concept and it would spoil the Indian culture as it encourages indecent expression of love. These people damagedhotels, shops and restaurants who were involved in celebrating the day and also beat the couples who went tosuch places and parks. As a consequence, there is loss of a stable community life.

Conclusion

Youth culture and globalization are inseparable from each other whereby each shapes the other in complex and sometimes in contradictoryways. There is profound impact of technology, media, fashion, music, and consumer products on the Youth. Globalization has not only led to the spread of technology, global media and consumer products but has also fostered the growth of various local youth cultures that oppose homogenization.It offers youth the opportunities of cross-cultural exchange andthere is also a challenge to preserve local identities. In this age of globalization, youth culture is a site of experimentation, resistance and innovation. It is here, that the youth of today assert their individuality and also cope up with a rapidly changing world. In this way, there is a dynamic relationship between globalization and youth culture.

Works Cited:

- Bauman, Z. *Globalization: The Human Consequences.* Columbia University Press, New York ,1998
- Castells, M. *The Rise of the Network Society.* Blackwell Publishers Ltd.Oxford ,1996
- Hall, S. "Cultural Identity and Diaspora". In P. Williams & L. Chrisman (Eds.), *Colonial Discourse and Post-Colonial Theor,* 1997
- Storey, J. *Cultural Theory and Popular Culture: An Introduction.* Routledge(8th Ed.),2018
- Bansal,P."Youth Culture: Influence of Media and Globalization" retrieved from
- https://egyankosh.ac.in/bitstream/123456789/65362/1/Unit-5.pdf
- https://en.wikipedia.org/wiki/Youth_culture

Chapter-8
Recurrentmotifs of Casteism and Societal Discrimination in Indian Popular Culture: Insights from Omprakash Valmiki's Joothan

Dr. Yasir Ahmad Khanday

Abstract

In common parlance a society is known by its priorities, preferences and what it adheres to. When a society starts fostering some specific ideas, practices and beliefs, which are accepted by the mainstream population, popular culture is constituted. Popular Culture or 'Pop Culture' is thus a widely accepted particular culture within a society. However, it is pertinent to state that the popular culture is always in flux. It keeps on changing as it showcases the constantly changing ideas, values, interests and the overall behavior of the society.This is what prevents popular culture from becoming overly monotonous and enhances the chances of its being relevant always. There are some capital propellants by which popular culture is nourished and disseminated and thus kept alive. These are the mass media, music and films, literature, globalization, work culture and the like. This paper is going to highlight how literature can play a pivotal role in propagating and advocating Popular Culture. It will also explore casteism and societal discrimination, the two dominant strands of Indian Popular Culture with reference to Omprakash Valmiki's autobiographical memoir, Joothan.

Keywords: Foster, Casteism, Societal Discrimination, Flux, Evolve, Joothan

"Popular Culture is simply culture that is widely favoured or well-liked by many people" (Storey 5). This definition by Professor John Storey has made it obvious that Popular culture is based on priorities, interests and collective experiences of general masses. Popular culture is also defined by Professor Storey as 'mass culture'. Other terms used for popular culture are working-class culture and folk culture. To further simplify the term 'popular culture', here is one more definition: "Popular culture consists of the traditional practices and beliefs or way of life of a specific group; and, finally the most wide-ranging definition of all, popular culture is simply the practices of everyday life" (Brien & Imre 2). Popular culture acts as the mirror of a society as it reflects current ideas, trends, norms and collective shared experiences. It can be instrumental in assessing a society as it underscores the people's areas of inclination and their preferred goals. For instance, in societies where topmost priority of the people is the government job, a culture of late marriages can be seen developing. So here popular culture becomes a placard or a signboard for a society having the issues of late marriage and accordingly, low fertility rate. Due to emerging global trends, popular culture keeps on evolving and crosses cultural borders in terms of societal preferences.Multiple reasons are there for which popular culture is a welcoming entity. It encourages innovation and creativity, thus preventing life from becoming outdated and boring. "The products and processes of popular culture continually change over time" (Huq 4). It propagates borderlessness in terms of nationality as it encourages crossing borders of cultural barriers. It thus fosters social connectivity. It creates an aura of friendliness and universal brotherhood because it drives people to connect more and more in terms of trade, cultural exchange and boost the world economy. "In a true inquiry environment, all people with assumptions about popular culture- even, and perhaps especially, teachers- need to make room for new information and a variety of perspectives…"

(Moore 186).

Literature has much to say in advocating popular culture

and taking it to a larger audience. The vogue of philosophy of 'art for life's sake' and the rejection of the doctrine 'art for art's sake' is quite relevant here. The litterateurs advocating the principle of art for life's sake were making every possible effort to keep literature relevant to life by choosing the contemporary issues as the subject matter for their novels, poems, plays, essays, etc. The writers who were at the forefront in this regard are G. B. Shaw, H. G. Wells, Rudyard Kipling, etc, who used to believe that art/ literature doesn't come out of a vacuum and must be didactic in nature and thereby enhance life. Literature and life can never be divorced:

Literature is the expression of life and its appeal lies in this fact...this means that the artist presents his interpretation of life. The artist, in this sense is called an interpreter of life. It is his own interpretation, of life as he saw it. Thus, literature is an interpretation of life as seen and interpreted by the writer." (Nimavat4)

Motifs of casteism and societal discrimination have had a significant place in Indian English literature. These have been recurrently used to highlight class-conflicts, hierarchies and injustice within a cultural context. Some noteworthy books dealing with the theme of casteism and societal discrimination are: Mulk Raj Anand's *Untouchable* (1935), *The God of Small Things* (1997) by Arundhati Roy, *The Annihilation of Caste* (1948) by B. R. Ambedkar, Baburao Bagul's *When I Hid My Caste* (1958), Aravind Adiga's *The White Tiger* (2008) and the one which is scrutinized here is *Joothan: A Dalit's Life* (1997) by Omprakash Valmiki. This popular trend of exploring casteism and societal discrimination is in vogue in the current times as well. We have witnessed some seminal texts published in recent years, like *Tomb of Sand* (2022) by Geetanjali Shree, Arun Sagar's *The Inheritance of Words* (2023), *Speaking of Caste* (2022) by Suraj Yengde etc.

Popular Culture: Shades and Shadows

***Joothan:** A Dalit's Life* is considered a pioneering achievement in Indian Literature. Omprakash Valmiki, the author of this autography, was born in Muzaffarnagar, Uttar Pradesh, in a Dalit community. Right from the days of his infancy, he used to be perturbed by his status as an outcast. Inspired from the struggle of Dalit emancipation led by Dr. Ambedkar, Omprakash associated himself with Dalit activism, and throughout his life he remained dedicated to the cause. Omprakash Valmiki is deemed to be a prolific writer in the oeuvre of Dalit literature. Dalit literature, which is chiefly composed by Dalit writers, depicts their ages-old suffering, subjugation and humiliation. Dalit literature aims to give voice to voiceless Dalits. Writers endeavour to ensure worldly dignity, freedom, andholistic individuality for the Dalit community. They have a quest for an egalitarian society and challenge the existing social setup that has oppressed and marginalized Dalits for centuries. Dalits were forced to do menial and demeaning jobs like cleaning latrines and carrying the headloads of human excreta, skinning of dead animals and their disposing, forced labour in agricultural fields with minimal wages or no wages at all, laundry work and unpaid domestic chores in the houses of landlords, removing cow dung from the cow sheds and making of cow dung cakes. These menial tasks assigned to Dalits were purely based on caste discrimination. Arundhati Roy paints a ghastly picture of this catastrophic injustice and discrimination in her essay, "The Doctor and the Saint", published as an introduction to the annotated edition of B. R. Ambedkar's *Annihilation of Caste* (2014):

According to the National Crime Records Bureau, a crime is committed against a Dalit by a Non-Dalit every sixteen minutes; every day, more than four Untouchable women are raped by Touchables; every week, thirteen Dalits are murdered and six Dalits are kidnapped. In 2012 alone, the year of the Delhi gang-rape and murder, 1574 Dalit women were raped (the rule of thumb is that only 10 percent of rapes or other crimes against Dalits are ever reported) and 651 Dalits were murdered. (14)

However, Omprakash Valmiki seems pioneering in highlighting this inhuman treatment perpetrated against Dalits. His *Joothan* articulates the trauma of living in a society marked by extreme caste hierarchies. It serves as the manifesto in the evolution of Dalit literature. *Joothan: A Dalit's Life* was originally composed in Hindi and was englished in 2003 by Arun Prabha Mukherjee, professor of English at York University. Valmiki, who was born in a Dalit family, documents his upbringing as an untouchable and his day-to-day experience as a low caste. At the very outset of the book, Omprakash portrays the picture of his childhood days and the unhygienic surroundings he was living in. All the human welfare policies of the government were not meant for Dalits, who were completely marginalized. The derogatory name given to Dalits was Chuhras. The village women, including young girls, older women and even the newly married brides, used to sit in an open space for defecation. These open-air latrines were not considered a matter of shame even in the broad daylight. The congested life with extensive families, having little to eat and almost nothing to wear, was what the Dalit life encompassed. There was stench everywhere: children and pigs comforting themselves in the mucky water of the nearby pond to avoid the scorching heat of the sun in summers. The mud houses, naked children with dogs around, daily fights and a slum-like environment all were a part of Valmiki's childhood. Dalits were never called by their names; instead, every type of abusive language was used for them. They were not considered humans by the upper caste people. Untouchability was deep-rooted in Indian popular culture. Omprakash says:

Untouchability was so rampant that while it was

considered all right to touch dogs and cats or cows and buffaloes, if one happened to touch a Chuhra, one got contaminated or polluted. The Chuhras were not seen as humans. They were simply things for use. Their utility lasted until the work was done. Use them and then throw them away. (2)

The word 'joothan' itself has a powerful connotative meaning which can be associated with poverty, affliction, antipathy and humiliation. Literally, it denotes the left-over food meant to be thrown away. But this left-over food is symbolic in highlighting the helplessness of Dalits. It is for this left-over foods Dalits had to beg at the doorsteps of the landlords so that they could escape starvation. They used to eat this jhootan with great relish which otherwise is quite abominable. Omprakash Valmiki recollects:

During a wedding, when the guests and the baratis, the bridegroom's family, were eating their meals, the chuhras would sit outside with huge baskets. After the baratis had eaten, the dirty pattals or leaf-plates were put in chuhras baskets, which they took home, to save the joothan sticking to them. The little pieces of pooris, bits of sweetmeats, and a little bit of vegetables were enough to make them happy. The joothan was eaten with a lot of relish. (10)

It was for this joothan, Dalits had to do every menial job in the houses of upper caste landlords. A chuhra family comprised of twelve or twenty members who used to work in the fields or the houses of upper castes throughout the year would not even earn enough to eat. Most of the times what they would be given for their labour was a volley of abuses. These poverty-stricken people are often the victims of medical carelessness. Omprakash recalls how his family was struck by lightning when his elder brother, Sukhbir died at a young age because of the lack of medical attention. Sukhbir was a primary support of the family and was always at the forefront in getting the basic needs of the family fulfilled.

He left behind a young wife and a one-and-a-half-year-old son. The societal discrimination is best described by Omprakash in terms of education facilities. There were no schools meant for low castes and the schools so-called open for all didn't admit Dalit children. Omprakash was the only child among his siblings who received formal education. But his educational journey was not a cake walk. He had to bear a lot of discrimination, injustice and humiliation. Initially he was denied the admission by a local government primary school. It was only after his father ran between the pillar and the post that Omprakash was granted admission. The school environment was not quite conducive for him. He was asked to sit at the back of the class where from he could hardly see anything written on the black board. The routine of Omprakash was comprised of the bullying by upper caste boys, their taunts, their abuses and a lot of humiliation. He was beaten by teachers on daily basis without any reason. This inhumane treatment was meant to force Omprakash to leave the school for ever. Omprakash reminiscences how he was forced to sweep the entire school and the ground for three consecutive days:

The playground was way larger than my small physique could handle and in cleaning it my back began to ache. My face was covered with dust. Dust had gone inside my mouth. The other children in my class were studying and I was sweeping. Headmaster was sitting in his room and watching me. I was not even allowed to get a drink of water. (5)

In conclusion, Omprakash Valmiki's autographical work, *joothan* has proven a success in elucidating the aspects of casteism and societal discrimination, which are recurrently used in Indian English literature.These motifs have been kept in limelight by other mediums like films, arts, work culture etc. but literature has immortalized these prevailing social realities. *Joothan* emphasises that a reconstruction of ideologies is needed. A society cannot lead towards progress and prosperity, unless it does not privilege the principles of egalitarianism. This work though written in Hindi is translated into multiple languages and thus reached to a wider audience.

References:
- Anand, S. *Annihilation of Caste: The Annotated Critical Edition of B. R. Ambedkar*. Navayana Publishing Ltd, 2014.
- Brien, Susie O, and Imra Szeman. *Popular Culture: A User's Guide*. Blackwell Publications, 2017.
- Haq, Rupa. *Making Sense of Suburbia Through Popular Culture*. Bloomsbury Publications, 2013.
- Moore, David Cooper. "Rethinking Popular Culture and Media." Journal of Media Literary Education, 4:2, 2012, pp. 184-186.
- Nimavat, B. S. *Hudson: An Introduction to the Study of Literary*. Prakash Book Depot, 2010.
- Storey, John. *Cultural Theory and Popular Culture: An Introduction*. Longman Publications, 2008.
- Valmiki, Omprakash. *Joothan: A Dalit's Life*. Translated by Mukherjee, Arun Prabha, Columbia University Press, 2003.

Chapter-9

Everyday Ironies: Satire and Pop Culture in Contemporary Indian Poetry with Reference to Nissim Ezekiel, Eunice de Souza, and Meena Kandasamy

Dr. Supriya Mandloi

Abstract
Culture is shaped not just by great works of art, but also by the everyday meanings people create and share. Popular culture, found in films, ads, media, and social rituals, plays a strong role in how we think, speak, and engage with the world. While Indian English poetry often appears literary or reflective, it also connects deeply with these cultural currents. This paper examines how satire and popular culture come together in the poetry of Nissim Ezekiel, Eunice de Souza, and Meena Kandasamy. Each poet draws from everyday language to question social norms, middle-class ambitions, and gender roles. Ezekiel adds humour and irony to the routines of urban India, influenced by borrowed English and Bollywood dreams. De Souza's sharp, understated voice highlights the subtle pressures women face from cultural and religious expectations. Kandasamy, with a bolder tone, employs pop-cultural symbols to challenge caste, patriarchy, and erasure. Together, their poems show how popular culture can serve as both a mirror, reflecting who we think we are, and a mask, hiding deeper social tensions. Through satire, these poets uncover the complexities and contradictions beneath the familiar surface of culture.

Keywords: Satire and Popular Culture, Middle-Class Aspirations, Gender and Identity, Caste and Resistance, Media Influence, Cultural Critique, Postcolonial Urban Life

Popular Culture: Shades and Shadows

Arts express the human soul. All forms of art, whether literature, dance, music, or theatre, provide creative and meaningful reflections of human thought. When these forms are shared and shaped by society at a certain time, they morph into culture. Culture promotes connectivity; it strengthens social bonds and brings harmony among differing practices, beliefs, and thought systems. As Storey notes, "Culture is how we live nature (including our own biology); it is the shared meanings we make and encounter in our everyday lives... created from the production, circulation, and consumption of meanings." To share a culture means interpreting and making sense of the world in similar ways.

Popular culture, as a part of culture, is fluid and constantly changing. It is not fixed but shaped by its context, emerging uniquely in specific places and times. According to Kidd, it represents "a complex of mutually interdependent perspectives and values that influence society and its institutions" (Kidd 12). Popular culture includes practices, beliefs, and items that reflect a society's most widely shared meanings. It also becomes a way to make cultural narratives accessible to a broad audience, often through media such as television, film, advertisements, and now digital platforms.

Nissim Ezekiel is often credited with shaping modern Indian English poetry, not just through form and language, but also through the topics he chose to examine. His poems provide sharp, often humorous views into the everyday lives of urban, middle-class Indians. What makes his work unique is the blending of satire with elements of popular culture—drawing from familiar voices, borrowed English, and references that echo cinema, television, and advertisements. This paper focuses on two of his dramatic monologues, "The Railway Clerk" and "Goodbye Party for Miss Pushpa T.S.," both of which show how pop culture seeps into language, behaviour, and social identity.

Popular Culture: Shades and Shadows

Next the focus shifts to the poetry of Eunice de Souza and Meena Kandasamy, whose voices are sharper and more political but similarly grounded in the everyday. De Souza's work subtly challenges the cultural roles expected of women, while Kandasamy's poems boldly speak from the margins, confronting both caste and gender violence. Across their poems, satire and references to popular culture serve not only to entertain but to reveal, making visible the contradictions, performances, and pressures of modern Indian life. This paper examines these poets together to show how satire, informed by pop culture, becomes a way to resist, question, and sometimes laugh at the worlds they inhabit.

Nissim Ezekiel: Representation of Pop Culture in "The Railway Clerk" and "Goodbye Party for Miss Pushpa T.S."

Nissim Ezekiel, often regarded as the father of modern Indian English poetry, used satire, irony, and everyday language to depict the realities of urban, middle-class Indian life. Two of his most popular dramatic monologues, "The Railway Clerk" and "Goodbye Party for Miss Pushpa T.S.," address different yet connected aspects of this environment—bureaucratic monotony and social ritualism—deeply influenced by popular culture. Through his characters' voices, Ezekiel critiques language, routine, aspiration, and social behaviour, highlighting how middle-class India adopts and performs ideals promoted by Bollywood, television, and advertisements.

"The Railway Clerk"

"The Railway Clerk" is a dramatic monologue that gives voice to a lower-middle-class clerk stuck in the dull and uninspiring world of Indian bureaucratic life. The poem critiques the mundane routines of these jobs and explores how postcolonial modernity and popular media shape our cultural goals. The speaker begins with a flat, almost indifferent description of his job:

Popular Culture: Shades and Shadows

> I am a clerk in the railways, and live in a railway quarter,
> My work is very responsible and I am always busy with it.. (Ezekiel, lines 1–2).

These lines express a sense of dull pride in routine, reflecting the middle-class glorification of stable government jobs, a theme reinforced in both Indian serials and films since the Nehruvian era. The focus on "responsible" work shows how tediousness is dignified. The clerk clings to hopes of moving up through exams:

> If I pass B.A. and work for the railway exams,
> I will rise (Ezekiel, lines 4–5).

This shows the deep belief in meritocratic success promoted in Bollywood films like *Do Bigha Zamin* and *3 Idiots*, where education represents a way to prosperity. The clerk's faith in gradual progress emphasizes how popular culture values endurance over radical action. The speaker acknowledges his despair but chooses to accept it:

> Sometimes I am very miserable and sit in the office for long hours,
> I am thinking of my future and decide rightly in the end
> That one has to adjust (Ezekiel, lines 8–10).

The phrase "one has to adjust" is common in Indian culture. One often hears it in family dramas and motivational ads. It means accepting changes instead of resisting them or trying to change things. The poem also emphasizes the financial instability that challenges the speaker's stoicism:

> My wife is always asking for money.
> Money, money—where to get it from? (Ezekiel, lines 11–12).

These lines reveal the gap between the ideal of the stable provider, which is prevalent in popular media, and the economic realities of the urban working class. The clerk's frustration mirrors the economic mediocrity glorified in popular narratives as "simple living, high thinking." "The Railway Clerk" transforms into more than a portrait of a civil servant—it reflects the collective mindset of postcolonial Indian urban life, filled with aspirations modelled after films, television, and advertisements. The poem subtly mocks how routine and resignation are romanticized, showcasing a protagonist trapped in a cycle of hope, disappointment, and passive endurance—a distinctly middle-class pop narrative.

"Goodbye Party for Miss Pushpa T.S."

Ezekiel's "Goodbye Party for Miss Pushpa T.S." presents another humorous dramatic monologue delivered in Indian English, imitating the language and tone of a middle-class farewell speech. The poem captures the mechanical nature of social politeness, the awkwardness of postcolonial linguistic identity, and the aspirations connected to going "abroad." The poem opens with an exaggeratedly polite and awkward tone, filled with grammatical quirks typical of Indian English:

Friends,
our dear sister
is departing for foreign
in two three days,
and we are meeting today
to wish her bon voyage.(Ezekiel, lines 1–6)

This passage humorously mimics formal farewell speeches in Indian social settings, where borrowed customs awkwardly mix with local expressions. The phrase "departing for foreign" satirizes how odd English phrases, common in Bollywood films and Indian media, have become normalized. It also points to the long-standing dreams and obsession of Indians with things that are essentially 'foreign'—foreign returns, foreign-made items, *phirangi bahu, phirangi* boy, etc. Ezekiel uses these language features to show how artificial and performative such gatherings can be. The speaker's overly emotional praise of Miss Pushpa,

Popular Culture: Shades and Shadows

while vague and repetitive, highlights how people tend to exaggerate qualities in these situations.

> She is most popular lady
> with men also and ladies also. (Ezekiel, lines 10–11)

This type of superficial flattery reflects how reality shows, office events, and school functions in Indian pop culture often feature insincere displays of emotion and affection. The sarcasm in the phrase "of ladies too" points out the stereotypical jabs often exchanged among women during conflicts. The repetition and generalization satirize the social obligation of showing gratitude over genuine feelings, a theme frequently seen in Indian soap operas and middle-class gatherings. The entire occasion revolves around Miss Pushpa's travel "abroad," which is treated as an achievement in itself:

> You are all knowing, friends,
> what sweetness is in Miss Pushpa?" (Ezekiel, lines 7–8)

"I am always appreciating the good spirit
pushing and pushing
wherever she is needing. (Ezekiel, lines 16–18)

The speaker lacks many details about her, yet he crafts an ideal image of her determination. He playfully critiques how Indian pop culture lifts the act of going abroad. Media, including films like *Dilwale Dulhania Le Jayenge* and various ads, have often celebrated the West as a place of success, freedom, and higher status. Ezekiel critiques this blind admiration, unveiling it as superficial and performative. He employs the structure of a farewell address to highlight the emptiness of middle-class customs. The poem illustrates society's fixation on surface appearances, whether in language, decorum, or the allure of Western influence—elements that prioritize rituals over genuine emotions. By mimicking Indian English, Ezekiel comments on the lingering effects of colonialism and shows how popular culture makes these modes of expression seem appealing, despite their lack of true depth.

Eunice de Souza: "Pop Culture and Gender in "Bequest", "Advice to Women", and "Sweet Sixteen"

Eunice de Souza is known for her straightforward yet sharp poetry, which highlights the contradictions women face while navigating patriarchal, religious, and middle-class expectations in India. Her writing takes on a restrained and ironic tone to challenge the morality, hypocrisy, and gender roles present in cultural systems, including those from popular media, religion, and home life. De Souza critiques how pop culture shapes female desire, behaviour, and identity using plain language, sudden tone shifts, and subtle irony.

"Bequest":

In "Bequest," the speaker grapples with the internalized need to stay emotionally guarded in a world that punishes female vulnerability:

I've made my commitments now.
This is one: to stay unmarried.(de Souza, lines 1–2)

This statement is both personal and political; it questions the belief that women find fulfillment through marriage, a common theme in Bollywood films, soap operas, and advice columns. The poem dismantles the stereotype of the self-sacrificing, emotionally giving woman.

I don't want to get hurt.
I don't want to hurt others. (lines 8–9)

This self-protective attitude directly challenges the romanticized suffering of women common in films, songs, and serials. It replaces that idea with self-containment and agency.

"Advice to Women":

This poem, deceptively simple, begins with advice:
Keep cats
if you want to learn to cope with

the otherness of lovers.(de Souza, lines 1–3)

Here, the speaker uses irony to highlight the emotional labour and compromise that women are expected to perform in relationships. The suggestion to choose pets over partners critiques the notion that women must always adapt, a sentiment echoed in romantic films and advertisements that glorify female patience, forgiveness, and nurturing roles. By advocating for detachment instead of submission, de Souza rewrites the common narrative of female devotion.

"Sweet Sixteen":

This poem delves into the confusion and guilt placed on adolescent girls by religious doctrines and pop-cultural expectations regarding purity and rebellion:

I remember the commands
of my teacher, Sister Letitia:
'Never go out alone!'
'Never trust a man!' (de Souza, lines 2–5)

These warnings, delivered in a Catholic school, reflect a wider cultural fear surrounding female sexuality. At the same time, popular culture bombards young women with hypersexualized images, beauty ideals, and fantasies of love—a contradiction the speaker faces directly:

And all the time I was being told
how good God was.(lines 6–7)

This moral contradiction—between divine love and human distrust—mirrors the media's portrayal of the "good girl" versus the "bad girl." The title, "Sweet Sixteen," is a pop culture label often linked to idealized innocence and sexual awakening, evident in magazines, teen films, and music. De Souza breaks down this romanticization by shedding light on the fear and repression behind it.

In her three poems, de Souza uses simple language and irony to reveal how popular culture both supports and hides patriarchal values. Her use of irony acts as a powerful tool—through mock-advice, quiet sarcasm, and pithy lines, she uncovers the absurdity of societal expectations and questions media-driven ideas of femininity, sacrifice, and virtue. The straightforwardness of her language masks a complex critique, reflecting the tone of self-help columns, school rules, and moralistic teachings—mediums that often shape young women's actions within pop culture and institutional settings. Furthermore, de Souza's refusal to glorify love, marriage, or submissiveness effectively challenges the romantic myths perpetuated by Bollywood and teen culture, where female identity often hinges on male attention or acts of sacrifice.

Eunice de Souza's poetry serves as a feminist response to the popular culture of middle-class India, exposing the fractures beneath the idealized images of womanhood promoted by films, religion, and media. In "Bequest," "Advice to Women," and "Sweet Sixteen," she contests the cultural scripts imposed on women, advocating for autonomy over conformity, realism over romanticism, and resistance over resignation. Her poetry urges readers—especially women—to recognize the performative traps of pop culture and reclaim the right to define their identities.

Meena Kandasamy: Resistance through Pop Culture

Meena Kandasamy is a Dalit poet, translator, and activist known for her bold political voice that addresses issues of gender violence, caste oppression, and media complicity. Her poetry features a raw, confrontational tone that often critiques mainstream cultural narratives that silence or glamorize oppression. Writing from the intersection of feminism, caste resistance, and pop culture critique, Kandasamy reclaims the language of power and visibility. Her work does more than challenge norms—it reveals how popular culture contributes to perpetuating systems of inequality, especially regarding how women's bodies, beauty, and suffering are consumed and commercialized.

In "Mascara," Kandasamy reveals how beauty standards

Popular Culture: Shades and Shadows

pushed by media and fashion industries shape and distort women's identities. The cosmetic item—mascara—serves as a metaphor for masking pain, oppression, and authenticity.

Mascara runs when you cry. So, I wear kohl. (Kandasamy, line 1)

This opening line rejects Western beauty standards in favour of an indigenous, resistant aesthetic. It plays on the language of advertising and self-care culture, but with a subversive twist: kohl becomes a symbol of cultural pride and emotional strength, unlike the fragility linked to mascara. Her critique targets how pop culture urges women to beautify rather than empower themselves, to conceal rather than confront:

I wear kohl / so the world knows I am capable of fury, too. (lines 3–4)

In this context, Kandasamy reframes makeup as more than just decoration; it becomes a political statement—a form of battle armour. This serves as a clear challenge to media portrayals that equate beauty with submissiveness and flawlessness, frequently sidelining the anger of women, especially those from marginalized backgrounds.

In "Dead Woman Walking," Kandasamy addresses the spectacle of violence against women, particularly how such suffering is often sensationalized or erased in mainstream narratives.

She walks, a dead woman, / headlines having failed her. (Kandasamy, lines 1–2)

These lines indicate that media coverage tends to be biased, often neglecting incidents that do not fit the prevailing political or aesthetic narratives. The "dead woman" symbolizes not just victims of violence but also those who remain overlooked due to a lack of journalistic interest and societal numbness.

Kandasamy employs a tone reminiscent of news reports, reflecting how newspapers list acts of violence without engaging with their causes or effects. She critiques the objectification of trauma:

> Her blood doesn't / stain prime-time news. (lines 4–5)

This text critiques how the media focuses only on certain types of victimhood that resonate with middle-class values or attract viewership. It shows how popular culture often presents violence against women as entertainment while failing to address the need for justice or real change. Kandasamy's writing style is intentionally demanding. She avoids romanticizing oppression and does not glamorize tough topics. Her poetry features direct language, utilizing short, straightforward sentences that resemble protest slogans or social media posts. Additionally, she incorporates pop culture references to criticize beauty ads, fashion trends, and news cycles that shape modern women's lives. In poems like "Mascara," she employs performance and reversal by repurposing consumer language, transforming beauty products into powerful symbols of resistance.

By reclaiming narrative power, she highlights the experiences of Dalit and marginalized women—individuals often ignored in mainstream pop culture, where they are viewed only as victims or symbols. In her poems "Mascara" and "Dead Woman Walking," Kandasamy strongly resists the dominant stories in popular culture. She critiques how the media celebrates female beauty while overlooking the pain women face, particularly issues related to caste and class. Her bold voice, use of cultural symbols, and refusal to romanticize suffering turn her poetry into a tool for activism. It seeks visibility and questions a culture that treats silence as grace. Kandasamy's work encourages readers to look beyond the surface of pop culture to see the genuine stories and struggles behind it.

In different ways, Nissim Ezekiel, Eunice de Souza, and Meena Kandasamy use poetry to reflect society. What connects them is how they draw from popular culture, not to celebrate it blindly, but to question what it reveals about who we are and how we live. Ezekiel's poems subtly mock the routines, ambitions, and borrowed manners of the urban middle class. De Souza's work, while more restrained, sharply interrogates the expectations placed on women by society, religion, and media. Kandasamy's voice is more forceful, pushing back against the silencing and stereotyping of marginalised women in mainstream culture. Across these poets, satire becomes more than just humour—it uncovers truths often hidden beneath everyday speech, customs, or media images. Pop culture in their work is not merely background—it's a living part of the world they critique, shaping how people communicate, behave, and think about success, love, and respectability. By reading these voices collectively, we start to see how poetry can address the world around it with honesty, irony, and even anger. In doing so, it helps us question the cultural narratives we've come to accept, reminding us that what seems normal often deserves a second look.

Rreferences:
Ezekiel, Nissim. 'The Railway Clerk'. *Collected Poems (1952–1988)*. Oxford University Press, 2005.
De Souza, Eunice. 'Bequest', 'Advice to Women', and 'Sweet Sixteen'. *A Necklace of Skulls: Collected Poems*. Penguin Books, 2009.
Kandasamy, Meena. 'Mascara' and 'Dead Woman Walking'. *Ms Militancy*. Navayana Publishing, 2010.
Kidd, D. (2017, February 28). 'Popular culture'. Oxford Bibliographies. Oxford University Press.
https://doi.org/10.1093/obo/9780199756384-0193
Storey, John. Cultural Studies and the Study of Popular Culture. Edinburgh University Press, 2010.
https://doi.org/10.1515/9780748641666.

Chapter-10

Popular Culture and Indian Society: Reflections of Social Change

Dr. Vijay Kumar Banshiwal

Abstract

This paper explores the interplay between popular culture and social change in India, examining how evolving cultural practices reflect broader societal transformations. Popular culture, manifested through media, festivals, cinema, and digital platforms, plays a pivotal role in shaping public discourse and influencing social norms. The research delves into the influence of traditional and modern cultural forms, highlighting how they contribute to the shaping of gender, caste, and identity in contemporary Indian society. Through a comprehensive analysis of media, including television, cinema, and social media, the paper investigates the significant role of media and technology in the rapid dissemination of cultural trends, bridging the gap between rural and urban India. Additionally, it examines the shifting values around religion, community, and family structures, which are continuously renegotiated in popular cultural representations. The paper also highlights the economic and political implications of popular culture, including its role in marketing, consumerism, and public policy. Ultimately, this research provides an understanding of how popular culture functions as both a mirror and a driver of social change in India, offering insights into the complexities of identity, modernity, and tradition in an increasingly globalized world.

Keywords: Popular culture, social change, media, Indian society, gender, identity, festivals, digital platforms, cinema, technology.

Introduction

Popular culture, often referred to as "mass culture,"

encompasses the practices, beliefs, and objects that dominate the everyday lives of people in a society. It evolves through the interactions of individuals within various communities, shaped by influences like technology, globalization, and historical transitions (Storey, 2018). In the context of Indian society, popular culture represents a blend of tradition and modernity, reflecting the nation's diverse cultural, linguistic, and regional identities.

India's popular culture is deeply rooted in its rich heritage but has undergone significant transformation due to socio-economic changes and technological advancements. For example, the advent of cinema in the early 20th century marked a turning point, establishing a medium that would later define popular culture in the country (Rajadhyaksha, 2009). Over time, elements such as television, music, and digital platforms became integral in disseminating cultural narratives to a broader audience, creating shared experiences across different strata of society.

Social change and popular culture are intrinsically linked, with each influencing the other. Popular culture often mirrors societal values and trends while simultaneously shaping public attitudes and behaviours. For instance, Bollywood cinema, a key aspect of Indian popular culture, has played a dual role in reflecting and challenging societal norms. Films like *Mother India* (1957) highlighted traditional values, while later works such as *Queen* (2014) and *Pink* (2016) questioned gender stereotypes, illustrating evolving social ideologies (Kumar, 2016).

In recent decades, globalization and digitalization have further accelerated the impact of popular culture on Indian society. The penetration of social media platforms such as Instagram, YouTube, and TikTok has not only democratized cultural expression but also reshaped consumption patterns. Data from the Internet and Mobile Association of India (IAMAI) reveals a sharp rise in online content consumption, particularly among the youth, showcasing the profound role of technology in shaping cultural trends.

Historical Context of Popular Culture in India

The historical evolution of popular culture in India reflects the nation's complex socio-political and cultural transitions. Its roots can be traced back to ancient times when epics like the *Ramayana* and *Mahabharata* served as early forms of popular entertainment and moral instruction, shared through oral storytelling traditions (Sharma, 2012). Over centuries, these narratives evolved into folk art, theatre, and festivals that celebrated regional and religious diversity.

The colonial era marked a significant transformation in Indian popular culture. British rule introduced print media, which played a crucial role in shaping public discourse. Newspapers, periodicals, and novels, often published in vernacular languages, became accessible to a wider audience, fostering a sense of national identity (Chatterjee, 1993). For instance, works like Bankim Chandra Chattopadhyay's *Anandamath* not only entertained but also inspired early nationalist movements.

The introduction of cinema in the early 20th century brought a paradigm shift in India's cultural landscape. The silent film *Raja Harishchandra* (1913), directed by Dadasaheb Phalke, is often regarded as the birth of Indian cinema and an early representation of popular culture in a modern medium. As cinema evolved, it became a powerful tool for reflecting societal changes and bridging regional divides, with films increasingly addressing issues such as independence, social reform, and economic struggles (Rajadhyaksha, 2009).

Post-independence, Indian popular culture expanded rapidly with the advent of television in the 1980s. Doordarshan, the state broadcaster, played a pivotal role in disseminating cultural values through programs like *Ramayan* and *Mahabharat*. These televised epics attracted record-breaking viewership, showcasing the enduring influence of ancient narratives on modern platforms (Kumar, 2016).

Globalization in the 1990s introduced Western influences, reshaping popular culture further. The liberalization of the Indian economy led to increased exposure to global media, music, and fashion, fostering a hybrid cultural identity. By integrating traditional elements with global trends, Indian popular culture began to resonate with both domestic and international audiences.

Media as a Catalyst of Social Change

Media has consistently played a pivotal role in shaping and reflecting social change in India. From print to digital platforms, its evolution has redefined how people interact with cultural narratives, influencing public opinion and societal norms.

In the early 20th century, print media emerged as a powerful medium for disseminating ideas of social reform and independence. Newspapers like *Kesari* and *The Hindu* not only informed readers but also mobilized them towards collective action during the freedom struggle (Chatterjee, 1993). By reaching diverse audiences, print media laid the groundwork for using mass communication as a tool for social transformation.

The advent of cinema further amplified media's impact on Indian society. Films often acted as mirrors of societal aspirations and tensions, addressing themes like caste discrimination, gender inequality, and economic disparity. For instance, movies such as *Do Bigha Zamin* (1953) highlighted rural poverty and migration, while *Damini* (1993) emphasized women's rights and justice. These narratives created awareness about pressing social issues while also fostering empathy and dialogue among audiences (Rajadhyaksha, 2009).

Television revolutionized Indian media in the 1980s,

particularly with the rise of Doordarshan. Iconic shows like *Buniyaad* and *Hum Log* tackled issues of family dynamics, class struggles, and modernization, influencing societal attitudes at a grassroots level. Furthermore, televised epics like *Ramayan* and *Mahabharat* played a significant role in reinforcing cultural identity and moral values during a period of rapid urbanization (Kumar, 2016).

The digital era has exponentially increased media's influence on Indian society. With over 700 million internet users as of 2018, platforms like YouTube, Instagram, and Twitter have democratized cultural expression and allowed for real-time engagement with social issues (IAMAI, 2018). Campaigns such as #MeToo gained significant traction in India through digital media, highlighting the transformative power of online platforms in advocating for gender equity and justice.

Media, in its various forms, continues to act as both a reflection and a driver of social change in India. By amplifying marginalized voices and shaping cultural discourse, it underscores its indispensable role in navigating the complexities of a rapidly evolving society.

Cultural Representation in Indian Cinema and Television

Indian cinema and television have long been influential platforms for reflecting and shaping societal values. They serve as both mirrors of the country's complex cultural landscape and agents of change, addressing key social issues and fostering inclusivity.

Cinema, often referred to as the lifeblood of Indian popular culture, has continually evolved to represent diverse cultural, social, and regional identities. In the early decades, films such as *Mother India* (1957) and *Pather Panchali* (1955) showcased rural struggles and the resilience of Indian society. These narratives provided a lens through which audiences could engage with issues like poverty, migration, and gender roles (Rajadhyaksha, 2009). Over time, Bollywood and regional cinema began to adopt more nuanced approaches, portraying urbanization, globalization, and individual aspirations while still drawing upon traditional values.

Television emerged as a dominant medium in the 1980s, with serials like *Hum Log* and *Buniyaad* providing compelling portrayals of post-independence challenges, including class disparities and family dynamics. These shows not only entertained but also educated audiences about prevailing societal issues (Kumar, 2016). The rise of private broadcasters in the 1990s further diversified content, leading to an explosion of regional programming and the representation of underrepresented communities.

In contemporary times, the portrayal of women in cinema and television has become a significant focus, reflecting broader societal shifts. Films like *Queen* (2014) and *Thappad* (2020) challenge traditional gender norms, while television serials increasingly depict women in leadership roles, illustrating a gradual but impactful change in societal perceptions (Desai, 2018). Similarly, issues of caste, class, and LGBTQ+ representation have gained prominence, with films like *Article 15* (2019) and series such as *Made in Heaven* breaking stereotypes and fostering dialogue.

Regional cinema, too, has played a crucial role in preserving and promoting local cultures. Tamil, Bengali, and Marathi films have explored themes like cultural identity and historical narratives, resonating deeply with regional audiences while gaining international acclaim.

Indian cinema and television, through their dynamic storytelling, remain essential cultural platforms, capturing the essence of a society that is both rooted in tradition and open to change. Their role in bridging divides and fostering social dialogue continues to grow in relevance.

Impact of Globalization on Indian Popular Culture

Globalization has profoundly influenced Indian popular culture, reshaping its contours by blending traditional values with global trends. This transformation reflects the dynamic interplay between cultural preservation and adaptation, driven by economic liberalization, technological advancements, and increased global connectivity.

The liberalization of the Indian economy in 1991 marked a turning point, enabling the influx of international brands, media, and cultural products. This economic shift led to the widespread availability of foreign content through cable television and later, streaming platforms. Channels like MTV India and Star World introduced global music, fashion, and lifestyle trends to Indian audiences, significantly impacting youth culture (Mehta, 2015).

Cinema has also been a key arena where globalization's impact is evident. Bollywood, while retaining its quintessential song-and-dance formula, has increasingly incorporated international filming locations, collaborations, and themes that appeal to global audiences. Films such as *Dilwale Dulhania Le Jayenge* (1995) and *Zindagi Na Milegi Dobara* (2011) reflect the aspirations of a globalized middle class while maintaining a connection to Indian cultural values (Gokulsing & Dissanayake, 2013).

The music industry has similarly experienced a fusion of global and local influences. Bollywood soundtracks now frequently feature elements of hip-hop, EDM, and reggae, catering to a more cosmopolitan audience. Independent music, propelled by platforms like YouTube and Spotify, has allowed Indian artists to experiment with global genres while incorporating regional flavors.

Digitalization has further accelerated the globalization of Indian popular culture. Social media platforms such as Instagram, Facebook, and TikTok have facilitated the dissemination of global trends, fostering a hybrid cultural identity among the youth. As of 2018, India had over 250 million Facebook users, showcasing the extent of digital penetration and its role in shaping cultural narratives (IAMAI, 2018).

However, globalization has also sparked debates about cultural homogenization and the erosion of traditional values. Critics argue that the dominance of Western cultural products risks overshadowing India's indigenous heritage. Nonetheless, Indian popular culture has demonstrated remarkable resilience, adapted global influences while celebrated its distinctiveness.In sum, globalization has transformed Indian popular culture into a vibrant amalgamation of the local and the global, illustrating its adaptability and relevance in a rapidly changing world.

Evolving Narratives in Contemporary Indian Literature

Contemporary Indian literature has undergone a significant transformation, reflecting the changing social, political, and cultural realities of a globalized and dynamic society. These narratives highlight the complexities of identity, tradition, and modernity, providing a nuanced understanding of India's multifaceted experiences.

Post-liberalization, Indian literature witnessed a surge in themes addressing globalization, migration, and urbanization. Authors like Arundhati Roy in *The God of Small Things* (1997) and Jhumpa Lahiri in *The Namesake* (2003) explore the intersections of personal and societal transformations, delving into issues of class, caste, and diasporic identity (Mukherjee, 2014). These works encapsulate the impact of socio-economic changes on individual and collective lives, resonating with both domestic and global audiences.

Regional literature has also played a vital role in shaping contemporary Indian narratives. Written in vernacular languages such as Tamil, Malayalam, and Bengali, these works delve deeply into regional histories, folklore, and socio-political issues. For example, Perumal Murugan's *One Part Woman* (2010) examines themes of gender, tradition, and societal expectations in rural Tamil Nadu, sparking critical discussions on cultural orthodoxy (Rao, 2018).

Indian English literature has increasingly addressed previously marginalized voices and perspectives. Writers like Dalit authors Bama and Yashica Dutt have foregrounded caste-based oppression, offering raw and authentic insights into systemic inequalities. LGBTQ+ themes have also gained prominence, with works such as *A Life Apart* by Neel Mukherjee and *The Ministry of Utmost Happiness* by Arundhati Roy portraying the struggles and resilience of queer individuals in a conservative society (Chopra, 2019).

The advent of digital platforms has further diversified Indian literature. Self-publishing platforms, blogs, and e-books have democratized storytelling, allowing emerging writers to share their voices without traditional gatekeeping. As of 2018, digital readership in India grew exponentially, particularly among the youth, creating new avenues for experimental and genre-defying narratives (IAMAI, 2018).

Contemporary Indian literature thus reflects the country's evolving ethos, blending traditional storytelling with bold, innovative perspectives. By embracing diversity and addressing pressing socio-political issues, it continues to contribute to a richer understanding of the Indian experience in the 21st century.

The Role of Festivals and Rituals in Shaping Indian Society

Festivals and rituals hold a central place in Indian society, serving as a nexus for cultural identity, social cohesion, and intergenerational continuity. These events transcend their religious origins, becoming powerful expressions of community life and instruments for cultural transmission.

Indian festivals, such as Diwali, Holi, Eid, and Christmas, are deeply embedded in the nation's cultural fabric. Diwali, for instance, represents the victory of light over darkness and is celebrated across religious and regional boundaries, reflecting the nation's pluralistic ethos (Kumar, 2017). The festival's economic impact is also significant, with consumer spending during Diwali accounting for a substantial portion of annual retail sales, driving both rural and urban economies (Saxena, 2018).

Rituals associated with these festivals often foster a sense of belonging and social harmony. Holi, known for its vibrant use of colours, symbolizes the breaking of social hierarchies as individuals from various castes and communities come together to celebrate. Similarly, Eid gatherings emphasize shared meals and charitable giving, reinforcing communal ties and promoting inclusivity (Ahmed, 2016).

Apart from major festivals, regional and tribal celebrations add to India's cultural diversity. Events like Pongal in Tamil Nadu, Bihu in Assam, and the Hornbill Festival in Nagaland highlight agricultural cycles and environmental stewardship. These celebrations not only preserve traditional practices but also contribute to regional tourism and cultural exchange (Sharma, 2018).

Rituals such as weddings, birth ceremonies, and funerary rites also play a pivotal role in societal structuring. They mark life transitions and reinforce family and community bonds. For example, the "seven vows" in Hindu weddings encapsulate shared responsibilities and mutual respect, values central to Indian familial structures (Sen, 2017).

In contemporary times, festivals and rituals have also adapted to modern sensibilities. Environmentally sustainable practices, such as eco-friendly Ganesha idols and cracker-free Diwali celebrations, reflect a growing awareness of ecological concerns (Deshpande, 2018).

Through their multifaceted roles, festivals and rituals remain integral to Indian society, weaving together tradition and modernity, fostering social integration, and nurturing cultural pride across generations.

The Influence of Indian Popular Culture on Social Behaviour and Values

Indian popular culture plays a significant role in shaping social behaviour and values, serving as a medium for both reflecting and influencing societal norms. Through various forms of entertainment—films, music, television, and digital media—it addresses and amplifies themes central to Indian life, such as family, tradition, love, and socio-political issues.

Cinema, particularly Bollywood, has been a cornerstone of popular culture in India. Films often depict familial bonds and moral dilemmas, reinforcing traditional values while simultaneously challenging outdated norms. For example, movies like *Kabhi Khushi KabhiGham* (2001) celebrate familial unity, while *Dil Chahta Hai* (2001) represents a shift towards individualism and modernity among urban youth (Ganti, 2012). Bollywood also influences social attitudes through its portrayal of gender roles, relationships, and cultural practices, with progressive films like *Queen* (2014) promoting female empowerment and independence (Mishra, 2017).

Television soap operas, with their widespread reach, similarly impact everyday behaviour and value systems. Shows like *Balika Vadhu* have sparked discussions on issues such as child marriage and women's education, encouraging shifts in societal perceptions (Kumar, 2016). Reality TV and talent shows further promote aspirations and provide a platform for social mobility, resonating particularly with younger audiences.

Music has been another influential medium. From devotional songs to Bollywood soundtracks, music has shaped cultural expressions of love, spirituality, and nationalism. Contemporary genres, blending traditional Indian music with global influences like hip-hop and EDM, appeal to a younger demographic, shaping their cultural and behavioural preferences (Roy, 2018).

Digital platforms have amplified the impact of popular culture, with social media emerging as a powerful tool for shaping societal values. Influencers and online content creators have created trends that redefine beauty standards, lifestyles, and political discourse. The viral reach of memes, reels, and campaigns has enabled rapid dissemination of ideas, bridging generational and geographical divides (IAMAI, 2018).

However, critics argue that popular culture occasionally reinforces stereotypes and consumerism, prompting debates about its ethical responsibilities. Despite such concerns, Indian popular culture continues to be a dynamic force, shaping individual and collective behaviours while reflecting the evolving values of Indian society.

The Role of Media and Technology in Propagating Popular Culture

In the contemporary Indian context, media and technology play a crucial role in shaping and propagating popular culture, significantly altering how cultural norms, trends, and narratives are disseminated. The proliferation of digital platforms, television, radio, and cinema has transformed India into a media-saturated society, allowing for the rapid spread of cultural influences from both within and outside the country.

Television has historically been the most powerful medium for reaching mass audiences in India. Since the early 1990s, with the advent of cable television, shows like *Ramayan* and *Mahabharat* captured the national imagination, broadcasting cultural and moral values to millions. Over time, the content on television evolved to include entertainment channels, news broadcasts, and reality shows, catering to a wide range of interests and demographics. For example, popular reality shows such as *Bigg Boss* and *India's Got Talent* have shaped popular culture by bringing diverse forms of entertainment and personal stories into the public eye, often influencing fashion trends, beauty standards, and even social issues (Chopra, 2019).

The digital revolution has further expanded the reach and impact of media, making content more accessible across socio-economic divides. Platforms like YouTube, Instagram, and TikTok allow individuals to create and share content, bypassing traditional media channels. This democratization of media has given rise to new forms of entertainment, such as viral videos, influencer marketing, and online web series, contributing to the rapid spread of global and localized cultural trends. Social media influencers, for example, now play a pivotal role in shaping fashion trends, lifestyle choices, and even political opinions among youth (IAMAI, 2018).

Furthermore, the accessibility of smartphones and affordable internet has ensured that millions of Indians, particularly from rural and semi-urban areas, can engage with popular culture. The widespread use of apps like WhatsApp and Facebook has fostered new forms of communication and interaction, allowing cultural content to circulate quickly and influencing public opinion and social behaviour (Mehta, 2017).

While the influence of media and technology on popular culture has been overwhelmingly positive, fostering greater cultural exchange and social awareness, it has also raised concerns about issues like misinformation, privacy, and the loss of traditional cultural practices. Nonetheless, the symbiotic relationship between media, technology, and popular culture continues to shape Indian society in profound and multifaceted ways.

Conclusion

Indian popular culture, in its diverse manifestations, continues to be a dynamic force influencing societal values, behaviours, and identities. Through films, television, music, festivals, rituals, and the burgeoning digital landscape, popular culture serves as a reflection of social changes, simultaneously shaping public consciousness and facilitating the expression of evolving norms. From traditional festivals that foster community bonding to modern narratives in literature and cinema that challenge social conventions, popular culture is intricately linked to the broader societal transformations occurring in India.

The role of media and technology in the dissemination of cultural content has further intensified, making it easier for individuals and communities to access, adapt, and participate in cultural dialogues. The intersection of traditional and modern elements in contemporary Indian media has led to the formation of new, hybrid identities, often challenging previously held notions of class, caste, and gender. However, this evolution also comes with its challenges, including the commercialization of culture and the rise of digital misinformation.

As India continues to grapple with these complexities, popular culture remains a powerful tool for social commentary, a space for questioning prevailing ideologies, and a means of collective expression. Whether it is the depiction of gender equality in Bollywood or the rise of regional content challenging national narratives, the conversations prompted by popular culture are central to understanding the shifting socio-political fabric of Indian society. In this context, popular culture not only entertains but also educates, advocates for change, and strengthens the country's cultural diversity. The future of Indian society will undoubtedly be shaped by its ongoing engagement with the global and local forces of popular culture, making it an ever-evolving area of study.

References:
Ahmed, I. (2016). Social integration and communal harmony: An analysis of Eid celebrations in contemporary India. *South Asian Studies, 33*(2), 145-163.
Chatterjee, P. (1993). *The nation and its fragments: Colonial and postcolonial histories.* Princeton University Press.
Chopra, R. (2019). The evolution of Indian television: From mythological to reality shows. *Journal of Indian Media and Culture, 45*(1), 56-74.
Desai, N. (2018). Gender representation in Indian cinema: A critical review of contemporary trends. *Journal of Media Studies, 32*(4), 89-104.
Deshpande, A. (2018). Eco-friendly practices in Indian festivals: A shift towards sustainability. *Environmental Studies Review, 25*(3), 201-218.
Ganti, T. (2012). *Bollywood: A guide to popular Indian cinema.* Routledge.
Gokulsing, M., & Dissanayake, W. (2013). *Indian popular cinema: A narrative of cultural change.* Trentham Books.
IAMAI. (2018). The impact of social media on youth culture in India. *Internet and Mobile Association of India.*
Kumar, P. (2016). Changing values and the role of television in shaping social attitudes in India. *Media Studies Journal, 28*(1), 74-88.
Kumar, R. (2017). Festivals of India: A cultural and economic perspective. *Journal of Cultural Economics, 29*(4), 92-107.
Mehta, A. (2015). Globalization and the transformation of Indian youth culture. *Journal of Digital Culture, 5*(1), 45-61.
Mishra, S. (2017). Feminism and Bollywood: A critical

analysis of gender roles in contemporary Indian cinema. *Feminist Media Studies, 17*(3), 347-359.

Mukherjee, S. (2014). Post-liberalization literature in India: Themes of globalization and identity. *Indian Literary Review, 12*(2), 112-129.

Rajadhyaksha, A. (2009). *Indian cinema in the time of celluloid: From Bollywood to the emergency.* Indiana University Press.

Rao, N. (2018). Regional narratives in Tamil literature: An analysis of Perumal Murugan's works. *Journal of South Asian Studies, 35*(2), 55-78.

Roy, P. (2018). Popular music and youth culture in contemporary India. *Journal of Popular Music Studies, 15*(2), 219-237.

Saxena, P. (2018). The economic impact of Diwali on Indian retail sales. *Economic and Political Weekly, 53*(16), 34-41.

Sen, A. (2017). Hindu weddings and the role of rituals in shaping social norms. *Journal of South Asian Culture, 22*(1), 65-83.

Sharma, M. (2012). The oral tradition and its evolution in Indian epics. *Asian Cultural Studies Journal, 19*(3), 101-120.

Sharma, M. (2018). Regional festivals and cultural preservation in contemporary India. *Indian Journal of Anthropology, 34*(2), 140-156.

Storey, J. (2018). *Cultural theory and popular culture: An introduction* (8th ed.). Routledge.

Chapter-11
The Kaleidoscope of Culture: Popular Culture's Reflection and Reflection of Indian Culture

Dr. Shruti Srivastava,
Ms. Srishti

Abstract

Culture is a term that embodies components such as customs, beliefs, social norms, laws, arts, literature and institutions accepted by a group of people or human societies. The cultural practices which are shared worldwide through mass media resources such as radio, television, print and movies and are popular among the masses for a particular span of time are termed under popular culture. The components of popular culture may change with the change in the global trends.

Indian culture comprises of diverse traditional values, customs, beliefs, arts and literature accepted by the natives of India. It is a land of cultural diversity; therefore the set of cultural practices accepted by the natives may vary from one region or state to another. Since ancient times India is deep rooted with a cultural heritage, the reflection of which can be still seen in the practices prevalent in the times at present.

In the era of globalisation, the nations are influenced by different cultural practices of one another. A nation may embrace another's music, arts, cuisines, religious beliefs and other practices. This widespread sharing is made possible through literature, Internet and other hot and cold media.

India's music, dance forms, theatre, arts, crafts, rites and rituals have already been enlisted in the intangible cultural heritage of India, recognized by UNESCO. Some of these practices are appealed by people all across the globe.

Popular Culture: Shades and Shadows

Navroz, a spring festival is a part of the intangible cultural heritage of India and is also celebrated in twelve counties such as Afghanistan, Iran and other Central Asian nations. Vedic chanting, Yoga and folk dances of India are also highly acknowledged all over the globe. India is also highly influenced by the popular culture prevalent in the times. We have embraced Pop music, reality shows, OTTs, social media platforms, fashion, cuisines of different parts of the world.

While the nations embrace and acknowledge one another's cultural practices, the cultural legacy should remain intact and be not at stake. The awareness to maintain the cultural authenticity can be done through education, media literacy and creative expression.

Keywords: Culture; popular culture; education; media; technology; globalisation; evolution; cultural hybridity.

Culture is a term that embodies components such as customs, beliefs, social norms, laws, arts, literature and institutions accepted by a group of people or human societies. The cultural practices which arepracticed and gain popularity as per the needs of its consumers are classified under popular culture and shared worldwide through mass media resources such as radio, television, print and movies and are popular among the masses.

India is nation of great cultural diversity in terms of its traditions, customs, beliefs, language, attire, music, dance, theatre and festivals. These elements vary from one region to another.India's music, dance forms, theatre, arts, crafts, rites and rituals have already been enlisted in the intangible cultural heritage of India, recognized by UNESCO. Some of these practices are appealed by people all across the globe. Navroza spring festival, is a part of the intangible cultural heritage of India and is also celebrated in twelve counties such as Afghanistan, Iran and other Central Asian nations. Epics such as Ramayana and Mahabharata are gained

Popular Culture: Shades and Shadows

worldwide recognition and acclaim. Indian ethnic wear such as Sarees, suits are embraced all over the world. The Indian paintings such as Madhubani, Warli art, Tanjore paintings and many others have also been popular worldwide. Vedic chanting, Yoga and folk dances of India such as *Garba* and *Dandiya* are also highly acknowledged all over the globe. India is also highly influenced by the dances all over the globe.

India is also influenced by the popular culture prevalent in the times. We have embraced Pop music, reality shows, OTTs, social media platforms, fashion, cuisines of different parts of the world. Earlier it was limited to Bollywood, advertisements and cricket in India. But due to technological advancements it has extended its range and has imprinted its influence on different areas such as songs, music, theatre, sports, education, jobs, food, lifestyle, family values, fashion, communication, social media and many more to count. There has also been a trend of reality shows, YouTube channels, talk shows, podcasts, TedTalks, reels, shorts and live streaming.

India is also influenced by other dance forms such as salsa, tango, hip-hop and contemporary dance. The reflection of these dance forms can be seen in the choreography of Indian Bollywood songs. The trend of dance reality shows has also been a platform where one can witness the fusion of Indian dance forms with foreign dance forms.*NaatuNaatu* is one of the best examples to represent a dance fusion of pop,*dappankuthu* and western classical. This song became a global hit and won the best original song award at the Academy Awards, and the Golden Globe Award for the best original song.

The components of popular culture may change with the change in the global trends.

India has a plethora of rich music. The different musical genres practiced here include; Indian Classical music with its

Popular Culture: Shades and Shadows

categories – Hindustani and Carnatic. Some other forms of classical music are *Dhrupad, Thumri,Khyal*. This music has been made accessible to a wider audience through Bollywood.The songs of different Indian musical genres are blended with global musical genres to create new renditions.Illaiyaraaja is an Indian music composer who has blended classical music with jazz and electronic genres. Other notable music composers known for this transition include A.R. Rahman, R.D. Burman and S.D. Burman and many others. Nescafe Basement and Coke Studio are one of the most popular and leading platforms to present the music popular culture. Some popular renditions of Indian folk music presented in Coke Studio include *Aajbirajmeinhori re rasiya;ChaapTilak*by AbeedaParveen and many more. In these platforms the singers and musicians from different regions and nations collaborate, compose and present musical performances of different musical genres or fusion of the genres. Some of their songs are different renditions of the original songs that were popular on a regional or national level. The blending of different musical genres with each other and the usage of musical instruments highlight the versatility of music. This not only appeals to the music listeners of that genre but also interests the enthusiastic listeners of other musical genres as well. Some songs and their videos also highlight the cultural diversity of the world. Some examples include, Sayonara representing the Japanese language; *Kersariya Balamaayo re* representing the homecoming. *Sandeseaatehain* highlight the soldiers' nostalgia, *SasuralGenda Phool* adapted in the movie Delhi 6 is a Chhattisgarh folk song sung in marriages and *"bannoteriankhiyan","rangeelomarodholna", "bajre da sitta"* are some widely popular songs sung and played during Indian wedding celebrations and many other represent different festivals celebrated in India.

Musical bands are another example of popular culture. There are different types of musical bands. The band is

Popular Culture: Shades and Shadows

formed with people having same musical taste, excelling in different categories such as vocals, instruments, sound, song writing and others.At present we have different regional, national and international level bands which are nationwide and globally popularamong people. The live performances of the bands captivate the audience.

Popular culture has also influenced the fashion trends of the world. In India, previously its influence was only limited to Bollywood. People were influenced by the celebrity outfits in movies. The outfits were mostly ethnic wears. But with the changing time and pace the fashion also evolved and western outfits were in vogue. This was how hybridity in the fashion was introduced and still prevails. Mall Culture also took over the conventional setup of a clothing store. Malls provide us a number of options in terms of brands, styles and other factors to look into and compare before buying a product. At present different fashion brands from all over the world are promoted and endorsed through celebrities to facilitate a global reach. The evolution from clothing stores to online shopping apps has also introduced people with a number of national and international clothing brands. One may choose from enormous brands as per one's needs and choices. Mall culture is not only confined to follow the fashion trends but has also took over the grocery, gadgets, beauty products and other stores to shop from. The online shopping destinations such as Amazon, Flipkart, Myntra are some leading examples.

Advertisements arefew examples which rule our minds. Earlier the advertisement of the products had jingles sung by singers but a considerable transition has been observed in that aspect as well. Some popular advertisement jingles are Washing Powder Nirma, Dhara Jalebi, Amul, Alpenliebe candy commercial, Coca Cola, Maggi and many other examples. The products are now endorsed by the celebrities to obtain a commercial success. People are less likely to see the ingredients used during the manufacturing of the product and the first preference for them remains the celebrity promoting the product. The celebrities are also made the brand ambassadors of different products to enable a wider recognition and reach.

    Every innovation and advancement carries merits and demerits with itself. Although every mode of communication, knowledge or entertainment is one click away from us but this has paved way for our emotional distress. Social media was introduced to make communication easier but we also find ourselves comparing one another and that shakes our mental peace at some extent. Our happiness now also depends on the likes, reactions and comments that we have on our photos and videos posted on the platforms such as Facebook, Instagram etc. when the responses do not meet our expectations it affects us negatively. Our connectivity with our acquaintances has now been limited to social media. It has highly affected our lifestyle and mental peace.

    Popular culture has both positive and negative impact on youth and education. Teens are very likely to be affected by cinema, music and theatre. Artificial intelligence is one of the latest emerging popular cultures in the entire world. AI was introduced to reduce human error, decrease the time required to complete different tasks and increase efficiency and output. But with the time passing by some of its disadvantages are also visible. It has somewhat made man dependent on the various beneficial features offered by it and get the desired outcome.

    Education was previously imparted through conventional teaching methods used by the teachers. Eventually the conventional classroom setup turned into audio-visual classrooms. Later on information and communication technology also started to play an important role in evolving the educational facilities by introducing different features such as projectors, PowerPoint presentations paperless classrooms, spreadsheets, online teaching and learning, paperless classrooms, Google forms and many other benefits. All these technological advancements and evolutions have made teaching and learning interesting, interactive and effortless.

Another emerging and leading popular culture and an initiative of Artificial Intelligence is ChatGPT. This chatbot provides numerous features such as human like conversations through responses and simplifies various tasks of different demands such as write essays, poetry and articles, songs, stories and tales, provide business ideas, translate, perform mathematical operations and help in computer programming. It has also lessened the human efforts required to complete assignments, projects and many such benefits. It also helps in providing creative learning methods and study plans to the students. All these features offered are beneficial on one hand but also pose a threat to the academic performance and learning and critical thinking of the students. Most of the students at present want their academic needs to be done merely by using the chatbot and not putting up their planning and efforts. It must be kept in mind that a technology has been introduced to lessen the human efforts but we are turning ourselves out to be its slave.

Book reading is on a decline according to a survey by National Endowment for the Arts. This decline is mostly observed in the age group between 18 to 34 years. Increased screen time on social media, online games, over-the-top platforms and other digital distractions are the major reasons behind it. Some genres are still very popular among the youth at present. These include campus novels. These highlight the socio-cultural and political issues prevalent in college life. Some also reflect on the coming of age aspect. Some best seller and immensely popular campus novels of India are Five Point Someone, 2 States and so on. Amish Tripathi is also the best-selling author of genres such as mythological fiction and historical fiction. Although mythology is considered as not a much popular genre among the readers but Amish's narration of the stories in the modern style and a reimagined perspective is totally praiseworthy. His commendable work"The Shiva Trilogy" is one of the fastest selling book series in the history of Indian publishing.

Significant changes have been observed in the work culture and environment as well. Strict working hours to flexible working management; in-office work to work from home or from anywhere transformation; assigned desks to flexible seating arrangements; landline phones, limited computer access to high speed internet and real-time collaborations are some notable examples of evolution in the work culture.

Video games replaced the conventional outdoor and indoor games played decades back. The introduction of online video games is also a form of popular culture. They are highly popular among adolescents and young adults. The time invested on these games drastically affects the health and other behavioural aspects of the players.

Indian culture mainly followed the joint family setup since ancient times. It highlighted the concept of strength in unity, oneness and the unbreakable bonding among the family members. But with evolving time and pace, members started to migrate from one place to another to seek better employment opportunities and other benefits for themselves. They also had to settle far away from their home when offered a different job location. Some members also leave their home due to domestic conflicts arising as a result of different perspectives and opinions. This may result into a single or a nuclear family concept.

Marriages in India are considered as a pious ceremony and institution but a change can also be seen in this concept. The recent years have witnessed a change in the outlook towards marriage. The concepts such as Big Fat Wedding,

Popular Culture: Shades and Shadows

Pre Wedding photo shoots, destination weddings are getting highly popular.

Cuisines are also one of the evolving examples of popular culture. The eating choices and patterns of the people of the world have transformed. Fast foods and packed food items were introduced and became immensely popular among the people of different age groups and restaurants were also set up to provide the fast food services to the customers. Currently food-tech and e-commerce industries such as Zomato and Swiggy are highly popular among people. In this competitive scenario both the male and female members in a family are employed. Therefore, they find less time to engage in the cooking habits due to their hectic schedule. This gave rise to a new initiative known as cloud kitchen. In a cloud kitchen the food is prepared for door step delivery and takeaway purposes only. It helps in generating employment opportunities for cooking enthusiasts and they may have their own business orstart up at a minimal cost. One may also start a cloud kitchen from their home or any desired place.

The beneficial side of such initiatives is its widespread reach not only at regional but also at national and international level. At present no dish is limited to its regional boundaries but has reached all over the globe as the chefs and cooking enthusiasts upload the cooking videos with the introduction of platforms such as Facebook, YouTube and Instagram so that they can be accessed by any enthusiastic learner at his own place.

Popular culture also gives rise to the concept of consumerism and as this culture remains in vogue as per the demands of its consumers. It can be short lived and long lived as per the change in demands and choice. This also has given a pathway to an increase in a materialistic approach in the individuals. India is a country, embraced and appealed for its rich cultural legacy and moral values. But with the rise in globalisation, people tend to judge one another on the basis of the materialistic possessions held by them. It seems that a person's values and virtues are turning secondary in the name of successful person.

We are currently living in a Global village where we are connected to one another through media and technology. Our social connection is now mainly through web and social media platforms. The real time conversations and meetings in person have considerably reduced. The faraway conversations which were mainly through letters PCOs, telephonic calls has eventually been substituted by to the point phone call conversations, text messages and e-mails.

It is an undeniable fact that the technological advancements, innovations and globalisation helps in sharing culture, skills and knowledge and strengthen cultural unity among nations. While we acknowledge and embrace the cultural practices of one another, the cultural legacy of one's nation should remain intact and not at stake. The awareness to maintain the cultural authenticity can be done through education, media literacy and cultural expression.

References:
Joshi, Priyanka, Cultural Ethos: Understanding popular culture, Nyra Publishers 2024.
Prakash, Om, Cultural History of India, New Age International, 2005.
Sarvabhootanand, Swami, The Perennial Values of Indian Culture, Ramkrishna Mission Institute of Culture, Kolkata, 2008.
Srinivasan, R, Facets of Indian Culture, BhartiyaVidyaBhawan, 1999.
Storey, John, Cultural Theory and Popular Culture: An Introduction, Taylor& Francis 2018.

Chapter-12
Fermented Flavors: Exploring Food Culture and Resistance in Axone

Devika. S. Raj

Abstract

This research paper explores the themes of food culture and resistance in the film *Axone* (2019), directed by Nicholas Kharkongor. The movie centers around a group of Northern migrants in Delhi who attempt to prepare a traditional dish called *Axone* (fermented soybeans) for a wedding celebration. The preparation of *Axone*, known for its pungent smell, becomes a symbol of cultural identity and resistance against the backdrop of racism and discrimination faced by the characters in the city. This study examines how the film portrays food as a medium of cultural expression and resistance, highlighting the challenges of preserving cultural heritage in a multicultural urban environment. Through a detailed analysis of the film's narrative, characters, and visual elements, the paper investigates the intersection of food, identity, and power dynamics. It also explores the broader implications of culinary practices as acts of resistance and the role of food in negotiating cultural boundaries. By situating *Axone* within the context of postcolonial studies and cultural anthropology, this research aims to contribute to the understanding of how food culture can serve as a site of resistance and identity formation in contemporary society.

Keywords: Axone, Food Culture, Cultural Identity, Discrimination, Culinary Practices

Introduction

In the rich tapestry of Indian cinema, *Axone* (2019), directed by Nicholas Kharkongor, stands out as a poignant exploration of cultural identity and resistance through the lens of food. Set against the vibrant yet challenging backdrop of Delhi, the film centres on a group of Northern migrants who attempt to prepare a traditional dish called *Axone*, made from fermented soybeans, for a wedding celebration. This seemingly simple act of cooking becomes a powerful symbol of cultural resistance and identity preservation in the face of racism and social marginalization. Discuss the broader context of migration within India, focusing on the movement of Northern communities to urban centres like Delhi. Explain the socio-economic and cultural reasons behind this migration and its impact on the migrant lives. The cultural stereotypes and misconceptions that Northern communities often face in other parts of India. Discuss how these stereotypes contribute to the marginalization and discrimination depicted in the film. The role of food in preserving cultural identity and heritage. Highlight how traditional dishes like *Axone* serve as a link to the migrant's homeland and as a medium for maintaining cultural continuity. Emphasize the interdisciplinary nature of your research by mentioning how it draws on postcolonial studies, cultural anthropology, and food studies. How this approach allows for a comprehensive analysis of the film's themes

Food, often seen as a mundane necessity, holds profound cultural and political significance. In *Axone*, the preparation and consumption of traditional dishes act as a form of resistance against the dominant cultural narratives and discriminatory attitudes prevalent in the city. The pungent aroma of *Axone*, which provokes strong reactions from the local community, metaphorically underscores the clash between cultural preservation and assimilation.

This research paper delves into the complex interplay of food culture, identity, and resistance depicted in *Axone*. Analysis of *Axone*, such as highlighting the importance of food culture in cultural resistance and shedding light on the experiences of marginalized communities. By situating the film within the frameworks of postcolonial studies and cultural anthropology, this study aims to uncover the deeper meanings behind the characters' culinary practices and their struggle to maintain their cultural heritage. The analysis will highlight how *Axone* uses food as a medium to challenge social hierarchies, assert cultural identity, and resist marginalization in a postcolonial urban setting and also "How does *Axone* use food to portray cultural identity and resistance?" or "What role does food play in the characters' struggle against marginalization and discrimination?"

Need of this Study

Food is a fundamental aspect of cultural identity. By studying *Axone*, we can gain insights into how Northern migrants in India use food to preserve their cultural heritage and assert their identity in a multicultural urban setting. The film sheds light on the racism and discrimination faced by Northern communities in metropolitan cities like Delhi. This study helps to bring attention to these social issues and promotes awareness and understanding of the challenges faced by marginalized groups. *Axone* within the context of postcolonial studies allows us to understand how colonial legacies continue to impact contemporary cultural practices and social dynamics. It provides a nuanced perspective on the ongoing effects of colonialism on food culture and identity. This study contributes to the field of cultural anthropology by examining how food acts as a medium of cultural expression and resistance. It highlights the role of culinary practices in negotiating cultural boundaries and maintaining community bonds. The act of preparing and sharing traditional food in the face of opposition is a form of cultural resistance. This study explores how food can be a powerful tool for resisting cultural assimilation and asserting one's cultural heritage. This research adds to the existing literature on postcolonial studies, cultural anthropology, and food studies. It provides a case study of how film can be used as a medium to explore and highlight complex cultural and social issues.

Research Methodology

The fundamental methodology for this research study is combination of qualitative research methodologies to effectively analyse and interpret the themes and cultural nuances presented in the film. Conduct a comprehensive review of existing literature on postcolonial studies, cultural anthropology, food culture, and films. This will provide a theoretical foundation for my analysis and help contextualize the research within the existing body of knowledge. key themes in the film, such as cultural identity, resistance, racism, and the significance of food. Focus on how these themes are portrayed through the narrative, dialogues, and visual elements. Explore the cultural practices and traditions of Northern communities, particularly their culinary customs, to understand the significance of *Axone* (the dish) as a symbol of cultural identity and resistance. Analyse the use of visual and audio elements in the film, such as cinematography, sound design, and mise-en-scène, to understand how they contribute to the portrayal of cultural identity and resistance.

Data and Sources of data

Primary Sources film *Axone* (2019) directed by Nicholas Kharkongor. Take detailed notes on key scenes, dialogues, and characters that highlight themes of food culture and resistance. Secondary Sources Academic Articles and Books "Bamboo Shoot in Our Blood: Fermenting Flavors and Identities in Northeast India" by Dolly Kikon. This essay explores how identities are mediated through fermented food in Northeast India. "Ethnic Fermented Foods and Beverages of India" by Jyoti Prakash Tamang, Namrata Thapa, Tek Chand Bhalla, and Savitri. This book discusses the diversity of ethnic fermented foods and beverages in

India "Microbial Quality and Safety of *Axone* -Akhuni, a Fermented Soybean Food of Nagaland" by Bhoj Raj Singh et al. This study analyses the microbial quality and safety of *Axone*, a fermented soybean food from Nagaland.

Theoretical Framework

Postcolonial theory examines the cultural, political, and social impacts of colonialism and the ways in which colonial legacies continue to shape contemporary societies. Key concepts from postcolonial theory that can be applied to your analysis include Hybridity This concept, developed by Homi K. Bhabha, refers to the mixing of cultures resulting from colonialism. In the context of *Axone*, you can explore how the characters' culinary practices reflect a hybrid identity, blending their Northern heritage with the multicultural influences of urban Delhi. Resistance and Agency Postcolonial theory also focuses on the ways in which marginalized groups resist and negotiate colonial power structures. Analysing how the characters use food as a form of cultural resistance against discrimination and social exclusion can provide insights into their agency and resilience. Cultural Identity: The theory emphasizes the construction and assertion of cultural identity in postcolonial contexts. You can examine how the preparation of *Axone* becomes a means for the characters to assert their cultural identity and maintain their heritage in a hostile environment. Cultural Anthropology studies the cultural practices, beliefs, and social structures of different communities. Relevant concepts from cultural anthropology for your analysis include Food as Cultural Symbol Anthropologists study food as a key element of cultural identity and social relations. In *Axone*, you can explore how the dish *Axone* symbolizes the characters' cultural identity and serves as a medium for expressing their connection to their homeland. Rituals and Traditions Cultural anthropology examines the role of rituals and traditions in maintaining cultural continuity. Analyse how the ritual of preparing and sharing *Axone* is depicted in the film and its significance for the characters' sense of community and belonging. Migration and Adaptation: Anthropologists study how communities adapt to new environments while preserving their cultural practices. Investigate how the Northeastern migrants in *Axone* navigate their cultural identity in the multicultural setting of Delhi, adapting their culinary practices to their new context. Power Dynamics and Social Hierarchies: Cultural anthropology looks at the power relations and social hierarchies that shape cultural practices. Analyse the power dynamics depicted in the film, focusing on how the characters' culinary practices challenge social hierarchies and resist marginalization. By applying these theoretical frameworks, you can conduct a comprehensive analysis of how *Axone* portrays food culture as a site of resistance and cultural expression. This approach will allow you to explore the deeper meanings behind the characters' culinary practices and their struggle to maintain their cultural identity in a postcolonial urban setting. Using postcolonial theory and cultural anthropology as your theoretical framework provides a robust foundation for analysing the themes of cultural identity, resistance, and the significance of food in *Axone*. This dual approach offers valuable insights into the complexities of cultural practices and the ongoing impact of colonial histories on contemporary societies.

Post-Colonialism and Cultural anthropology

The film portrays the Northern characters as the "other" within their own country. This reflects the post-colonial theme of internalized colonial attitudes, where Northern people are often seen as outsiders in other parts of India. This movie highlights the racism and discrimination faced by Northern which is a direct consequence of colonial-era stereotypes and prejudices. The character struggle to cook Axone, a traditional dish, in a Delhi neighbourhood exemplifies this. The act of cooking Axone becomes a symbol of resistance and cultural identity. The character determination to prepare the dish despite societal pressures showcases their resilience and commitment to preserving their heritage. The film provides a rich depiction of Northern cultural practices, including food preparation and communal living. This anthropological perspective helps viewers understand the cultural significance of Axone and other traditional practices. The interactions between the Northern characters and the local Delhi residents offer insights into the social dynamics and power structures. The film explores how cultural differences can lead to misunderstandings and conflicts. It also emphasizes the importance of community and solidarity among Northeastern. The characters support for each other in the face of discrimination highlights the strength of their cultural bonds. Axone provides a nuanced exploration of the challenges faced by Northers in India and the importance of cultural preservation and resistance. cultural anthropology is represented in the through **Food as Cultural Expression** *Axone* showcases the preparation of the traditional Northern dish Axone (fermented soybean) as a central cultural practice. The meticulous process of preparing this dish highlights the significance of food in cultural expression and heritage preservation. The film depicts various rituals and traditions associated with Northern culture, such as communal cooking and celebrations. These rituals reinforce community bonds and serve as a way to maintain cultural continuity in a diasporic context. By portraying the daily lives of the Northern characters, the film provides insights into their social practices, values, and norms. This includes their interactions, hospitality, and the importance they place on communal living. The interactions between the Northern characters and the local Delhi residents shed light on the social dynamics and power structures at play. These interactions often involve misunderstandings, prejudice, and conflict, reflecting broader social tensions. Cultural anthropology examines how communities support each other in the face of adversity. *Axone* highlights the solidarity among Northern migrants as they navigate challenges and discrimination, showing the strength of their community bonds. The film explores the characters' struggle to maintain their cultural identity while living in a different cultural environment. This reflects the anthropological concept of identity negotiation, where individuals and groups navigate their sense of belonging in a multicultural setting. The experiences of racism and discrimination faced by the Northern characters are central to the film's narrative. Cultural anthropology looks at how marginalized communities resist and respond to such power dynamics. The act of cooking Axone in the face of opposition serves as a form of cultural resistance. The characters determination to preserve their culinary traditions despite societal pressures highlights their resilience and agency. The film also shows how the Northern characters adapt their cultural practices to fit their new urban environment. This reflects the dynamic nature of culture and how it evolves in response to changing contexts. By examining these aspects through the lens of cultural anthropology, *Axone* provides a rich depiction of how cultural practices, social dynamics, and identity are maintained and negotiated in the face of marginalization and discrimination.

Analysis

Axone uses the preparation of traditional Northern food as a lens to explore cultural identity and the hybrid nature of postcolonial societies. According to Homi K. Bhabha's concept of hybridity, cultures blend and evolve as a result of colonial and postcolonial interactions. In *Axone*, the characters culinary practices reflect this hybrid identity, blending their Northern heritage with the multicultural influences of urban Delhi. The dish *Axone*, with its strong smell and distinct preparation method, symbolizes the characters attempt to maintain their cultural roots while navigating a new and often hostile environment. The film highlights the struggle of Northern migrants to assert their cultural identity in the face of discrimination and stereotyping. The characters' determination to prepare *Axone* despite opposition from their neighbours and landlords demonstrates their resilience and agency. This act of cooking becomes an assertion of their identity and a way to resist cultural assimilation. By preparing *Axone*, the characters are not only maintaining a connection to their homeland but also asserting their right to cultural expression in a city that often marginalizes them.

The act of preparing and consuming *Axone* in *Axone* serves as a powerful form of cultural resistance. According to postcolonial theory, resistance involves reclaiming and asserting cultural identity in the face of dominant power structures. The characters in the film use food as a means to resist the social and cultural pressures to assimilate into the dominant culture of Delhi. The pungent aroma of *Axone*, which provokes strong reactions from the local community, metaphorically underscores the clash between cultural preservation and assimilation. The neighbours' complaints about the smell reflect the broader social intolerance towards Northern cultural practices. The characters refusal to abandon their culinary traditions in the face of this opposition is a form of resistance against cultural erasure. Through food, they challenge the dominant narratives that seek to marginalize and silence their cultural identity.

Axone vividly portrays the racism and discrimination faced by Northern migrants in Delhi. The film depicts instances of verbal abuse, physical altercations, and social exclusion that the characters experience due to their ethnic background. The hostility they face is often directed at their culinary practices, which are seen as foreign and unwelcome by the local community. The preparation of Axon becomes a focal point for these tensions, highlighting the cultural and social boundaries that Northern migrants navigate daily. The characters determination to cook *Axone* despite these challenges underscores their resistance to the systemic racism and discrimination they face. The film thus uses food as a lens to critique the social hierarchies and power dynamics that marginalize Northern communities in urban India. Cultural anthropology emphasizes the role of rituals and traditions in maintaining cultural continuity. In *Axone*, the ritual of preparing and sharing traditional food plays a central role in the characters' efforts to preserve their cultural heritage. The wedding celebration for which they prepare *Axone* is a significant cultural event, symbolizing the continuity of traditions across generations and geographical boundaries. The film highlights the importance of culinary rituals in reinforcing cultural identity and community bonds. By engaging in the ritual of cooking *Axone*, the characters reaffirm their connection to their cultural roots and to each other. This act of cultural preservation becomes a form of resistance against the pressures of assimilation and cultural homogenization.

The experiences of Northern migrants in *Axone* reflect the broader dynamics of migration and adaptation in a multicultural urban setting. Cultural anthropology examines how communities adapt to new environments while preserving their cultural practices. The film portrays the challenges of maintaining cultural identity in a new and often hostile environment, as well as the ways in which migrants negotiate their identities in response to these challenges. The characters culinary practices serve as a means of adapting to their new context while preserving their cultural heritage. By preparing *Axone* in Delhi, they navigate the complexities of cultural preservation and adaptation, reflecting the hybrid nature of their postcolonial identity. The film thus underscores the significance of food in negotiating cultural boundaries and maintaining a sense of belonging in a multicultural urban environment.

In *Axone*, the characters' culinary practices challenge the social hierarchies and power dynamics that marginalize Northern communities in Delhi. The film critiques the dominant cultural narratives that seek to exclude and silence Northern voices, highlighting the power of food as a medium of resistance and cultural expression. The characters determination to prepare *Axone* despite opposition from their neighbours and landlords demonstrates their resistance to the social hierarchies that seek to marginalize them. By asserting their right to cultural expression through food, they challenge the dominant power structures and assert their agency. The film Cultural anthropology also examines the power dynamics and social hierarchies that shape thus highlights the role of culinary practices in resisting social and cultural marginalization.

Examine specific scenes where the cultural practices of the Northern characters come into conflict with those of the local Delhi community. These clashes reflect broader social tensions and the difficulties of intercultural coexistence. Intercultural Dialogue Highlight moments in the film where dialogue between characters from different cultural backgrounds leads to greater understanding or conflict resolution. This can underscore the potential for intercultural dialogue to bridge cultural divides, Social Cohesion and Solidarity Community Support by Analyse this in terms we can see how the characters support each other within their close-knit Northern community. Discuss how shared cultural practices, such as cooking and eating *Axone*, strengthen social cohesion and provide a sense of belonging. The Acts of Solidarity Explore scenes that depict acts of solidarity among the characters, such as standing up for each other against discrimination. Discuss how these acts reinforce their collective identity and resistance to marginalization.

Gender and Food Culture Examine how gender roles and expectations are depicted in relation to food preparation and cultural practices. Analyse whether the film challenges or reinforces traditional gender roles within the context of Northeastern culture. Empowerment through Cooking Discuss how female characters in the film use cooking as a means of empowerment and cultural expression. Highlight moments where cooking becomes a tool for asserting autonomy and resisting patriarchal norms. Urban vs. Rural Dynamics Rural Nostalgia Explore how the characters express nostalgia for their rural homeland through their culinary practices. Analyse how the film contrasts rural and urban life, particularly in terms of cultural preservation and adaptation. Urban Adaptation Discuss the challenges and opportunities that urban life presents for the characters, particularly in terms of maintaining their cultural identity. Analyse how the film portrays the adaptation of traditional practices in an urban setting. Symbolism of Ingredients and Cooking Methods Symbolic Ingredients Examine the symbolism of specific ingredients used in the preparation of *Axone*. Discuss how these ingredients represent cultural identity, heritage, and the connection to the Northeastern homeland. Cooking Methods Analyse the traditional cooking methods depicted in the film and their cultural significance. Discuss how these methods serve as a link to the past and a means of preserving cultural knowledge.

Impact of Modernity on Tradition Modern Influences: Discuss how modernity and globalization impact the characters' cultural practices. Analyse scenes that depict the tension between traditional practices and modern influences. Cultural Adaptation: Examine how the characters adapt their traditional practices to fit into their modern urban context. Discuss the implications of this adaptation for their cultural identity and heritage. By incorporating these additional points into your analysis, you can provide a more comprehensive and nuanced understanding of the themes of food culture and resistance in *Axone*. This will further strengthen your argument and demonstrate the depth and complexity of the film's portrayal of cultural identity and marginalization.

This research paper has thoroughly examined the themes of food culture and resistance in the film *Axone*, demonstrating how culinary practices serve as a powerful medium for asserting cultural identity and challenging social marginalization. By applying the theoretical frameworks of postcolonial studies and cultural anthropology, this study has shown that the preparation of *Axone*, a traditional Northern dish, becomes a symbolic act of cultural resistance against the backdrop of discrimination and racism faced by Northern migrants in Delhi. The analysis of the film's narrative, characters, and visual elements has revealed the deeper meanings behind the characters culinary practices, highlighting their resilience and agency in preserving their cultural heritage. The concept of hybridity, as posited by Homi K. Bhabha, has been employed to illustrate how the characters navigate their identities in a multicultural urban environment, blending their Northern traditions with the influences of their new context.

The paper has explored the significance of rituals and traditions in maintaining cultural continuity and community bonds, emphasizing the role of food as a cultural symbol. The preparation of *Axone* for a wedding celebration underscores the importance of culinary rituals in reinforcing cultural identity and resisting assimilation. Through a detailed analysis of *Axone*, this research has proven that food culture is a crucial site of resistance and cultural expression for marginalized communities. By reclaiming and asserting their culinary practices, the characters in the film challenge the dominant cultural narratives and power structures that seek to marginalize them. This study contributes to a deeper understanding of postcolonial food culture, cultural identity, and resistance, highlighting the enduring impact of colonial histories on contemporary societies and the ongoing struggle for cultural preservation and recognition.

Acknowledgement

I would like to extend my heartfelt gratitude to everyone who contributed to the successful completion of this research paper. First and foremost, I would like to thank my academic advisors and mentors, whose guidance and support have been invaluable throughout this study. Their insightful feedback and encouragement have helped shape this research into its final form. I am deeply grateful to the filmmakers and the cast of *Axone* for creating such a poignant and thought-provoking film, which served as the primary source for this research. Their work has provided a rich and engaging context for exploring the themes of food culture and resistance.

I would also like to acknowledge the contributions of the scholars and authors whose works have informed and inspired my research. Their studies in postcolonial theory, cultural anthropology, and food culture have provided the theoretical foundation for my analysis. Finally, I extend my sincere thanks to my family and friends for their unwavering support and encouragement throughout this process. Their understanding and patience have been instrumental in allowing me to dedicate the necessary time and effort to this research.

References:

Academia.edu. "Academic Papers and Essays on Food Culture, Postcolonialism, and Cultural Anthropology." Accessed 11 Nov. 2024, www.academia.edu.

Malhotra, Simi, Kanika Sharma, and Sakshi Dogra, editors.

Food Culture Studies in India: Consumption, Representation and Mediation. Rawat Publications, 2020.

Rasool, Sabahat, and Manjinder Kaur Wratch. "A Study on the Theme of Resistance: Food as Metaphor and Cultural Identity in Chimamanda Ngozi Adichie's Purple Hibiscus." Research Journal of English Language and Literature, vol. 6, no. 4, 2018, pp. 101-109.

ResearchGate. "Research Studies and Publications Related to Fermented Foods and Cultural Identity." Accessed 11 Nov. 2024, www.researchgate.net.

Singh, Bhoj Raj, et al. "Microbial Quality and Safety of Axone -Akhuni, a Fermented Soybean Food of Nagaland." Journal of Food Safety, vol. 34, no. 3, 2014, pp. 245-255.

Whitt, Jennifer Burcham. "An Appctite for Metaphor: Food Imagery and Cultural Identity in Indian Fiction." Master's Thesis, Appalachian State University, 2007.

Chapter-13
Indian Eco-Fiction and Popular Culture: A Study of Environmental Narratives in Literature and Media

Dr. Ashwini Ashok Kadam

Abstract

Environmental degradation, global warming and climate change are urgent global concerns that influence various cultural and literary expressions. In the Indian context, with its vast and diverse ecological landscape, these issues find resonance in literary texts, cinema, folklore, and digital media. Indian eco-fiction and popular culture not only serve as artistic representations of environmental issues but also act as powerful tools to create awareness and advocate sustainable development. This study explores the evolution of Indian eco-fiction, from mythological storytelling to contemporary climate fiction, to examine how literature and media portray ecological crises, anthropocentrism, and sustainability challenges. It investigates conversions of literary narratives with popular culture in shaping India's environmental consciousness. Additionally, the research investigates the way films, web series, and folklore reflect ecological anxieties and encourage environmental activism. Through an ecocritical lens, this study highlights the role of storytelling in influencing public discourse, catering to the urgent need for a symbiotic relationship between humans and nature. By bridging eco-fiction and popular culture, this research speaks for a more environmentally conscious masses to create an egalitarian society.

Keywords: Eco-fiction, Indian literature, popular culture, climate change, environmental narratives, Consumerism, anthropocentrism.

Popular Culture: Shades and Shadows

Introduction

The Contemporary era has given rise to an indispensable discourse on climate change, global warming, deforestation, and depletion of natural resources. This discourse is reflected in various cultural and literary expressions. Indian eco-fiction and popular culture serve as artistic endeavors and act as critical commentaries on environmental issues prevailing in these days. From Amitav Ghosh's *"The Hungry Tide"*(2004) to the cinematic representations in *"Kadvi Hawa"* (2017), the Indian ecological curiosity spans folklore retellings, dystopian futures, and contemporary realistic fiction.

This study critically examines the evolution of Indian eco-fiction and environmental themes in popular culture, with the aim to enquire how literature and media have shaped awareness of masses and environmental activism. The 21st century has witnessed an unprecedented environmental crisis, with climate change, deforestation, water scarcity, and biodiversity loss threatening the planet's ecological balance. India has experienced particular environmental issues because of its diverse ecosystems, which range from the drought-prone areas of Rajasthan to the delicate mangroves of the Sundarbans. Indian eco-fiction and environmentally conscious popular culture are products of these problems' growing centrality in literary and cultural discourse.

Eco-fiction, broadly defined, as a literary work that explores the relationship between human beings and ecosystem Eco-fiction often emphasizes the issues like environmental degradation and conservation efforts taken for sustainability of ecological justice. In the West eco-fiction has been studied all across, ranging from Rachel Carson's *Silent Spring* (1962) to contemporary climate fiction (cli-fi). Since then, Indian eco-fiction has evolved with its own unique perspective, and deep characteristic expressions in mythology, folklore, colonial histories, and modern socio-political concerns.

Indian eco-fiction is an important subgenre of environmental literature as it dynamically depicts how nature is perceived in Indian traditions and culture. The ancient Vedic texts, for instance, respected rivers like the Ganga and Yamuna as goddesses, while epics like the *Ramayana* and *Mahabharata* emphasized the ultimate importance of forests. These ancient narratives have been influencing contemporary eco-fiction that blend spiritual and ecological themes all together.

The Intersection of literature and the themes of environmental awareness in India are being witnessed in various literary forms. It is the realistic depiction of ecological crisis that asks for attention towards the environmental themes in Indian literature. Writers such as Amitav Ghosh, Shubhangi Swarup, and Perumal Murugan have thought over the urgency regarding environmental concerns and have contributed to mainstream literary fiction from the eco-centric perspective. Amitav Ghosh's *The Hungry Tide* (2004) describes the delicate balance between conservation and human survival that takes place in the Sundarbans. Secondly, Shubhangi Swarup's *Latitudes of Longing* (2018) renders a blend of geological and ecological narratives that takes place on islands, mountains, and oceans. While Perumal Murugan's *Poonachi* (2018) is an allegory about the exploitation of animals and the agrarian crisis in India. Through such and many more literary works, Indian eco-fiction not only narrates stories but also challenges the lack of consciousness of political and corporate sectors toward environmental degradation.

Popular culture in the contemporary era can be a mirror which reflects ecological conditions in India. So apart from literature, Indian cinema, folklore, and digital media too have played an important role in creating and shaping eco-consciousness. For instance, films like *"KadviHawa"* (2017) and *"Jal"* (2013) straightly address the issue of climate change and problems like water scarcity. Secondly, the Web series and documentaries have gradually started highlighting environmental activism, for instance *"Delhi Crim"* (Season 2, 2022), which features illegal mining. While folklore traditions like the legend of Bon Bibi in the Sundarbans talks about indigenous environmental ethics, which highlights the coexistence of human beings and wildlife.

This study aims to explore how Indian eco-fiction evolved from mythology-based storytelling to contemporary climate fiction. It serves toanalyze the role Indian films, web series, and folklore play in raising environmental awareness. It aims to study critically how do eco-fiction and popular culture contribute to public discourse and environmental activism. Additionally, by observing Indian eco-fiction and its representation in popular culture in forms like literature or media this study seeks to highlight how narratives have the power to shape eco consciousness and inspire masses to take steps towards sustainability.

Rob Nixon's *Slow Violence and the Environmentalism of the Poor* (2011) have introduced the notion of "slow violence," which points out the gradual and unnoticeable environmental study of immediate, catastrophic events. This concept is important as it brings attention to the long-term consequences of environmental exploitation, especially in postcolonial and developing-world contexts.

In Indian literature, ecocritical studies have explored various themes, including folklore, colonial exploitation, and contemporary climate change and ecological crises. Traditional narratives, like the *Bon Bibi* legend of the Sundarbans, depict indigenous ecological ethics and conservation efforts taken by a community. Such narratives emphasize the harmonious relationship between humans and nature, highlighting the importance of local traditions in environmental sustainability.

Colonialism and Ecological Exploitation is yet another theme reflected in Amitav Ghosh's *Ibis Trilogy* (*Sea of Poppies*, *River of Smoke*, and *Flood of Fire*) which explores the ecological aftermath of colonial rule, specifically from the perspective of the exploitation of natural resources and indigenous people. His literary works reveal the way imperial economic policies resulted in environmental destruction, deforestation, and agricultural crisis in colonial India.

The theme of Water Crises and Agrarian Distress is witnessed in contemporary Indian literature which highlights the environmental issues such as droughts, deforestation, and farmer suicides. Literary works like *Jal* (2013) for example explores the ramifications of water scarcity, on the other hand, Perumal Murugan's *Poonachi* depicts environmental degradation and resulting rural hardship by allegorizing the life of a goat. Such texts highlight the struggles of marginalized communities facing ecological challenges. Through such a variety of themes and perspectives, eco-fiction in both global and Indian contexts plays an important role in raising awareness about environmental issues, by critically depicting unsustainable practices of society, and by advocating ecological justice.

Eco-fiction in Indian context is a writing that engages with environmental issues, nature, and ecological issues. It typically explores the relationship between human beings and the natural world, exploring themes such as anthropocentrism, the impact of industrialization, climate change, environmental degradation, and the importance of preserving biodiversity. In Indian literature, eco-fiction also observes the diverse landscapes, cultural practices, and indigenous knowledge systems, with critical analysis of the conflict between modernity and traditional environmental values.

There are several Key Characteristics of Eco-Fiction in the context of Indian Literature. Firstly, Nature is considered as a central character in eco-fictions where often the natural world is not just a backdrop in the narrative but a protagonist in itself, playing an important role. Writers treat the environment as an active participant in shaping the narrative of human struggles and experiences. Secondly, Indian Eco-fiction often highlights the symbiotic relationship between humans and environment. It focuses on the dependency of human beings on the natural environment, and it also criticizes how exploitation of these natural resources leads to ecological destruction. Pollution, overconsumption and deforestation are some of the highlighted themes in eco-fiction, describing anthropocentric actions that hamper landscapes and ecosystems.

Thirdly, Many Indian eco-fictions foreground traditional knowledge systems, such as the ways in which forests, water, and natural entities were worshiped and conserved. The ecological wisdom is often contrasted with the careless exploitation of the environment in modern times of popular culture. Fourthly, Eco-fictions in India condemn industrialization because the rapid growth of India's industrialization, has triggered the negative impact of development on the environment such as deforestation, air pollution, and the displacement of local communities. Further, Climate Change is one of the prominent themes in Indian eco-Fiction which often deals with the issues like changing weather patterns and its effect on agriculture, biodiversity, and livelihoods in rural India. Several literary works in eco-fiction discuss the cultural attachment to specific landscapes and how environmental degradation affects local traditions and ways of life. For instance, the environmental issues around the Narmada River and the protests against the construction of dams are often explored in eco-fiction narratives. Such narratives focus on the depiction of rivers, endangered species, and deforestation.

Indian eco-fiction is a constantly growing genre that contemplates on the country's deep-rooted connection to its landscapes and environment, it also focuses on environmental challenges in the contemporary times. It provokes critical thoughts about sustainability, the consequences of industrialization, and the importance of sustainable development with ecological responsibility. As environmental issues become more urgent globally, eco-fiction in Indian literature continues to offer rich insights and calls for action.

Popular culture that encompasses cinema, television, digital media, folklore, and music is highly influential in building societal attitudes including perceptions of the environment. In India, where oral traditions, mythology, and visual storytelling hold significant cultural value, popular culture plays a crucial role in influencing environmental awareness, activism, and policy discussions. Indian literature, especially eco-fiction, often reflects and criticizes these cultural narratives, offering nuanced perspectives on environmental crises and sustainability.

Popular culture is a powerful medium that can either promote sustainable practices or reinforce ecologically harmful behaviors. Popular culture has the power to create awareness about environmental issues, however it can also contribute to environmental degradation through commercialization, hyper consumerism, and overconsumption. The mass media, industry, and festivals tend to promote lifestyles that encourage excessive consumption, leading to consequent environmental harm. Popular culture can sometimes support and promote behaviors that are detrimental to the destruction of the environment, because of large-scale events, wasteful production practices, and glorified media narratives that result in unchecked industrialization.

Hyper consumerism and waste generation is a

significant means by which popular culture impacts the environment negatively. The entertainment industry, particularly Bollywood, is known for its extravagant film sets, lavish costumes, and high-budget productions, many of which generate substantial waste. Additionally, music concerts, awards shows, and cultural festivals frequently result in the overuse of plastic, food waste, and high energy consumption. Mass celebrations such as the festival of Ganesh Chaturthi in India, have contributed to severe environmental destruction. Traditionally, idols were immersed in rivers and ponds resulting in water pollution and harming aquatic life because of non-biodegradable plaster of Paris and toxic chemicals of paints. In the contemporary period popular culture plays a vital part in shaping behavior of masses, and when such wasteful practices get normalized, it reinforces unsustainable over consumption patterns.

Glorification of resource exploitation is yet another way in which popular culture adversely impacts the environment. This happens largely because of romanticization of industrialization and urbanization while ignoring their ecological negative consequences. Great deal of films and advertisements celebrate rapid economic upturn, construction booms, and promote luxury lifestyles without paying heed to the environmental destruction resulting from these developments. For instance, movies depicting the transformation of rural landscapes into urbanized landscapes frame this change as a sign of progress, often neglecting the deforestation, loss of biodiversity, and increased pollution that come with urbanization. Similarly, advertisements frequently promote high-consumption lifestyles and media reinforces the notion that economic success is tied to material wealth, further triggering unsustainable consumer behavior.

In this era some aspects of popular culture have started

to embrace sustainability and eco-conscious behaviors, many are ignorant and continue to exploit resources by overconsumption. Addressing these problems needs a change in mindsets to be conscious about how the media portrays environmental sustainability and the consequences of anthropocentric activities on nature. By integrating environmental sustainability into media, entertainment and cultural narratives, popular culture can evolve into a favorable force to bring ecological awareness.

Indian literature, especially eco-fiction, has played an important role in acknowledging the environmental narratives set by popular culture. The mainstream media mostly celebrates urbanization, industrial growth, and consumerism, whereas many Indian literary works challenge these perspectives by highlighting environmental degradation and promoting sustainable development. Some literary texts critically observe the failure of popular culture to address environmental concerns, on the other hand some reclaim indigenous environmental wisdom that has been overshadowed by commercialization of narratives. Furthermore, dystopian and satirical literature serve as an incisive commentary on the promotion of unsustainable trajectory by modern media.

This study observes literature as a criticism of unsustainable development. Indian eco-fiction always challenges the unsustainable practices promoted in mainstream popular culture. It offers a critical approach on industrialization, climate change, and environmental neglectfulness. Firstly, one of the most highlighting criticisms comes from Amitav Ghosh's *The Great Derangement* (2016), in which he debates that literature and cinema have largely ignored climate change as a major issue. Ghosh asserts that popular culture has normalized ecological neglect, failing to depict the urgent reality of environmental crises. His literary work demands a reimagining of narratives that foregrounds the climate emergency. Secondly, Perumal Murugan's *Poonachi* (2018) is a narrative in which a stranger leaves his baby goat in the possession of an old man living in the drought-stricken Odakkan Hill. They welcome the tiny goat, whom they name Poonachi, who becomes the center of their lives. However, slowly Poonachi realizes that she is treated just as a domesticated animal where she is constantly under pressure for birthing littles and providing milk. As the drought intensifies, the old man and woman become so poor, so gradually their relationships with their animal companions, including Poonachi, slowly rupture. This narrative serves as an allegory to criticize industrialization and its consequences. Through the narrative of a black goat the author showcases a world of exploitation, hence the novel subtly addressing the issue of the commodification of both animals and marginalized communities.

"Who can say what is in store for anyone? Even before birth, one's fate is predetermined. The only difference is, some can make a noise about it while others suffer in silence." (Murugan, 2018)

The quote connects to Poonachi's commodification, as she is valued only for her productivity. The narrative contemplates on how the broader impacts of modernization, and the pursuit of economic progress are often achieved at the cost of ecological and ethical concerns.

Shubhangi Swarup's *Latitudes of Longing* (2018) is structured into four sections: Islands, Faultline, Valley, and Snow Desert. Each section of the narrative is set in a different geographical landscape and time period across the Indian subcontinent. The novel begins in the post-colonial Andaman Islands, moves through politically charged Burma, explores tourist-heavy Nepal, and concludes in the snow-covered mountains of Ladakh. Though the stories unfold in distinct settings, they are linked by recurring characters who emerge from a central narrative and develop their own individual arcs. Swarup employs a unifying symbol *Pangea* in the novel, the prehistoric supercontinent that once held all of Earth's landmass. By using this metaphor Swarup highlights the interconnectedness of humanity further emphasizing the deep association between people, places, and histories despite geographical and political divisions. She also engages with themes of environmental consciousness, blending environmental histories with human stories. The novel explores the deep interconnections between nature and culture, questioning how popular narratives shape public perceptions of the natural world. By weaving together personal and ecological histories, Swarup challenges the mainstream depiction style of environment as just a backdrop to human ambition, instead presenting it as a powerful force. There she writes "*The earth was here before us, and it will outlive us. We are just passing currents in its eternal ocean.*" (*Swarup, 2018*), emphasizing the long-lasting power of nature beyond the capacity of human existence.

Indian eco-fiction attempts to reclaim and revive traditional environmental knowledge and wisdom that has been neglected or commercialized by mainstream popular culture. While deep ecological insights, emphasizing sustainable coexistence with nature rather than its exploitation is emphasized in many indigenous and folk narratives. Amitav Ghosh's *Jungle Nama* (2021) is a depiction of the Bon Bibi legend, a traditional tale from the Sundarbans that highlights the mutuality between human life and the natural environment. Through poetic verse, Ghosh seeks attention to the environmental destruction threatening the Sundarbans, a region highly affected by climate change and deforestation. The work can be both a cultural preservation effort and an environmental warning.

Similarly, Pankaj Sekhsaria's The *Last Wave* (2014)

further observes these themes through the facets of tourism and modernization in the Andaman and Nicobar Islands. By showcasing the ecological and cultural disruption resulting from commercial development, the novel criticizes the manner how popular culture often romanticizes tourism while ignoring the environmental destruction caused by the tourism industry.

"Tourists came and went, clicking pictures of the turquoise waters and white sand beaches, never stopping to think about what lay beneath the surface—lives uprooted, forests felled, traditions lost." (*Sekhsaria*, 2014).

This quote throws light on how popular culture, particularly the tourism industry, often presents the tranquil and enchanting version of nature but completely ignoring the deeper ecological and cultural disruptions it causes. It highlights the fragile relationship between nature and intervention of human beings, finally urging a more responsible approach to environmental stewardship.

Eco-fiction also utilizes satire and dystopian elements to criticize consumerism and the negligence towards environment resulting from popular culture. By exaggerating real-world vogues and trends, such literary works expose the insanity and dangers of unsustainable development. Jugal Mody's *Toke* (2012) is a comic yet biting criticism of inefficiency of government and corporate greenwashing. The novel depicts a group of stoners who end up with saving the planet The author by using satire highlights the failures of political and economic institutions in addressing climate change. Through its comedic tone, *Toke* highlights the contradictions in mainstream ecological discourse, where commercial companies and governments often prioritize profits over genuine responsibility towards sustainable development.

Similarly, Amitav Ghosh's *Gun Island* (2019) presents climate change as a force that reshapes human civilization, driving mass migration and social upheaval. The novel critiques the long-standing neglect of environmental issues in mainstream narratives, showing how industrialization and consumerism have contributed to an ecological crisis with far-reaching consequences.

"The Sundarbans are the frontier where commerce and the wilderness look each other directly in the eye; that's exactly where the war between profit and Nature is fought." (Ghosh 2019)

Here, Ghosh emphasizes the conflict between economically profitable pursuits and environmental conservation, a central theme in the narrative. By framing climate change as an unavoidable reality rather than a distant threat, *Gun Island* challenges readers to reconsider their perceptions of environmental urgency. Further, Sumana Roy's How *I Became a Tree* (2017) is an exploration through a philosophical approach, wherein the author's desire to escape the destruction of civilization and adopt the stillness and resilience of a tree. Through lyrical prose of nature writing, Roy observes that modernity is an unending pace and it brings alienation from the environment. The book is a contemplation on the environmental and psychological costs resulting from an unsustainable lifestyle, ultimately encouraging a deeper connection with the natural world.

Indian literature offers powerful and different narratives to the ecological complacency that find expression in popular culture. Whether through direct criticism, or the reclamation of indigenous wisdom, and even through dystopian and satirical reflections, eco-fiction challenges readers to confront the ecological consequences of commercial and anthropocentric attitudes of human beings. These works not only expose the shortcomings of mainstream flag bearers of popular culture but also promote more responsible and sustainable engagement and affinity with the environment. As environmental concerns have become increasingly urgent, literature continues to serve significantly for reimagining humanity's relationship with the environment. Ultimately, the impact of popular culture on the environment is a double-edged sword as it can either contribute to ecological destruction through uncontrolled consumerism or create a platform for meaningful environmental activism. Indian literature plays a crucial role in reflecting on these cultural dynamics, offering both critique and alternative pathways for a sustainable future.

Conclusion

So, to conclude, in contemporary times, bridging popular culture and eco-fiction is crucial to promote sustainable development. Both realms, popular media and literature, hold immense power in shaping public attitudes, perceptions, and behaviors towards the environment. Popular culture can either promote awareness or trigger unsustainable practices, on the other hand eco-fiction helps to contemplate so to examine these narratives, to be challenged or to be reimagined. The dynamic interplay between the two can foster a more eco conscious society.

The convergence of popular culture and eco-fiction can be an effective tool to foster eco consciousness. By incorporating narratives of sustainability into mainstream media with orientation of literary reflections on nature and climate change, a more holistic approach to environmental awareness can be accomplished. Films, television series, and social media campaigns could model themselves on eco-fiction, to portray environmental issues not merely romanticizing nature or depicting it as a backdrop. Simultaneously, literature can continue to challenge and refine the narratives emerging from popular culture, to ensure that they not only promote awareness but also yield action.

In an era where climate change poses a catastrophic threat, storytelling, both visual and literary, must work in tandem to inspire positive sustainable outcomes. Popular culture can bring environmental issues to mass audiences, while eco-fiction can deepen engagement and provoke critical thought. By bridging eco-fiction and popular culture-the two influential realms, masses can foster a more responsible approach towards sustainable development, to ensure that eco consciousness becomes intrinsic in both entertainment and intellectual discourse.

Further, Indian eco-fiction and popular culture serve as critical reflections on the environmental crises shaping contemporary India. Literature, mythology, cinema, and digital media have all played roles in raising awareness and critiquing unsustainable development. Future research can explore how regional eco-literature and indigenous narratives contribute to a more sustainable environmental ethos.

Works Cited:
Bhushan, K. *Ecology and Development in India: A Critical Perspective.* Routledge, 2020.
Chakraborty, Nirajana, and Samata Biswas. "Latitudes of Longing: An Ecocritical Exploration of Our Geopolitics." *Journal of Ecocritical Studies*, vol. XX, no. XX, 2021, pp. XX–XX.
Ghosh, Amitav. *The Great Derangement: Climate Change and the Unthinkable.* University of Chicago Press, 2016.
---. *Gun Island.* Penguin Random House, 2019.
---. *Jungle Nama: A Story of the Sundarbans.* HarperCollins, 2021.
---. *The Hungry Tide.* HarperCollins, 2004.
Murugan, Perumal. *Poonachi: The Story of a Black Goat.* Context, 2018.
Nixon, Rob. *Slow Violence and the Environmentalism of the*

Poor. Harvard University Press, 2011.

Roy, Sumana. *How I Became a Tree.* Aleph Book Company, 2017.

Sekhsaria, Pankaj. *The Last Wave: An Island Novel.* Harper Collins, 2014.

Swarup, Shubhangi. *Latitudes of Longing.* HarperCollins, 2018.

Chapter-14
The Undercover Over Screen: A Study of Real Life Espionage Narratives in Indian Cinema

Dr. Shruti Dubey

Abstract

The paper focuses on the Indian movies based on real life incidents loosely adapted from the legends of Indian spies and attempts to study the movies Raazi (2018) and Mission Majnu (2023) as popular on-screen delineations of the real-life covert operatives and focus on how through this delineation a larger narrative has been knit so as to bring to the fore the sentiments of national pride, belongingness and supreme devotion to the nation. The portrayal of the real life unsung heroes and all that they faced is done so as to resonate with the patriotic fervour and the pride of belonging to the nation esteemed with producing such larger than life real heroes. The delineation of the protagonists is studied against the theoretical backdrop of nation, nationalistic allegiance and identity and the subtle ways the latter is manoeuvred in the aforementioned scenario to provide an answer to the question of why, in today's time, the cult of spy thrillers/adaptations of real life thrillers have gained prominence and are a sure formula for a 'box-office blockbuster'.

Keywords: Espionage, Spy-Thrillers, Undercover, Identity, Patriotism.

Cinema, they say, is one of the 'languages through which the world communicates itself to itself.'

(Comolli qtd. in Branigan and Buckland, *Routledge Encyclopedia of Film Theory* 30)

Any movie enthusiast would relate to the fact that the

most beloved of her movies resonate and are replete with the experiences of the world that she must have felt and experienced in some or the other phase of her life. This quality of cinema to relate to the viewer, to be able to give expression to the sentiments quite closely, is one of the features that has led to the undeniable and unquestionable popularity of the medium. It has also become the most preferred medium in the hands of the makers who wish to convey a perspective through an intricate plotline. The *Routledge Encyclopedia of Film Theory* quotes the eminent critics Comolli and Narboni in response to the question of what cinema is as follows:

...what is a film? They [Comolli and Narboni] specify two aspects, which relate almost as signifier and signified...the film is an industrial product sold for profit, and it is an ideological vehicle. ... 'Because every film is part of the economic system it is also part of the ideological system.'(Branigan and Buckland 285)

The entry also enumerates certain characteristics of films which contribute to making them an appropriate medium of delineating the desired. Whatever the audience views on the screen is a sort of dynamic interplay of many factors including financial, interpersonal, socialand behavioural among others. Certain features among these render movies an appropriate medium for generating, affecting, diverting and changing the pre-existing views and opinions of a large chunk of the intended audience. Precisely for this reason we find movies as one of the most popular modes of communicating a world-view or voicing one's vision on a particular phenomenon.Branigan and Buckland are of the view that popular culture has efficiently been disseminating the desired ideology through its aesthetic allure:

Two qualities of films make them especially favourable to conveying ideology. First, because they require teamwork, they typically mobilize economic forces and are tied to monopoly suppliers like Kodak. Second, cinema has the reputation of being a realist medium, tied by technology to what later critics would refer to as indexicality: a privileged relation to the world based on the involuntary physics of light and light-sensitive film-stock. (243)

But according to the critics, herein lies the crux of the matter as the movies stand as a statement not of an objective stance but of the very heartfelt perspective of the maker/the team or human factors involved in the making. These perspectives can vary based on a variety of factors like the gender, age, cultural background and others as such. An individual having an association with any of these might have different sentiments and feelings from someone who might not share the same factors. Also, one's age and the times that one is surviving in would make or mar one's views on a particular aspect or phenomenon as the social and cultural as well as educational conditioning also affects the process of meaning making as well as creative responses to the happenings in the society and world at large. Undoubtedly, popular culture possesses the power to shapereality in accordance with that ideological context:

However, they argue that 'concrete reality' is an eminently ideological idea. The cinema typically reproduces not things as they are but as they appear, and therefore according to the relationships established between people and their world under actually existing social and historical conditions. (243)

Speaking of the types of movies in the Indian cinema, one cannot claim of any genre that is left untouched and unexplored by the industry. With a humongous amount of releases per year, now also expanded to OTT platforms, the Indian film industry can boast of a variety of genres being utilized, explored and being served to cater to a very large amount of audiences with varying tastes and interests. One amongst these is the genre of spy thrillers, both fictitious as well as those based on the accounts of the real life spies, either adapted from the news and legends or those from biographies and documented experiences. What makes this genre especially interesting is the fact that not a lot of the workings of the people involved in this profession is evidently available, for even in the real life these personnel remain away from the public eye and avoid any public displays of heroism as such. Known to be the unsung heroes behind many of the crucial military victories that the country can boast of, these key figures operate in shadows without expecting any public renown or praise. The focus of this analysis is twosuch movies from the genre. This analysis is strictly restricted to those based/claimed to be adapted from real life narratives of such operatives who have played an invisible yet crucial role before, during and after the 1971 truce between India and Pakistan. The movies namely Raazi (2018) and Mission Majnu (2023) have been selected for the same.

The significance of selection of these movies, as the primary texts for investigation in this research work, is due to the deeply interwoven past shared by the two nations. Furthermore, the current geopolitical situation of the subcontinent also underlines the scholarly relevance of this research endeavour. The profound value held by one's geographical neighbours, be it in politics, national ideology or popular culture is indisputable. "It is a reality to us....Pandavas could not choose relatives... we can't choose our neighbours. Naturally, we hope good sense prevails ..." ("Just as Pandavas," *Times of India*). This statement by our honourable External Affairs Minister S. Jaishankar during the launch of his book entitled *The India Way* in January, 2023 speaks volumes about the strained relations between India and the neighbouring Pakistan, ever since the two were separated on the lines of religious affiliations. The two state heads have ever since been at loggerheads regarding a variety of issues which both have been constantly voicing at international platforms; the most important amongst these being the issue of the neighbour funding and protecting terrorism and terrorist activities which have been the cause of the unfortunate loss of many innocent Indians. Mumbai, Pathankot, Uri, and now Pahalgam, the neighbour has time and again proved that its policies and evil tactics are focussed on spreading terror amongst our countrymen. But this time we Indians, under a strong leadership and a dedicated defence force, have proven our mettle and responded accordingly. The way Operation Sindoor was conducted made every Indian proud of our defence forces. This graceful yet strong Indian response was celebrated in wide variety of ways from the icon of Amul honouring the Indian military officers with the tagline 'Send them pakking' to Sand Art being dedicated to it to parents naming their babies born on the 6-7 May, 2025 as Sindoor.

It is well evident that this sense of enmity with our neighbour who has been responsible for many a bleeding hearts of the nation every now and then combined with our Indian ideals of non-violence and a preference for peace and larger good of the humanity have led us to celebrate every successful interaction with Pakistan. Be it the victory in the cricket matches or any other sport wherein we register a victory over the Pakistani opponent or be it the wars of 1971 and Kargil, we Indians rejoice in the fact that our players, defence forces, diplomats, government leaders are a righteous step ahead of the adversary and our cinema is not lagging behind in making the most of this sentiment and delineating it on the screen. Ever since the tussle has gained momentum,Indian cinema has responded in a myriad ways and presented a variety of issues related to India-Pakistan ties. Movies like *Veer-Zara, Bajrangi Bhaijaan, Happy Bhag Jayegi, LOC Kargil, Lakshya, Border, Uri: The Surgical Strike, War, Skyforce* are among some recent examples of the same.

Popular Culture: Shades and Shadows

Raazi is a 2018 Indian spy thriller loosely adapted from the book *'Calling Sehmat'* (2008) by Harinder Sikka that has been directed by Meghna Gulzar and produced by Junglee Pictures and Dharma Productions of Karan Johar, Hiroo Yash Johar, Apoorva Mehta and Vineet Jain starring Rajit Kapoor, Alia Bhatt and Vicky Kaushal in lead roles. According to Sikka, the book is inspired by the real life account of a Research and Analysis Wing (RAW) operative named Sehmat, an alumnae of the Delhi University, who is trained and sent to Pakistan as a spouse of a defence officer just before the India- Pakistan truce of 1971, being the one whose secret inputs aided the naval movement during the war, eventually leading to India's victory and Pakistan's surrender. Soon after the release the movie reported high box-office collections and also rose to become one of the most successful films with a female lead, as reported across newspapers. *Mission Majnu* is a 2023 Indian spy thriller directed by Shantanu Bagchi and produced by Amar Butala, Ronnie Screwvala and Garima Mehta starring Sidharth Malhotra, Rashmika Mandanna, and Rajit Kapur in lead roles. According to the makers of the film, it is based on the real life of a Research and Analysis Wing operative who during the decade of 70's resides in Pakistan and uncovers the secret facility involved in the production of Nuclear Weapons which eventually leads to exposing Pakistan's secretive attempts and the consequent global humiliation that the authorities had to face. Released on an OTT platform the movie soon rose to the top ten not only in the country but also among global audiences.

Both the movies delineate the protagonists navigating through tough lines where they try to lead normal lives as a part of the social setup and under this façade they try to operate in the best interest of their motherland. Going by the major theoretical postulate of Tim Edensor that "the national is constituted and reproduced, contested and reaffirmed in everyday life" (20). Trying to analyse the delineation of the protagonists according to this backdrop, we can observe that in both the cases the characters find themselves accepting the national and cultural mandates and functioning according to their standing in the family as well as the society. We find our protagonists in situations where they are to perform the 'everyday' in total allegiance to the rival state and its rules in order to be able to conduct their covert operation. Sehmat, the younger daughter-in-law of the family of her spouse Iqbal Syed performs all the familial duties to perfection so much so that she ends up winning the hearts of the family as well as other well-wishers. It is only the old family servant Abdul who is apprehensive of the girl and her intentions and he ends up finding the tools she has been using to convey sensitive information ever since she became a part of the family, an incident due to which Sehmat is compelled to eliminate this threat of exposure. On the other hand, Amandeep Singh resides in Pakistan under the alias Tariq Hussain and works as a tailor at a workshop that deals in taking contracts for stitching the army uniforms. After he meets Nasreen who is blind he falls in love with her and marries her after having convinced her family for the same. Once married, he takes care of her wife and they live a blissful conjugal life. But what he keeps concealed is his actual work which the lady, though blind, somehow senses. These protagonists are shown to be well versed and all engaged in their day to day lives in the rival country. Their works, their actual task, nowhere seems to disrupt the normalcy of their lives. But with eventual snowballing of incidents, they end up being exposed which leads to their loss, familial and relationships, in both the cases. Despite the huge personal loss in both the cases, the operation they are involved in turns out to be successful and the outcome is in favour of the motherland.

Speaking about the issue of 'identity' in context of a routine life, Edensor enumerates three traits that serve as the basic requirements for any individual to be able to keep up with and enjoy belongingness towards the nation state. The foremost among these is that of "popular competencies" which are defined as "everyday practical knowledge which enables people to accomplish mundane tasks; the ability of citizens to carry out the formal requirements necessary to get things done" (93).The protagonists are delineated as undergoing rigorous training wherein they acquire and cultivate all the traits of tradecraft, not only in the physical domain but also in mental and emotional domains, so as to be able to navigate a constant interaction with the adversary in typicalculturally specific and politically correct manner. Also there exists a backstory, a prior motive and patriotic allegiance to the motherland that provide a personal interest to the same igniting the passion manifold. A basic mandate is that they should resemble and be one with the individuals of the rival state so as to allow for a maximum functionality.

Another similar trait, as enumerated by Edensor, is that of "embodied habits" or "the forms of bodily hexis and social interaction, often criss-crossed with class, gender, ethnicity and age"(94). Sehmat utilizes her special position in the family as well as the social circle of the Army wives association and partakes actively in the social gatherings which help her in gaining access to the families of other key army officials which she uses for her own benefit. An assistant to a tailor, Amandeep (Tariq) makes the most of the limited opportunity to visit the headquarters to deliver a bulk order of stitched uniforms and tries to elicit crucial bits of information that eventually help him to bring the bigger picture together.

Finally, an allegiance and loyalty to the national symbols along with what Edensor terms as "synchronised enactions of everyday life", which he defines as "the complicated construction of national time includes the important element of cyclical time, the enduring repetition of daily, weekly and annual routines, and entrenched notions about when particular actions should be carried out" (96). Both the protagonists adhere to the norms of nationalist and cultural celebratory modes. Sehmat helps a group of school students prepare a song for the performance on the eve of Pakistan's Independence Day celebrations the eve of the celebration of their independence. The lyrics of the song deserve special mention. "Ae watan, watan mere, aabaad rahe tu," (Oh beloved country of mine, wish you to keep thriving) ("Ae Watan," Raazi). "Main jahan rahun, jahaan me yaad rahe tu" (Wish you to be revered/remembered wherever I live in the world). "Tu hi meri manzil hai, pehchan tujhi se/Pahunchu main jahaan bhi/Meri buniyad rahe tu" (You are my final destination and I owe my identity to you, wish my existence to be enrooted in your grandeur irrespective of the heights that I might achieve in my life.While the performance of the song and the efforts of Sehmat undeniably appear in the honour of Pakistan, her real sentiments attached to the lyrics are meant for her own motherland.

The utilization of such lyrics is intended to add to the sentimental appeal of the characterization and to convey the sense of utmost patriotism and the consequent ability to sacrifice everything in the name of nation. A song from *Mission Majnu* entitled "Matti ko Maa Kehte Hain" (we address our land as mother) composed by Manoj Muntashir expresses the sentiments of an undercover operative fully well and played along with the visuals of the protagonist struggling for the sake of motherland, the lyrics serve as an apt medium of conveying the patriotic fervour and have the potential of touching audiences' hearts.With the claims that we Indians are the only one in the entire world to reverently address our country as mother, the song stirs the pride in every Indian heart; "...hum tere aanchal tale rahete hain/Duniyaa mein hum hee akele hain jo maati ko "maan" kehthe hain" ("Matti ko Maa Kehte Hain," *Mission Majnu).* The final wish of the patriot/son of the soil is just one -

though it can be expressed in myriad ways:

Sar tera unchaa rahe, ai vatan, koyi jaane naa jaane hamein

Ho, khushboo ke jaise hawaon mein hum gumnaam se behate hain

Jismon pe vardi na kaandhe sitaare

Na jhande jhukenge zikar pe hamaare

Par jaan-nisaari ki jab baath hogee

Aage milenge qataaron mein hum.("Matti ko Maa Kehte Hain")

The protagonist here is presented to be working on minute details, bringing all split-ends of the big picture together, for which many a time he has to encounter a life threatening situation. But through all of these, he manages to steer clear and finally have atleast his family rescued from the evil eyes of the authorities, risking his own life in exchange. Even the end shows him not losing hope, despite the situation turning adverse, and giving a tough fight to the adversaries.The intentional addition of the action-sequences in quasi-realistic fight scenes might leave one wondering of them having happened in the real life, but as the makers of the film have stated that those have been used as devices to add on to the mass appeal of the characterisation and in response to the need of the scene. Director Shantanu Bagchi underscores this idea as follows:

It's based on a true story which actually happened. In this story the spy is an intelligent guy who is thinking laterally, he is not snooping on somebody and figuring it out. He is trying to find something and it's an interesting story of a spy with a bright mind, adhering to a kind of realistic situation, rather than many other spy films that you have seen. They are glorified, almost like superheroes. Of course, there are some action sequences (in *Mission Majnu*) which are not as realistic but...I think they will add to the thrill. (Biswas, "Mission Majnu is realistic...")

Similarly, Sehmat's father (played by Rajit Kapur) in *Raazi* addresses his darling daughter when she is departing from the home post her wedding with the hope that the adverse situations would soon get rectified. The metaphorical expression of the melting of snow and the consequent ripening and thriving of fields, "Mere dilbaro/Barfein galengi phir se/Mere dilbaro/Fasalein pakengi phir se/" while showering his daughter with blessings"Tere paaon ke tale/Meri dua chalein" is the sentiment that conveys the Indian ideal of striving for a better future for the entire humanity where peace reigns supreme("Dilbaro,"*Raazi*). The daughter is delineated endeavouring towards the ideal for which she ends up paying a dear price as we see her fainting and collapsing towards the end as soon as she returns to the Indian territory after having lost her spouse, her familial and emotional bonds and more importantly her humanity.

To conclude, both the movies are replete with elements that add to their popular appeal and lead them to be appropriate delineations of real-life unsung heroes whose presence is conspicuous through their absence. The staging of such a character adds to the thrill of the movie and along with compelling lyrics the makers aim to make the most of the sentimental value of an invisible life being offered at the altar of the motherland. All these add up to a formula for the consequent success of the creative venture where we have a real life documented, a nationalist undertone, emotional play, a tragedy followed by a national victory and a popular star cast, all come together.

References:

"Ae Watan." *Raazi*, directed by Meghna Gulzar, music by Shankar–Ehsaan–Loy, lyrics by Gulzar, performance by Arijit Singh. Junglee Pictures and Dharma Productions,

2018.

Biswas, Sneha. "Mission Majnu is realistic, no answer for those still comparing to Raazi: Director Shantanu Bagchi." *Hindustan Times*. 25 Jan. 2023. https://www.hindustantimes.com/entertainment/bollywood/mission-majnu-is-real-no-answer-for-those-comparing-to-raazi-shantanu-bagchi-101674584486105.html. Accessed on 15 May 2025.

Branigan, Edward, and Warren Buckland, editors. *The Routledge Encyclopedia of Film Theory*. Routledge, 2014.

Braudy, Leo, and Marshall Cohen, editors. *Film Theory and Criticism: Introductory Readings*, 7th ed., Oxford University Press, 2009.

"Dilbaro."*Raazi*, directed by Meghna Gulzar, music by Shankar–Ehsaan–Loy, lyrics by Gulzar, performance by Harshdeep Kaur, Vibha Saraf, and Shankar Mahadevan. Junglee Pictures and Dharma Productions, 2018.

Edensor, Tim. *National Identity, Popular Culture and Everyday Life*. Berg, 2002.

Hermes, Joke. *Re-reading Popular Culture*. Blackwell Publishing, 2005.

"Just as Pandavas could not choose their relatives, India can't choose its neighbours: Jaishankar on Pakistan." The Times of India, 28 Jan. 2023, http://timesofindia.indiatimes.com/articleshow/97405578.cms?utm_source=contentofinterest&utm_medium=text&utm_campaign=cppst. Accessed on 2 May 2025.

"Maati Ko Maa Kehte Hain."*Mission Majnu*, directed by Shantanu Bagchi, music by Rochak Kohli, lyrics by Manoj Muntashir, performance by Sonu Nigam. RSVP Movies and Guilty By Association, 2023.

*Mission Majnu.*Directed byShantanu Bagchi, performances bySidharth Malhotra, Rashmika Mandanna, and Rajit Kapur.RSVP Movies and Guilty By Association, 2023.

Storey, John. *From Popular Culture to Everyday Life*. Routledge, 2014.

Strinati, Dominic. *An Introduction to Theories of Popular Culture*. 2nd ed., Routledge 2004.

Raazi. Directed by Meghna Gulzar, performances by Rajit Kapoor, Alia Bhatt and Vicky Kaushal. Junglee Pictures and Dharma Productions, 2018.

Sikka, Harinder. *Calling Sehmat*. Penguin Random House India, 2008.

Chapter-15
Modernistic Unveiling of Myth in Popular Culture in Salman Rushdie's *The Ground Beneath Her Feet*

Dr. Dimple Dubey

Abstract

Classical myths have always been an inspirational source and considered a benchmark in literature, furnishing us with narratives and archetypes tat persist to reverberate through the eras. These myths, originating from ancient Rome and Greece, have been revised and redefined in prismatic ways to replicate the virtues and apprehensions of different periods. In modern literature, authors have reframed these ancient mythical tales to probe and critique contemporary social and cultural concerns, transforming the mythological personages and providing a substance to readdress prevailing societal implications. Salman Rushdie in *The Ground Beneath Her Feet* has repurposed a classical myth and reimagined it in the light of pop culture and global relevance.

Keywords: Myth, Pop culture, globalization, Rushdie, Postmodernism.

Cultural theorists and scholars have often claimed that myths of a culture can be discerned as natural phenomenon as they serve to explicate what societies cannot. They reinforce the origin and refinement of societal beliefs and customs and even the ubiquitous experiences shared by the citizens of a community. Myths are not anomalous to any specific culture, rather they convey critical components of culture from prehistoric oral tradition to modern narrative scaffolds. Each culture has its own sets of myths that impel in setting the ethical and moral tone of the society, binding the citizens and promoting a sense of concerted community. Albeit, myths or mythologies generated out of myths are customarily believed to be tales of antiquity but what characterizes them as a narrative is the presence of incredible protagonists and their distinctive relation to gods and deities, their extraordinary achievements and their implausible deeds. Mythical narratives have offered wisdom, knowledge, insights and a sense of comfort by depicting and demonstrating, moral and ethical behaviors suited to the practical world enforcing an exuberant understanding of the human spirit in all its detailed codification of their perplexing experiences. The myths that have been told, why they have been told so and what are they saying to us in terms of both purpose and endeavors is what fosters their magnitude and substance.

The fascination for myths and mythologies has been in vogue since ancient times. The Hebrew, Greek and Roman civilizations have been the representors of classical myths encompassing tales of human survival, supernatural phenomena, loss of love and various other conflicts. As these mythological tales have spread through manifold cultural epochs, the actual events and personages have changed over time exhibiting an obvious parallel with the stories of modern times. The ancient classical tales have now transformed into contemporary crafts due to cultural exchanges with frequently visiting civilizations, put differently, the effects of globalization and transnationalism. Nevertheless, several ancient Greek and Roman mythical tales have been pristinely restored and adapted in modern storytelling with contemporary attribution, romances and characters. These tales have an enduring appeal in modern storytelling contributing in debunking its effectualness to connect with readers at the premise of shared human experience, addressing fundamental probes of existence, identity and ethics.

Popular Culture: Shades and Shadows

Every new century has reproduced the antiquated network of mythologies and created new ones and have somewhat validated its constant presence in the culture, and restructuring, as a stable element of social communication. Anthropologists, philosophers, psychologists and cultural scholars have affirmed that the process of myth-making is regarded as an approach to creating a mythological message and in modern times, the modern myth functions as a double reality. The multiple repetitions of the mythological messages construct a hyper real image and value and has changed its historical objective appearance but it prevails to be an important form of culture. The latter half of 20th century has witnessed major transformations in myth-making via manipulation techniques in digital and mass media communication, advertising, culture and politics. This approach has led to a broad understanding that myths and mythologies do not exist outside of the locus of society and social communication, fixating the conception that there is a substantial affinity between myth and language and that modern culture has its own distinctive ways of popularizing myth and mythologies on a global rank. The modern myth can be measured as a consciously constructed myth that becomes an instrument to evaluate the popular trends vise music, fashion, everyday life, etc.

French philosopher and theorist Roland Barthes has defined myth as a derivative semiological system that is created by the "deformation" of the natural language. In his book "*Mythologies*," he expounds that "myth is a system of communication, that it is a message. This allows one to perceive that myth cannot possibly be an object, a concept, or an idea; it is a mode of signification, a form... since myth is a type of speech, everything can be a myth provided it is conveyed by a discourse" (90). Myth cannot explain anything on its own but it aids in implying formulation that facilitate in creating an explanation and generate clarity. Barthes affirms, "myth is a type of speech defined by its intention... much more by its literal sense; and that in spite of this, its intention is somehow frozen, purified, eternalized, *made absent* by this literal sense" (104).He further argues that myth as a double-structure encloses within it "a perpetual alibi," as "its signifier has two sides for it always to have an 'elsewhere' at its disposal" (104). Barthes' theory proposes that mass culture contributes to the construction of modern myth, and that this "double-structure of myth" allows society to propagate its ideological meanings whilst at the same moment allowing for a denial of this procedure (123).

When these myths come across with the modern refinement of culture and civilization, their re-creation and extensiveness of a new genre is challenged based on certain fundamental paradigms. Hence the mythologies prevalent today are regardless to the cultural evidence of the axiomatic system of the past. Theorists and scholars hold a firm belief that there is a myriad to unravel in every mythological system since these chimerical revisions are an unconventional and path- breaking ways of discerning the old by the inclusion of modern settings and integrated perceptions banishing various genres. The multiple revisions of mythical narratives necessitates the creation of a new genre. The process of retelling mythical narratives and the fragments obtained by the application of certain philosophies verify that the preceding conventions have slowly and steadily evolved out of old-time cultural fixations to an alternative kind of restructuring.

Retelling primarily focuses on culture, it's confirming with authority, and aptitude to reformulate mythology, based on its association to the mythical perceptions. Modern myth does not symbolize closure and order, but disclosure and openness. They are more like metaphors that create correlation between apparently distant worlds that invoke novel and always shifting meanings. It is then imperative on cultural theorists to study the ancient myths in all their complex forms and formulations and analyze the probable cultural and social contexts in which it gets manifested in the contemporary mythological echelons. The authors extend the scope for contradictory and anticipatory segments of essentiality while commuting with the fusion of past and present. Since the 60s and 70s with the rise of technological and digital platforms there has been a transformed dynamic representation of myth with various reshaping practices for traditional storytelling. In popular culture, mythology has influenced art, music, films, etc, enabling eternal stories to resonate with the new audiences. In music and art, myths have continued to thrive via experimental genres like rock, pop and hip-hop. These fusions have highlighted the adaptability of myths and capability to connect across generations. The credit for such remarkable representation of an ancient classical myth through the agency of popular culture can be bestowed on the celebrated postcolonial author Salman Rushdie in his novel *The Ground Beneath Her Feet* (1999). This novel explores the legendary myth of Orpheus and Eurydice in a speck with rock' n' roll as its cardinal axis. But before we proceed with the recounting of the myth in the context of the novel, let us explore the myth in its originality.

The grandeur of Greek cultural aspects have always been a great source of allure and enchantment for contemporary authors and artists. From modern to postmodern era authors have scoured for a new mythology. Presumably the new mythology is to be found in the impingement of cultures, religion, histories and arts, and possibly it was to be occasioned through the stimulus of popular culture. As mentioned by Mikhail Bakhtin in *The Dialogic Imagination*, "The Greek romance is a very malleable instance of the novelistic genre, one that possesses an enormous life-force" (107).

He then furnishes his viewpoint firmly by dispensing the essence of Greek-romance intrinsically:

Popular Culture: Shades and Shadows

It is nevertheless a *living human being* moving through space and not merely a physical body in the literal sense of the term. While it is true that his life may be completely passive– "Fate" runs the game- he nevertheless *endures* the game fate plays. And he not only endures - *he keeps on being the same person* and emerges from this game, from all these turns of fate and chance, with his *identity* absolutely unchanged. (Bakhtin105)

Bakhtin claimed that protagonists of ancient romances endured the shattering events in the quest of life and forgot nothing. Resultantly they passed the test of durability and continuity and this constituted the ideological and artistic meaning of Greek romance.

Salman Rushdie extensively uses classical mythology and Greek and Latin cultural forms in his 1999 novel, *The Ground Beneath Her Feet*. He has rewritten the mythical story of Orpheus and Eurydice, using katabasis (the trope of the descent into Hell), inspired from Dante's *Inferno* suggestively criticizing the destabilizing effects of globalization on culture and art and also revealing the essence of creativity lying hidden in the unconscious of the artist.

In different periods of history Orpheus' myth has acquired different meanings but the most beguiling characteristic is his liminality, his amplitude to move in-between life and death, between art and culture of all times, between imagination and reality, therefore composing himself as a myth model. The Orpheus myth is a befitting choice for this novel as Rushdie rewrote it in the context of globalization. Rushdie questions in one of his essay "Globalization" in his non-fictional work *Step Across This Line*, "Do cultures exist as separable, pure, defensible entities?Is not mélange, adulteration, impurity, pick' n' mix at theheart of the idea of the modern, and hasn't it been that wayfor most of this shook-up century? (297)

Popular Culture: Shades and Shadows

The novel chronicles the lives of two prominent rock stars OrmusCama and VinaApsara and of their ill-fated tragic love. Their story is narrated by Umeed Merchant, aka Rai, an internationally renowned photographer who was connected to Ormus and Vina since childhood and was a part of their lives from India to America. The novel begins with Vina's death in an earthquake in Mexico in 1989, during her very first solo musical tour. The rest of the book just looks back on the lover's lives and of those related to them.

As per Greek mythology, the myth of Orpheus and Eurydice has manifold interpretations that deliver into Orpheus' voyage for the pursuit of lost love, healing and finally his garnering of Eurydice from the Underworld from where no mortal had ever reverted. Ancient Greek culture has many times been glorified throughout western history and has also been wielded for inspiration. Virgil and Ovid, two famous Roman poets had perused this myth in their bodies of work. Virgil recited this story in the fourth book of the *Georgics*. Orpheus who was the son of Apollo, the Greek god of sunlight, poetry and music, falls in love with a nymph, Eurydice. The next morning of their wedding, Eurydice dies due to snakebite. Overwhelmed with grief Orpheus decides to travel to the world of the dead and bring her back. He persuades Hades and his wife Persephone to release her. It is agreed upon at the prerequisite of not turning back to look at her until they return back to the living world. Unfortunately he loses her by turning around and the journey persists to be incomplete. In Virgil's version however there is an inconsiderable reference to Aristaeus, a minor god, who attempts to capture Eurydice in malice, along the banks of a river and she in her struggle to free from him gets bitten by a snake and dies. In Ovid's version of the myth in *Metamorphoses*, Orpheus and Eurydice are to be married without the provocation of Aristaeus, and she simply steps on a snake at the riverbank and dies.

Rushdie chose Virgil's document of Orpheus' myths in this novel, which constituted the segment of bees -keeper, Aristaeus. Rushdie drew on the katabatic myth to describe the westward relocation of the three characters to intensity on the allusion of selfhood so that the characters collide into each other in their journey establishing strange and mismatched connections. Every character thereupon is a little Orphic in this novel as they all elude their hearts desire and are immersed in searching of an *underworld* for a new sense of self.

Through this novel Rushdie attempted to create a modern epic that determined mythology as the backdrop of the commonplace, the mundane and the trivial. He foraged for the mythic in the modernistic reality. The novel is a kind of a voyage of ordinary beings who desire to be modern-day heroes with the status quo of celebrity, exhibiting "a knowledge of the mythic, the overweening, the divine" (*GBHF* 575). These celebs in the novel parade "Consummate mythologies of themselves" (*GBHF* 92), since their identities are constructed largely by the requisites of the global market. In fact the novel is an amalgam of the occurrences of metamorphosis in the ancient and the new age mythic representation of the Greek romance of Orpheus and Eurydice. The transformations are a part of the endeavors taken by the characters that comprise of dying and coming into being and Rushdie has always justified of the disorientation that we experience as to be oriented towards Dis (Hades) as death. The challenge is however,the approach to respond to loss—either to adhere to transformations or resist. Rushdie's protagonists in the novel endure varying stages of transformations as opposed to exclusive Dantean conversion. There is a certain infusion of erratic transformation due to the global and cosmopolitan intimidations when Ormus and Vina complete their "journey to the center of the earth" (*GBHF* 373), how they possibly find a disfigured "Pleasure Island" (*GBHF* 372) instead of a

Popular Culture: Shades and Shadows

Dantean torture chamber.

Bakhtin reinitiated the theme of metamorphosis in *The Dialogic Imagination* as primarily human transformation of human identity, and that individuals are inked from the pre-class world folklore cache. Bakhtin affirmed:

Metamorphosis or transformation is a mythological sheath for the idea of development - but one that unfolds not so much in a straight line as spasmodically, a line with "knots" in it, one that therefore constitutes a distinctive type of *temporal sequence*. The makeup of this idea is extraordinarily complex, which is why the types of temporal sequence that develop out of it are extremely varied. (113)

Consequently in modern representations of classical myths according to Bakhtin:

We are offered various sharply differing images of one and the same individual, images that are united in him as various epochs and stages in the course of his life. There is no evolution in the strict sense of the world; what we get, rather, is crisis and rebirth. (115)

Maria warner in *Fantastic Metamorphoses, Other Worlds* discovered, "Metamorphic Writing" proliferates "in transnational places and at the confluence of traditions and civilizations" (18). Rai, the narrator in the novel too familiarizes to Vina that "Metamorphosis is what supplants our need for the divine" (461).

Rushdie picturized the descent into the underworld as a metaphor for crossing frontiers between cultures and between parallel worlds.He thereby enabled the exploration of the theme of migration and hence engrossed into the intricate inter-cultural mixings and movements distinctive to the process of globalization. Metamorphosis as a consequence of katabasis seems to be the kernel of the novel as all three, Ormus, Vina and Rai undertake this journey into the underworld of the unconscious, not just once but several times.

Popular Culture: Shades and Shadows

Rushdie remodeled himself into a homodiegetic narrator, in the embodiment of Rai in the novel who specifically rejects simple linearity in voicing the story. He shares:

Our lives disconnect and reconnect, we move on, and later we may again touch one another, again bounce away. This is the felt shape of human life, neither simply linear nor wholly disjunctive nor endlessly bifurcating, but either this bouncy-castle sequence of bumpings-into and tumbling apart. (*GBHF* 542)

Rushdie aimed at constructing a repetitive and roundabout– "Shape of human life" which is also progressive and advancing. Jorge Louise Borges' story *The Garden of Forking Paths* serves as an apt epigraph for this novel and its constant dallying with alternative dimensions, new world orders, modern representation of narrative and individual identities that work as a premise for an inversion of popular myth of rock' n' roll.

Rushdie has written of the ineffectiveness of the concept of a *line*, either as a mode of understanding lived experience or as an approach of structuring narrative. The labyrinth narrative fabricates such that the characters are attracted towards and yet drifted apart from the break downs and melt downs, by the gains and losses at life events in place of liner chronological sequence.

No, this is a story of a deep but unstable love, one of breakages and reunions; a love of endless overcoming, defined by the obstacles it must surmount, beyond which greater travails lie. A hurdlers love. The forking, fissured paths of uncertainty, the plunging low road of death itself: along these ways it goes. This is a human love. (*GBHF* 322)

We also read in the novel that:

The world is irreconcilable, it doesn't add up, but if we cannot agree with ourselves that it does, we can't make judgements or choices. We can't live. (*GBHF* 351)

Popular Culture: Shades and Shadows

Borges' short story happens to be Vina's favorite nineteenth century work that entailed the idea that infinite realities get created as people face crisis of decision. Each decision leads to a new path and the implications of those decisions create future opportunities for more choices that disintegrate into more new paths. The notion of non-linearity of time and reality contrives the novel to be highly intertextual. The archetypal protagonistwas drawn on the historical, and chronological parts of progression due to his descent in the underworld. In the postmodern representation of a migrant's life, Rushdie modified this pattern with the vivid experiences of a migrant crossing borders and frontiers and having had the sense of lived experience that is timeless and evolving. Rushdie annotates this in the novel:

There is that within us which believes us worthy of the stars. Turn right on this forking path and you find god; turn left and there is art, its uncowed ambition, its glorious irreverent over-reach. [...] Our creations can go the distance with Creation; more than that, our imagining- our imagemaking – is an indispensable part of the great work of *making real.* (*GBHF* 466)

We find *ground* on which to *make our stand*. (*GBHF* 54)

Rai, the narrator, declares that Ormus and Vina suffer a fundamental disorientation as they migrate from Bombay to the West, this "Loss of the East" (*GBHF* 176), is a kind of separation from the self, the loss of identity, a descent to hell as depicted by Rushdie in the novel. Ormus, Vina and Rai are themselves accountable for their apocryphal, geographical journey. Vina after reaching New York, makes an objection, "It can't be the edge as well as the center" (*GBHF* 378).

The Ground Beneath Her Feet recounts the story of lovers who journey into the modern underworld in search of love and truth. According to Rushdie, the modern underworld comprises any sort of failure in the fulfillment of desires and achievements of fantasies and dreams. Ormus' countless failures to pursue Vina, from the first drift in the middle of 1950s, after they meet in a record store in London when she was twelve and share love and passion for music, to losing her again after a car crash and being comatose in the middle of 1960's, to rising from it after her kiss and pledging to not touch her for ten years, to finally being married to her in 1970s yet failing to be in her companionship forever after her death in 1989 in an earthquake in Mexico, exquisitely sketches a fragile 'fabric of reality' that collapses in space and time, the "fabric of the surface" that is being "unwoven" from below (*GBHF*323).

The new-age katabatic journey draws a shift in the Orphic descent where Vina is the restorer of Ormus, even though they both lose each other at many times. Rushdie's endeavor to twist the myth of Orpheus where Vina rescues the lover three times, firstly at the age of twelve when she asks Ormus to start writing his own songs and create music and stop listening to the whispers of his dead twin brother Gayomart, secondly when he is in a three year comatose condition and is threatened of murder and finally when he gives up his desire to live and she returns from the dead to deliver him the message of eternal love. Suggestively Rushdie drew, "Many different versions of the first encounter between VinaApsara and OrmusCama…presently in circulation, thanks to the clouds of mythologisation, regurgitation, falsification and denigration that surrounded their story for years"(*GBHF* 92).

It is crucial to highlight that Rushdie crated a montage of multiple alternate realities to unfold the story of musicians and their craft. He reconstructed a new mythology and spawned it through the agency of pop culture. Rushdie hybridized the ancient Greek myth by infusing it with the contemporary mythos of rock' n' roll. He used the rationale of popular rock music to delve into the new-found proviso of the artist and the domination of the audience in the mass-media culture. It became a common ground that transgressed all sorts of divisions between reality and myth and crossed all borders-cultural, racial, mental, musical, and therefore cloaked as a catalyst of plurality and of collective understanding between people across the globe.

Culture has always been often delineated within the heterogeneous framework. The ethnic, racial, religious and other demographic interventions could be typically associated to it. Yet each cultural group or community has also designated itself to an ideology. These ideologies have created a spectacle in establishing a desirable array of audiences for various mass-media features such as advertisements, movies, musical concerts etc. Contrarily, popular culture did not associate with an upper class or high society audience that intended to appreciate culture narrowly nor was defined by a specific group or community with an unkempt range of vision. It was composed of unremarkable events, actions and objects that influenced a great number of people.

The postmodernist cultural theory affirmed that the former divisions of high and low culture had become superfluous and been supplanted since music as paragon transgressed the frontiers of culture, mind and metaphysics and had become the glossing unifying source of communion. Rai, the narrator gives an explanatory introduction to the infusion of music in the novel, "So, music, love and life-death: these three. As once we also were three. Ormus, Vina and I. We did not spare each other. In this telling, therefore, nothing will be spared" (*GBHF* 31).

Rushdie has described Ormus as the modern-day Orpheus, "a musical sorcerer whose melodies could make city streets began to dance and high buildings sway to their rhythm, a golden troubadour the jouncy poetry of whose lyrics could unlock the very gates of Hell" (*GBHF* 96-97). We discover that Ormus, "within moments of his birth began making the strange, rapid finger movements with both hands which any guitarist could have identified as chord progressions" (*GBHF* 32).

Ormus is pictured as the new-age embodiment of Elvis Presley, John Lennon and Freddie Mercury, the rock artists from 60s-80s.During these decades the western world had experienced a new form of transfiguration in the outset of pop stars and movie artists who become omniscient and garnered the status of a celebrity.As a genre, rock music originated in the United States in the late 1940s and early 1950s. It was not just a musical style but a cultural rarity that influentially shaped the identity of youth and society on a global stratum. Rock music resonated with the psychological states of different generations fusing in the impressions of rebellion, discontent, and empowerment of various kinds. The genre became more popular with themes of freedom, and individualism that reverberated with the youth, seeking to shape their identities, and made fans connect over shared struggles, experiences and ideals. Rock music, therefore, became a powerful impetus for emotional release and catharsis. In the novel Rushdie made it obvious, "If Ormus is the rock, Vina can be the roll" (*GBHF* 325).

In one of his interviews to Le Monde, Rushdie declared that, "this book is not a novel about rock' n' roll, but an attempt to respond to the evolution of world culture in the last half-century" (VI). Rushdie blended his polyphonic fiction and rock' n' roll offering a kind of "secret language" that would transcend distinctness, cut over frontiers and that withheld the enunciate capacity of being idolized. The update of Orpheus-Eurydice myth aligned well in his textual vivacity and the redundant rock' n' roll medium.

On the accepted popularity of rock' n' roll, Rushdie expressed his amazement to Charlie Rose in an interview thus:

> ...how easily the music travelled. There we were, these kids thousands of miles away from America, knowing nothing about American really ... And yet this music seemed to belong to us instantly. And it strikes me now that maybe that was happening everywhere in the world. It was probably happening in, you know, Patagonia and Yokohama. (255-6)

Since transnational movement is the central ethos to the novel facilitated by cosmopolitanism and globalization, global influences on music are clearly evident to substantiate the hybrid, heterogeneous world and to herald rock music as a globally shared culture. The charismatic personalities of the rock stars and the tangible melodies created by them charmed the audiences worldwide creating a flap of fandom. The music became a unifying force, transcending cultural and geographical boundaries, and advocating a sense of global community. Rushdie was compelled to efface local variations of music. He features Ormus breezing in other un-American influences to showcase the widespread popularity of music and its receptivity as a part of mass culture product. VTO's first album incorporates:

> ...the sexiness of the Cuban horse, the mind-bending patterns of the Brazilian drums, the Chilean woodwinds moaning like the winds of oppression, the African male voice, choruses like trees swaying in freedom's breeze, the grand old ladies of Algerian music with their yeaning squawks and ululations, the holy passion of the Pakistani qawwals. (*GBHF* 379)

Rushdie has proposed music as a stimulus of plurality and of universal understanding between people. The genre of popular music has upended numerous new musical forms partially due to electronic-media and mass culture that has been receptive to the acceleration of it. The popular music trend mingling with different sounds of different cultures is now referred to as "world music". Ormus and Vina's band

VTO holds concerts with anti-war songs that bring together millions of people of different religions, races and cultures. His specially created 'earthquake songs' were about conjoining the real and virtual worlds, the alternative realties, the double visions to achieve unification and thereby initiate one new world-order. Rai, the narrator offers a photographic view of the global regards and hail of VTO's peace ballads and anti-war messages in their songs that explicate the search and plea for universal peace. "Americans buy the Ballads by the wagonload, but the album's anti-war message causes a few subterranean rumbles" (*GBHF* 419).This is supposedly was strived through "Rock music, the music of the city, of the present, which crossed all frontiers, which belonged equally to everyone" (96). For both Ormus and Vina, popular music was a medium to cross borders of judgment, soul and mythical insights, kind of a "key that unlocked the door for them, the door to magic lands" (*GBHF* 95) and "the magic valley at the end of the universe" (*GBHF* 177).

To conclude, the novel depicts a space in which an age-old myth is relocated into a new form, shaped with complex identities and at the same time enriched with the rich narrative of pop music and culture as contemporary mythical impulses transcending envisages of global movements. Orpheus and Eurydice are metamorphosed into contemporary rock artists whose celebrity status escalates across the globe in a complex route of migration, from India to USA where they achieve global fame with their rock band named VTO, coarsely based on the Irish band U2.In one of the interviews after the publication of the novel, Rushdie mentioned that, "rock is the mythology of our time" (Kadzis 223). He clarified that, "It meant that there was a language of cultural reference…which people all around the world would easily get, just in the same way that people once might have got a range of classical or mythological reference…It was interesting to contrast it in the novel with that older mythology..." (Kadzis 223).He continued to explain his choice for the mythic aspect of the novel:

I think I am interested in the way in which culture use celebrities. In that respect they are quite like the old pantheons of gods, who, you know, behaved very badly. Ancient gods were not model examples, but simply instances of human beings enlarged to divine proportions. It was about how humans might behave if you removed all restraints and gave them great power. In that sense, celebrity is a kind of recurrence of that theme...Sometimes they behave very well, and sometimes they're destroyed by it. (Kadzis 225-26)

The new found cultural faculty challenged the conventional values of the time, enflaming arguments and triggering fears of moral descend but its anti-establishment sensibility advocated for social change and personal liberation. Rushdie incorporated variety of popular culture sources juxtaposing the fantastic and bizarre, reality and double vision within the text to mark it as characteristically incredible and of the postmodern order. Therefore, we can formulate that the Rushdieancarnivalesque space celebrates "hybridity, impurity, intermingling, the transformation that comes of new and unexpected combinations of human beings, cultures, ideas, politics, movies, songs" (*IH* 394)

Works Cited:
Bakhtin, M. Mikhail. *The Dialogic Imagination.* Translated by Caryl Emerson and Michael Holquist, edited by Michael Holquist. University of Texas Press. Austin: USA, 1981.

Barthes, Roland. *Mythologies.* Translated be Annette Lavers, publisher's name, 1991.

Borges, Jorge Luis. *The Garden of Forking Paths.* Trans.by Jorge Luis Borges and Norman Thomas Giovanni, Victoria Ocampo, 1931.

Kadzis, Peter. "Salman Speaks." *In Conversations with Salman Rushdie*, edited by Michael R. Reder, Literary Conversation Series, University Press of Mississippi, Jackson, 2000, pp. 216–227.

Maronis, P.Vergili. *Georgicon: Liber IV.*Edited by T. E. Page, Macmillan And Co. 1909.

Ovid. *The Metamorphoses of Ovid.* Trans. by Mary M. Innes, Penguin Books, 1953.

Rose, Charlie. "Rushdie Calls Rock Music First Globalized Cultural Event." *In Salman Rushdie Interviews: A Sourcebook of His Ideas,* edited by P. S. Chauhan, Westport, CT: Greenwood, 2001, pp. 255–265.

Rushdie, Salman. "Globalization." *Step Across This Line: Collected Non-Fiction 1992–2002*, edited by Salman Rushdie, Vintage, 2002, pp. 296–298.

———.*The Ground Beneath Her Feet.* Vintage Canada Edition, 2000.

———. *Imaginary Homelands: Essays and Criticism 1981-1991.*Granta Books, 1991.

———. Interview with Bruno Lesprit ("Salman Rushdie, enfant du rock "), Le Monde 1 October 1999 (review section): VI.

Warner, Marina. *Fantastic Metamorphoses, Other Worlds: Ways of Telling the Self.* The Clarendon Lectures in English, 2001. Oxford: Oxford University Press, 2002.

Chapter-16
Scintillating contours of Ecocinema: Addressing Environmental Concerns through Popular Culture in *WALL-E*

Dr. Siddhi Tripathi

Abstract

The contemporary environmental issues gaping at humanity are a reminder of the urgency with which such issues need to be dealt with. A thorough consideration on the vices of extreme consumerism and technological surplus, that is degrading our ecology, alerts us of the impending disaster awaiting us if we continue wreaking havoc on the sensitive balance established by nature. It is therefore essential to acquaint the young generation regarding these sensitivities as they will hold the reins of our planet's future, ensuring a sustainable development without destroying our invaluable ecology. Products of mass appeal, such as *WALL-E*, intimidate towards a horrifying prospect of a devastated biosphere overtaken by techno-toxic debris that has completely sterilized our planet. Today's children are tomorrow's hope of reversing what appears to be a grim reality of techno genic contamination and ecological collapse. This paper intends to investigate into the intersections of ecocinema and popular culture so as to understand how mass appeal reflects on environmental dilapidation. This film is emblematic of the fact that positive ecological ideology can be effortlessly propagated via popular culture.

Keywords: Ecocinema, Popular Culture, animation, environmental ethics, Anthropocene

Introduction

Contemporary times are a witness to the perilous impact

human activities have had on the ecology of our planet. This Anthropocene is a geological epoch in which one single species is responsible for altering earth's climatic order. Thus, the requirement of engaging in environmental advocacy has become imperative on the part of humans. The need to safeguard and maintain the ecological balance has never been so pronounced than today. However, it does not entail that our ancestors were oblivious to the impending ecological ramifications of unchecked industrial advancements over past decades. Engaging in the orthodox framework of ecological activism, our former cohorts took the assistance of various scientific reports, environmental recommendations and eco-activism to promote and popularize sustainability discourse. But these traditional forms of ecological advocacy often fail to reach the layman. Consequently, technological incursion continues its assault upon the delicate balance of nature, as the larger humanity remains oblivious to the consequences of its conduct. This Capital centric age requires a holistic approach to effectively address this issue, and to pursue this objective, people need to understand the magnitude of the crisis. The need of the hour is to foster comprehension of the layman on the environmental discourse. Popular culture emerges as an efficient tool that can effectively bridge this communicative disparity.

Cultural theorist Stuart Hall has discussed in detail about the significance of popular culture as a platform of negotiation, ideological deliberation and meaning-making that reflects contemporary anxieties. Dismissing popular culture as a mere frolic and escapist genre of amusement downgrades its didactic potential of transforming the narrative. It possesses an instrumental potential to decode complex ecological quandaries into engaging animated storytelling. It is a site of semantic creation that establishes an emotional resonance of the masses to climate-related problems which otherwise seem to be an extremely farfetched reality. This literary domain effectively translates the potential horrors of climate change, overconsumption and our collective apathy to environmental dilapidation.

Popular culture encompasses a wide array of diverse forms, namely: the film and television culture, musical trends, tabloid culture, gaming culture, fashion trends, digital dynamics on the internet, consumer culture propagated through brands, sports culture, culinary trends, digital comics and graphic novels, ecocinema, and so forth. In this vein, Stephen Rust, Salma Monani, and Seán Cubitt in their chapter "Cut to Green: Tracking the Growth of Ecocinema Studies" mention:

...that film can no longer be considered apart from its imbrication in the fabric of the world.... [I]t [is] difficult to miss the insistent ecological themes that filmmakers [have] returned to over and over in their onscreen messaging.... [The] new generation of Eco critical scholars [have] insisted that the cinematic apparatus, far from being divorced from nature, is in fact profoundly ecological.... [In their opinion] film as medium and cinema as a mode of experience are mediations that suture us back into a world that otherwise slips away... [T]he pedagogical and political compulsion to point out that the worst environmental damage has already happened or is about to happen, and cinema's obligation is to horrify its audiences, to force them to change or to help them envision some form of survival. (Rust et al. 1-3)

Hence, ecocinema operates within the purview of visual narratives and mass media, as one amongst the subgenres of popular culture, propagating environmental cognizance in the masses. Employing aesthetic strategies to engage in ecological themes, ecocinema aims at shaping the sensitivities of the multitude, to cater sustainability issues in mainstream mass media. The distribution of such environmentally sensitive cinematic production works to establish an emotional resonance of even the amateur with anthropogenic influences. In other words, ecocinema draws upon the communicative dexterity of popular culture to accomplish its eco-centric aspirations. Using realistic documentaries and dystopic films it imposes an obligatory action upon the masses regarding the eco-crisis gaping at us. It works at cultivating public imagination to address various eco-critical concerns. The vivacity of this cultural form lies in the fact that it possesses the didactic potential of successfully disseminating and deciphering multifarious ecological dilemmas through recreational pursuits.

Discussion

Emerging from the intellectual backdrop of mid-1990s, the scholarly discipline of ecocinema scrutinizes the interrelations between environment, cinema, human existence, and the prevailing ecological trepidations. Ecocinema is comprehensive and has the ability to ceaselessly adapt to the changing scenario, to accommodate global diversity and its multicultural aspect. This field of study evaluates a wide array of artworks dealing with ecological themes, be it overtly presented in the artwork or carrying covert environmental issues. The genre of ecocinema proliferates awareness regarding environmental concerns, by alchemizing storytelling, to equip various art forms in order to cultivate ecological advocacy through popular culture. By dramatizing the ecological anxieties, ecocinema stimulates the conviction of conservation in humans. Calling for the facilitation of a political action in the matter, it discourages the abstentious attitude of humans regarding the impact of their activities on nature. In Sheldon Lu's words:

[E]cocinema [is a] "cinema with an ecological consciousness. It articulates the relationship of human beings to the physical environment, earth, nature, and animals from a biocentric, non-anthropocentric point of view" (p. 2). (Lu qtd. in Ryan and Telles 5)

Engaging in the disruptions of human and non-human existence, ecocinema voices out the narratives centered on ruptures in ecology to initiate 'environmental justice' (Ryan and Telles 7). The scholars in favor of environmental humanities engage in fundamental considerations such as: the construction of Nature as an agent in that work of art, and the depiction of sociocultural outlook towards ecological issues situating it particularly in that national context. It also engages in thought-provoking inquires as to how the narrative reinforces or disrupts the aesthetic consumption of Nature, along with its constructive and transformative eco-value. This transformative facet of ecocinema comes out in the words of Chris Tong:

...the audience does not sit passively in front of the screen, but rather participates actively in the world of multimedia. In fact, there is no hard and fast boundary between actors and spectators, producers and consumers, senders and receivers, academics and fans. ("Ecocinema for all" 114)

Possessing the capacity of emotionally engaging with its viewers, ecocinema aids in soliciting responses to eco-crisis. Thus, we can plausibly argue that ecocinema acquires layers of meaning as its audience views and engages with the movies, comprehending and interpreting the discourse presented before them. This scholarly dialogue between the visual narrative and its viewers facilitates a collaborative semiotic process which analyzes the aesthetic as well as the sociopolitical dimensions of the work. This, in turn, fosters solidarity amongst the audience beyond geopolitical limits. Consequently, the openness of ecocinema champions for an ever-evolving, cumulative approach that creates awareness for ecological preservation of our planet. Ecocinema includes wildlife documentaries, and television series depicting the natural environs such as: *River Blue* (2016), *Minimalism* (2016), *Chasing Coral* (2017), *Blue Planet II*

(2017), *Night on Earth* (2020), and *Kiss the Ground* (2020). Ecocinema also includes feature films as *The Silent World* (1956), *The Day after Tomorrow* (2004), *An Inconvenient Truth* (2006), *Avatar* (2009), *Before the Flood* (2016), *Don't Look Up* (2021), and animated movies such as *Wall-E* (2008).

Walt Disney Pictures' creation *WALL-E* is a science fiction romance directed by Andrew Stanton and produced by Jim Morris. The narrative was penned down by Andrew Stanton and Pete Docter. The storyline depicts a robot's sui generis existence—a solitary being who is tasked to mitigate waste on an uninhabitable and deserted Earth. For the past centuries, Wall-E has been gathering, compressing, and stacking waste into smaller cubes so as to reduce the volume of the trash scattered on the planet's landscape. Depicting the timeline of 2805, the film shows its viewers a devastated planet with nothing in sight except debris. The planet's ecology is completely annihilated by overwhelming buildup of waste left-over by humans. Maria Bose in her research work "Immaterial Thoughts: Brand Value, Environmental Sustainability, and WALL-E" remarks that:

WALL-E's depiction of the ruined Earth is perhaps the film's clearest example of humankind's collective failure to fully apprehend physical environment and our interdependence with it.... WALL-E's trash is ... a figure for the hidden costs of production under purportedly immaterial value regimes, this trash is equally a spectre of our debt to the environment, a material reminder of capitalism's unsustainable practices and thus a sign of humankind's embeddedness within much broader material conditions (264)

Rampant consumerism, unchecked commercialization and environmental exploitation have left Earth's landscape utterly desolate, as depicted in the film. Due to the dehumanizing motivation of power hungry humans, earth gets converted into a wasteland which is no longer viable for habitation. The unrestrained power-driven exploitation of the planet's resources has transformed the environs to the extent that no life-form can survive on it. Resultantly, humans have fled into space and have been surviving on spaceships for the past few centuries. These spaceships are a commercial venture of a global capitalistic enterprise named Buy n Large (BnL). This multinational conglomerate has left behind several artificial entities, on planet Earth, to clean up the centuries old mess created and accumulated by human beings. Overtime, all the robots have become inoperative except Wall-E, i.e. Waste Allocation Load Lifter: Earth-Class; this automaton is able to survive by harvesting hardware from obsolete machines. This solitary automaton has acquired quasi-human traits exhibited through the fact that he keeps a cockroach as a pet and has named it Hal. This pet cockroach underlines Wall-E's deep desire of companionship and emotional connection in an utterly alienated existence. The choice of this pet also symbolizes Wall-E's quest of survival amongst the wreckage of an anthropogenic ruin. This atypical dynamics of interspecies foregrounds the themes of alienation, psychological estrangement, an impulse towards emotional affiliation, and an anthropomorphic depiction of human-like sentiments by humanizing the robot. This compassionate automaton develops an emotional connect with an Extra-terrestrial Vegetation Evaluator, also known as EVE. Living in a desolate planet, longing for emotional attachment, Wall-E becomes enamored by the arrival of EVE on the planet. EVE's objective is to scan and collect evidence for the existence and possibility of life on the planet. After spending an ample amount of time together, Wall-E presents his latest and most significant finding to EVE, a sapling recently discovered by him. This little plant according to Andrew Stanton is the "'key image,' which symbolizes the emotional core of the story" (qtd. in Hauser, *The Art of Wall-E* 11). The gravity of this symbolism is expressed as follows:

"It was the plant. It was the hope of this little spark of life against all the odds, against all this trash, all this decay, all this man-made stuff," he recalls. "It evolved from the inspiration you get when you see that dandelion pushing through the crack in the pavement in New York City. Against all odds, life is trying to happen, trying to be there for all the right reasons" ... The image represented not only hope for Earth's regeneration but also the revival of the human spirit... (Stanton qtd. in Hauser 11-12)

After witnessing the proof of Earth's environmental transformation, EVE activates the green signal to its starship Axiom. Resultantly, an unmanned rocket collects EVE and this plantlet, along with Wall-E clinging on to its outer frame. As the three of them arrive on spaceship, the viewers witness degenerated humans surviving on it. Due to lack of gravity and physical activity, humans have become completely dependent on automatons and have lost even the ability to walk without support. When humans sever their ties from Mother Nature and forget their true potential they are reduced to pawns in the hands of artificial intelligence units. This is another forewarning of human deterioration due to our unconstrained material desires that exploit our planet's non-renewable resources. The starship is under control of the autopilot named AUTO that happens to be a robot, trying its best to conceal, destroy, and discard the sapling brought from planet Earth by EVE and Wall-E. Its objective is to dissuade humans, living on Axiom, from returning back to Earth. Catering to its initial programming, autopilot is intent on destroying the plant "brought aboard the Axiom, believing, as did BnL's late CEO Shelby Forthright, that the Earth could only give off false signals of its habitability" (Bose, "Immaterial Thoughts" 265). Buy n Large (BnL) is an influential corporation in *Wall-E* that holds the reins of humanity and in turn the future of the planet.

This single corporate house has established its monopoly over the society and has contributed in the gradual erosion of human identity, institutional accountability, and democracy. It has served as a catalyst in cultivating the addictive behavior of constant consumption in humans blinding them towards the consequences of their actions. Its consumerist principles are solely responsible for the systemic collapse of waste governance on the planet. BnL's smiling logo is in striking opposition to its overreaching practices of absolute control over production as well as consumption. The friendly persona of this brand is a satirical critique of hegemonic corporations that endorse convenience while engendering social and ecological devastation. This ironic representation is indicative of the shortsightedness of humans regarding the true potential of Nature and its recuperating powers. After all its machinations fail, the evil robotic autopilot attacks both Wall-E and EVE, throwing them in a dumping chamber believing them to be destroyed. This compartment of the spaceship is designed to automatically dispose off the waste of the starliner into the space. However, both EVE and Wall-E are in a semiconscious state, they save themselves from that dumping space and return to their quest of saving humanity's existence.

At this point, Axiom's Captain—McCrea becomes aware of his first mate robot—AUTO's schemes and he decides to save the sapling. In a fierce battle to save humanity's existence, McCrea fights with AUTO to regain his control over the star liner. In this skirmish, AUTO momentarily gains an upper hand and tries to destroy the plant. It tries to close the Holo-Detector that is basically a scanning compartment, before EVE can safely place the sapling in it. This chamber is designed to determine the possibility of life on Earth, and in case Earth's atmosphere has become favorable enough to support life, it would automatically initiate the process of landing Axiom on the planet. Before the plant can be placed in the Holo-Detecter, AUTO sends a command to close the chamber but is unsuccessful in doing so as Wall-E steadily situates himself in the way. Wall-E's self-sacrifice obstructs the Holo-Detector from being completely shut. This pivotal decision of self-abnegation is an act of resistance indicative that in order to save ecology as well as humanity's future, humans need to look beyond their own well-being. By overcoming individual welfare and imbibing altruistic renunciation, we need to look at the bigger picture. This voluntary forfeiture might be detrimental in short-term but would prove to be quite beneficial in the long run. Wall-E's self-offering is a noble act for the greater good. After a lot of struggle by the Captain and Wall-E's sacrifice, McCrea switches the spaceship's control to manual mode making it impossible for AUTO to control it any longer. These happenings, situated in this paradigm, are reflective of profound conceptual frameworks of martyr-like dedication towards collective humanitarian welfare beyond constrains of atomized interests.

Once the Captain gains control over the Axiom, the plant is placed inside the Holo-Detector and all the residents of the space shuttle become aware of the scenario. Then, the process of going back to Earth gets initiated and as the spacecraft lands on Earth EVE desperately tries to save Wall-E whose systems are on the verge of complete collapse. The desperate attempts of EVE yield results; however Wall-E's memories are lost. EVE tries to recuperate his personality and memories by taking him to places where they created heart-touching memories but to no avail. Emotionally distraught at this loss, EVE bids Wall-E a final farewell giving him a mechanical kiss by touching his forehead with her own. This figurative kiss creates static electricity in Wall-E's circuits leading to a shock that ultimately revives his memories. On a deeper level, this

Popular Culture: Shades and Shadows

scene exemplifies the potency of emotional relations that can transform and rekindle even the most severe ruptures. A touch full of love and compassion can restore even the loss of one's essence; ergo, it materializes as a dynamic force of sanguinity and resurrection that can stimulate humanity. This scene reestablishes the essence of humanity—emotions and empathy. Merely being functional does not mean that we are alive; just as the humans living on Axiom in an obese, stagnant and socially isolated state were as good as not. Such an existence is equivalent to being non-existent. Indulged bodies and placated minds transform humans into passive prisoners who are mere audiences in their own lives. Overall, this film depicts the devastating impact of overdependence on technology along with the redeeming power of human perseverance and courage.

The minimal dialogues and virtually non-existent verbal communication in the film are symbolic of the gigantic destruction caused by human greed, thoughtlessness and unaccountable human pursuits. The scarce oral communication in the film is indicative of the mirroring effect which symbolizes the silence after a storm. When imprudent human activity crosses its threshold all discourses cease to be. Witnessing the robot cleaning the mess left behind by the humans is such a gloomy and heart wrenching sight that it is beyond articulation. Despite its disconsolate and dystopic framework, *WALL-E* has been a commercial success story:

... grossing $521.3 million worldwide and becoming the ninth-highest grossing film of 2008. It won the 2008 Golden Globe Award for Best Animated Feature Film, the 2009 Hugo Award for Best Long Form Dramatic Presentation, the final Nebula Award for Best Script, the Saturn Award for Best Animated Film and the Academy Award for Best Animated Feature with five additional Oscar nominations. The film was widely named by critics and organizations, including the National Board of Review and American Film

Institute, as one of the best films of 2008, and is considered among the greatest animated films ever made. ("WALL-E")

Notwithstanding its post-apocalyptic and dystopic themes, Eco cinematic creations such as *WALL-E* emerge as a commercial success attracting a wide range of audience from diverse age groups and cultural backgrounds. Regardless of the disturbing picture of ecology's collapse the narrative retains its aesthetic appeal. Its cinematic charm and emotional narration holds the attention of the audiences while engaging them in a critical consideration on issues like excess consumerism, disregard for waste mitigation, and an aggressive exploitation of environmental capital. The narrative tones down the intensity of ominous clouds, indicative of prospective uncertainty, by situating the dystopic scene in a chronologically extended projection— 2805. This grim picture of a probable future forces us to consider what is at the core of the discussion:

[T]he film ... relates this discussion of value to the broader dynamics of perception—namely, by staging the emergence of a responsible environmental subject willing to acknowledge the disjuncture between immaterial production and the very real violence being done to a material world. (Bose 264)

The apocalyptic vision of an uninhabitable planet due to an excess of material waste establishes the milieu for narrative progression engaging with the questions of value. Through its robotic characters, the film caters to the obligation of implementing action-oriented solutions to glaring ecological problems. The characters of Wall-E and EVE remind us to recognize the eco-social consequences of technological advancements stemming from consumer culture. The cost of this consumer culture tends to be conveniently disregarded. Humans have been turning a blind eye to the detrimental impact of consumer culture for past decades. It is therefore imperative that we undo our blunder by taking responsibility of our negligence and reestablish our connection with our environment. In this vein, the film serves as a medium of eco-awareness while simultaneously portraying the imminent ambiguity if these issues are left unaddressed.

Conclusion

Today ecocinema has become an instrument of change with its overarching messages heralding a structural transformation in human approach towards environmental issues that have been gaping at us since decades. It has been successful in alerting us of accessing and appropriately disseminating the destructive potential of unchecked human activity. Through its eco-conscious film making, it raises awareness regarding a sustainable tomorrow by decentering the anthropocentric perspective. As a captivating storytelling medium, it persuades us to move beyond our human supremacy so as to adapt bio-centric ethics. It is a form of popular media that establishes the significance of harmonious integration into the bio-chain. Only when humans refrain themselves from overriding the interests of other living beings can they truly assimilate into the biological continuum created by Mother Nature. We need to imbibe the idea that we are merely a part of this creation, and should not act as its masters. Ecocinema attempts to establish this viewpoint through commercial media productions, such as *WALL-E*, in contemporary times. These commercial productions intertwine ecocinema and popular culture blurring the boundaries between the genres to cultivate eco-consciousness via hybrid art forms. Ecocinema popularizes apocalyptic Sci-Fi creations by blending aesthetic pleasure with environmentally sensitive representations to stir a potent emotional response against the devastating prospect of ecological collapse. Pixar's production—*WALL-E* is one such effort to synthesize ecological pedagogy with cultural intermediation. Its dystopic themes combined with verbal silence, robotic emotions, and pathos remind us of what is at stake—our Future, our Existence.

Works Cited:
Bose, Maria. "Immaterial Thoughts: Brand Value, Environmental Sustainability, and *WALL-E*." *Criticism*, vol. 59 no. 2, 2017, pp. 247–277. *Project MUSE*, https://dx.doi.org/10.13110/criticism.59.2.0247.

Hauser, Tim. *The Art of WALL-E*. Chronicle Books, 2008.

Rust, Stephen, et al. "Cut to Green: Tracking the Growth of Ecocinema Studies." *Ecocinema Theory and Practice 2*, edited by Stephen Rust, Salma Monani, and Seán Cubitt, Routledge, 2023, pp. 1–16. DOI: 10.4324/9781003246602-1.

Ryan, John Charles, and Jason Paolo Telles. "Introduction: Environment, Media, and Popular Culture in Southeast Asia." *Environment, Media, and Popular Culture in Southeast Asia*, edited by Jason Paolo Telles, John Charles Ryan, and Jeconiah Louis Dreisbach. Springer Nature, 2022, pp. 1–30.

Tong, Chris. "Ecocinema for all: Reassembling the audience." *Interactions: Studies in Communication & Culture*, vol. 4, no. 2, 2013, pp. 113–128. Doi: 10.1386/iscc.4.2.113_1.

WALL-E. Directed by Andrew Stanton, performances by Ben Burtt, Elissa Knight, Jeff Garlin, and Fred Willard. Pixar Animation Studios, 2008.

"WALL-E." *Wikipedia: The Free Encyclopedia*, Wikimedia Foundation, 3 May 2025, https://en.wikipedia.org/wiki/WALL-E. Accessed 7 May 2025.

Chapter-17
The Interplay of Popular Culture and Indian English Literature

Dr. Pranali Milind kunar Jadhav

Abstract

Popular culture, with its dynamic and ever-evolving nature, has deeply influenced various domains of human life, including art, cinema, music, and literature This research paper explores the intricate relationship between popular culture and Indian English literature, emphasizing how the latter reflects, critiques, and reshapes cultural narratives. Indian English literature has evolved as a dynamic medium for addressing the complexities of India's socio-cultural fabric, incorporating diverse aspects of popular culture such as cinema, music, folklore, and digital media. Authors like Salman Rushdie, Arundhati Roy, and Chetan Bhagat have skilfully woven elements of mass culture into their narratives, creating relatable yet profound works that resonate with contemporary readers.

The paper examines how literature captures the aspirations, struggles, and contradictions of an evolving society, using popular culture as a lens to portray modernity, globalization, and identity politics. By integrating the influences of Bollywood, cricket, social media, and regional traditions, Indian English literature bridges the gap between elite literary forms and the mass appeal of popular culture. Furthermore, it critiques the commercialization of culture and challenges stereotypes spread by mainstream narratives.

The Paper emphasizes the dual role of Indian English literature as both a reflector and a transformer of popular culture, making it a critical tool for understanding India's cultural atmosphere in an era of rapid socio-political change.

Popular Culture: Shades and Shadows

Keywords: Popular Culture, Indian English Literature, Traditions, Modernity, Globalization, Digital Media.

Introduction

Popular culture, with its dynamic and ever-evolving nature, has deeply influenced various domains of human life, including art, cinema, music, and literature. In the Indian context, popular culture acts as a powerful medium that reflects societal trends, challenges, and aspirations. Indian English literature, a significant branch of global literature, has effectively embraced and critiqued popular culture, serving as a mirror to the complexities of Indian society. This interplay between popular culture and Indian English literature provides a fertile ground for exploring the narratives, identities, and cultural shifts within a rapidly modernizing India.

The rise of popular culture in India can be traced back to the post-independence period, where mass media, cinema, and consumerism began shaping the collective imagination. Parallelly, Indian English literature emerged as a strong voice, addressing the diverse realities of the nation. Writers like R.K. Narayan and Mulk Raj Anand focused on the various shades of everyday life, laying the groundwork for later authors to engage with the themes of popular culture more directly. By the late 20th century, authors such as Salman Rushdie, Arundhati Roy, and Chetan Bhagat began weaving elements of popular culture into their narratives, offering critiques of contemporary issues, from globalization to socio-economic disparity.

One of the significant aspects of popular culture in Indian English literature is its ability to represent the intersection of tradition and modernity. The texts often reflect how popular culture influences identity formation, societal values, and power dynamics in Indian society. For instance, in novels like Aravind Adiga's *The White Tiger*, the impact of consumerism, capitalism, and media on individual lives is vividly portrayed. Similarly, the works of Jhumpa Lahiri often explore the diaspora experience, showing how popular culture creates bridges and barriers between immigrant communities and their host nations.

Indian English literature also critiques the commodefication and homogenization that come with the rise of globalized popular culture. Writers highlight the tension between local traditions and the influence of Western ideologies, as seen in the works of Anita Desai and Kiran Desai. This literary engagement with popular culture allows readers to question and deconstruct the narratives spread by mass media, advertising, and the entertainment industry.

Moreover, Indian English literature provides a platform for marginalized voices, using popular culture as a lens to discuss issues such as caste, gender, and regional disparities. For instance, the popularity of regional films, music, and digital content in literature often symbolizes resistance against the dominance of mainstream, homogenized cultural products. Authors like Perumal Murugan and Meena Kandasamy interweave elements of local popular culture to depict the struggles and resilience of oppressed communities.

Popular culture in India is inherently pluralistic, encompassing cinema, music, television, folklore, festivals, and digital media. Unlike the exclusive connotations associated with high culture, popular culture is accessible and relatable to the masses. It reflects societal norms, aspirations, and conflicts, often becoming a vehicle for social commentary. From Bollywood's melodramatic narratives to viral content on social media, Indian popular culture has constantly reinvented itself to remain relevant in a rapidly changing socio-political landscape.

The postcolonial condition of India adds layers of complexity to its popular culture. As a society emerging from colonial suppression, India's cultural products often overlap the traditional and the modern, the local and the global. This duality is crucial in understanding the thematic and stylistic diversity within Indian English literature.

Popular culture encompasses the practices, beliefs, and objects that are dominant or prevalent in a society at a given time. It includes media, music, cinema, fashion, language, and other cultural expressions. Unlike high culture, which is associated with elite tastes, popular culture resonates with the masses and often mirrors societal trends, aspirations, and anxieties. WilliamsRaymondexplores how popular culture is intertwined with social structures and is not just a passive phenomenon but an active part of societal norms and practices.

"Popular culture is not an inert set of practices and meanings but a set of complex social relationships which are both lived and produced in specific social contexts."

(Raymond Williams (1974), *Television: Technology and Cultural Form,* 146)

In the Indian context, popular culture is deeply intertwined with historical, political, and economic transformations. The advent of globalization, the propagation of mass media, and the rise of consumerism have significantly shaped India's cultural landscape. Indian English literature engages with these elements, offering a platform to critique the forces driving popular culture and their impact on individual and collective identities.

Popular Culture as a Theme in Indian English Literature

Indian English Literature has evolved significantly, reflecting the nation's cultural shifts and societal transformations. One of the notable themes explored by Indian English writers is popular culture, which serves as a lens to understand the dynamic interplay between tradition and modernity in Indian society. From Bollywood to folklore, advertisements to cricket, and urban lifestyles to digital trends, popular culture influences and is influenced by the narratives crafted by Indian English authors. Terry

Popular Culture: Shades and Shadows

Eagleton discusses how culture, especially popular culture, serves as the medium through which societal values and meanings are constantly shaped and revised.

"Culture is the very substance of human life, it is what gives meaning to existence, and popular culture is the realm where that meaning is continuously renegotiated."

(Terry Eagleton (2000), *The Idea of Culture,* 35*)*

Indian English writers have frequently drawn from the wellspring of popular culture, using its idioms and imagery to craft narratives that resonate with readers.

Bollywood, as India's most influential cultural industry, has deeply impacted Indian English literature. Writers like Salman Rushdie, Arundhati Roy, and Ruchir Joshi have incorporated cinematic elements into their narratives. In Rushdie's *The Moor's Last Sigh* and *Shalimar the Clown*, the magnificence and melodrama of Indian cinema echo in the storytelling. Similarly, Vikram Chandra's *Sacred Games* delves into the dark side of Bollywood and its intersection with organized crime, exploring themes of morality and ambition.

Indian mythology and folklore, as enduring aspects of popular culture, have been reinterpreted in contemporary Indian English literature. Amish Tripathi's *Shiva Trilogy* and Chitra Banerjee Divakaruni's *The Palace of Illusions* present mythological characters in a modern, relatable context. These works have contributed to the revival of interest in India's mythological heritage, blending tradition with contemporary sensibilities.

The economic liberalization of the 1990s accompanied in a wave of consumerism, influencing both popular culture and literature. Authors like Chetan Bhagat and Anuja Chauhan depict urban middle-class life, marked by the aspirations and anxieties of a consumerist society. Bhagat's novels, including *Five Point Someone* and *The 3 Mistakes of My Life*, use colloquial language and relatable scenarios to mirror the experiences of India's youth, making his works a part of the broader cultural atmosphere.

Thus, Popular culture, as a theme in Indian English literature, serves as a powerful mirror to the societal changes, aspirations, and contradictions of India. By engaging with elements like Bollywood, cricket, mythology, consumerism, and digital culture, Indian English writers create narratives that resonate with diverse audiences. These stories not only celebrate India's cultural vivacity but also critique its evolving identity, making popular culture a pivotal theme in the literary exploration of modern India.

Representation of Popular Culture in Indian English Literature

The representation of popular culture in Indian English literature reflects the dynamic interaction between tradition and modernity, urban and rural landscapes, and local and global influences. This theme manifests through varied genres, narratives, and styles, capturing India's complex socio-cultural milieu.

Indian English literature often employs a hybrid linguistic style, blending English with regional languages and slang. This "chutnification" of language, a term popularized by Salman Rushdie, reflects the vibrancy and fluidity of Indian popular culture. It captures the linguistic diversity of India and resonates with readers familiar with such linguistic codes.

Indian English literature oscillates between stark realism and imaginative fantasy, mirroring the escapist tendencies of popular culture. For instance, the magical realism in Rushdie's *Midnight's Children* parallels the exaggerated narratives of Bollywood, while the persistent realism in Arundhati Roy's *The God of Small Things* exposes the harsh socio-political realities of India.

Cities like Mumbai, Delhi, and Kolkata frequently serve as the backdrop for narratives in Indian English literature.

Popular Culture: Shades and Shadows

These urban spaces, filled with cultural exchanges, encapsulate the essence of popular culture. Suketu Mehta's *Maximum City* provides a detailed exploration of Mumbai's multifaceted cultural landscape, while Jeet Thayil's *Narcopolis* delves into the city's underworld of drugs and decadence.

Thus, the representation of popular culture in Indian English literature showcases the nation's evolving identity, grappling with global influences and local traditions. By weaving contemporary cultural elements into narratives, writers create relatable, engaging, and thought-provoking works that resonate with a wide audience. This thematic exploration not only reflects society but also shapes it, making Indian English literature a critical space for cultural dialogue.

Popular culture, with its pervasive influence on societies, has become a significant subject of literary exploration. Indian English literature, in particular, offers a nuanced critique of popular culture by reflecting its complexities, contradictions, and the socio-political undercurrents that shape it. Thus the discussion shows that how Indian English literature analyses popular culture by examining its representation, interrogation of societal norms, and exploration of identity and power dynamics.

Indian English literature not only reflects popular culture but also critiques its shortcomings and contradictions. Issues such as the commercialization of culture, gender stereotypes, and the homogenizing impact of globalization are frequently addressed.

Indian English literature, as a body of work, has emerged as a powerful medium to interrogate and reflect upon cultural phenomena. Writers like Salman Rushdie, Arundhati Roy, Chetan Bhagat, and R.K. Narayan have engaged with popular culture, either as a backdrop to their narratives or as a central theme. Their works dissect the cultural atmosphere, highlighting the interplay between tradition and modernity, rural and urban spaces, and global and local influences.

Indian English Literature has played a significant role in enhancing and shaping popular culture by bridging the gap between traditional Indian ethos and the global modernity brought about by globalization and colonial encounters. Here's an overview of its impact:

Indian English literature captures the diversity, complexity, and vibrancy of Indian identity. By portraying everyday lives, struggles, aspirations, and traditions, it has brought Indian culture to the global stage. Works like R.K. Narayan's *Malgudi Days* and Arundhati Roy's *The God of Small Things* showcase quintessential Indian settings, traditions, and lifestyles that resonate with readers worldwide.

By writing in English, Indian authors have made Indian stories accessible to an international audience. Salman Rushdie's *Midnight's Children* and Jhumpa Lahiri's works have become ambassadors of Indian culture, enhancing its global appeal and contributing to a growing interest in Indian cinema, music, and festivals.

Indian English literature often reflects elements of contemporary popular culture, such as Bollywood, cricket, and Indian food. Authors like Chetan Bhagat and Anuja Chauhan incorporate urban Indian settings, youth aspirations, and modern relationships, blending traditional values with modern sensibilities. These narratives resonate deeply with young readers, influencing their perspectives on identity, love, and societal norms.

Indian English writers have challenged stereotypes about Indian culture and presented nuanced portrayals of societal issues. For instance, Aravind Adiga's *The White Tiger* critiques economic inequality and societal norms, reflecting a deeper and more complex version of modern

Popular Culture: Shades and Shadows

India than what is often presented in mainstream global media.

Literature in Indian English has also played a crucial role in amplifying the voices of marginalized communities. Works by Dalit writers like Bama (*Karukku*) and Mulk Raj Anand (*Untouchable*) challenge caste hierarchies and bring lesser-known aspects of Indian culture into popular discourse.

Indian English literature and popular culture intersect frequently, particularly with Bollywood. Movies adapted from Indian English novels, such as *The Namesake* and *Slumdog Millionaire* (based on Vikas Swarup's *Q&A*), have popularized literary themes. Similarly, music, dance, and visual arts inspired by literary works have further deep-rooted these themes in popular culture.

Indian English literature has significantly influenced how Indians view and use English, which has, in turn, impacted popular culture. Writers like Ruskin Bond and Khushwant Singh use accessible English to tell stories rooted in Indian contexts, making literature a powerful cultural bridge for urban and rural readers alike.

Indian English literature has explored subcultures such as, diasporic narratives (Jhumpa Lahiri), and feminist perspectives (Kamala Das, Anita Desai). By addressing these themes, it has expanded popular culture's scope to include narratives often excluded from mainstream discourses.

The growth of Indian English literature has also contributed to popular culture by the rise of literary festivals like the Jaipur Literature Festival. These platforms celebrate books, ideas, and authors, making literature an integral part of cultural consumption.

Thus, Indian English literature enhances popular culture by preserving and reinterpreting Indian traditions while embracing global modernity. By doing so, it not only enriches the cultural discourse within India but also brings

Indian culture closer to the world, fostering understanding and appreciation across boundaries. The interplay between literature and popular culture is thus a dynamic and mutually enriching process.

One of the critical ways in which Indian English literature critiques popular culture is by examining its role in identity formation. For instance, Arundhati Roy's *The God of Small Things* explores the influence of societal norms and cultural stereotypes on individual identities. The novel critiques the popularization of rigid caste hierarchies and patriarchal structures, exposing how they marginalize certain groups. Similarly, Salman Rushdie's *Midnight's Children* weaves the history of postcolonial India with the personal stories of its characters, critiquing how mass movements and political propaganda shape collective identities.

Popular culture often propagates stereotypes and homogenized identities, diverse voices. Indian English writers challenge these narratives, emphasizing the multiplicity of identities in a multicultural society like India. They highlight how popular culture—through cinema, advertisements, and social media—often reinforces gender roles, caste biases, and consumerist ideals. By doing so, they urge readers to question these constructs and advocate for a more inclusive and equitable cultural representation.

The rise of consumer culture, empowered by globalization, is another recurring theme in Indian English literature. Authors like Aravind Adiga and Vikram Chandra explore the intersection of capitalism, materialism, and societal values in their works. Adiga's *The White Tiger* critiques the aspirational culture spread by popular media, which glorifies wealth and success while ignoring systemic inequalities. The novel's protagonist, Balram Halwai, embodies the struggles and moral compromises of individuals striving to climb the socio-economic ladder in a globalized world.

Similarly, Vikram Chandra's *Sacred Games* delves into the connection of crime, politics, and popular culture in urban India. The novel critiques the commercialization of human relationships and the dehumanizing effects of unchecked consumerism. By portraying the dark ideof globalization, Indian English literature questions the celebratory narratives surrounding economic liberalization and its impact on Indian society.

Media and cinema, as dominant forces of popular culture, receive critical attention in Indian English literature. DouglasKellner focuses on the influence of media culture on individuals, highlighting how popular culture shapes personal identity and societal behaviour.

"The media culture provides a powerful system of representations that shape our experience of reality, guiding and regulating behaviour in everyday life."

(Douglas Kellner (1995), *Media Culture. 1)*

Writers often depict how these mediums influence public perception, shape cultural norms, and perpetuate ideologies. For instance, Shashi Tharoor's *Show Business* offers a satirical take on the Bollywood film industry, exposing its superficiality, commercialization of art, and moral compromises. The novel critiques the glamour and glitz of Bollywood, revealing its role in shaping societal values and aspirations.

Chetan Bhagat's novels, such as *One Night @ the Call Center* and *2 States*, engage with popular culture by reflecting contemporary youth culture and the influence of media on relationships and aspirations. While Bhagat's works are often criticized for their simplistic narratives, they highlight the growing impact of technology, social media, and consumerism on Indian society.

The tension between tradition and modernity is a recurring theme in Indian English literature. Popular culture often amplifies this tension by juxtaposing traditional values with modern lifestyles. Jhumpa Lahiri's *The Namesake* explores the challenges faced by Indian immigrants in reconciling their cultural heritage with the demands of modern Western life. The novel critiques the idealization of traditional values in popular culture, emphasizing the need for a balanced and detailed understanding of cultural identity.

Similarly, R.K. Narayan's *Malgudi Days* presents a microcosm of Indian society, where traditional values coexist with the forces of modernization. The stories critique the romanticization of rural life in popular culture, revealing its complexities and contradictions. By portraying the struggles of ordinary individuals, Narayan's works highlight the impact of socio-cultural changes on everyday life.

Indian English literature also critiques popular culture by subverting its narratives and offering alternative perspectives. Writers like Mahasweta Devi and Amitav Ghosh challenge dominant cultural discourses, giving voice to marginalized communities and their struggles. Mahasweta Devi's works, such as *Draupadi* and *Breast Stories*, critique the commercialization of women's bodies in popular culture, exposing the intersection of gender, caste, and class oppression.

Amitav Ghosh's *The Hungry Tide* explores the impact of environmental degradation and displacement on vulnerable communities, critiquing the romanticized portrayal of nature in popular culture. By foregrounding the voices of the dispossessed, these writers challenge the hegemonic narratives spread by mainstream culture.

The portrayal of women in popular culture, often reduced to stereotypes, has been interrogated by Indian English writers. Roy's *The God of Small Things* and Shashi Deshpande's *That Long Silence* challenge patriarchal norms embedded in cultural narratives. These works highlight the need for a more inclusive and nuanced representation of gender.

Globalization has led to the erosion of regional identities and the dominance of a homogenized, Westernized popular culture. Aravind Adiga's *The White Tiger* critiques the disparity between India's urban elite and rural poor, emphasizing the cultural and economic divides exacerbated by globalization.

Popular culture often intersects with politics, and Indian English literature has been instrumental in exposing this relationship. Works like Rohinton Mistry's *A Fine Balance* and Adiga's *Last Man in Tower* critique political corruption and social inequality, offering a counter-narrative to the glorified depictions in mainstream media.

The Digital Turn: Social Media and New Narratives

The advent of digital media has transformed the landscape of popular culture, influencing both the production and consumption of literature. Self-publishing platforms and social media have democratized literary expression, enabling new voices to emerge. Writers like Durjoy Datta and Ravinder Singh have leveraged digital platforms to reach a broader audience, blending literary themes with popular culture tropes.HenryJenkins speaks about the transformative power of convergence in popular culture, where technologies and media are continually reshaped by audiences and industries in a rapidly evolving media landscape

"Convergence is a process, not an endpoint... It transforms the relationship between existing technologies, industries, markets, and audiences."

Henry Jenkins (2006), *Convergence Culture,* 16 *)*

Moreover, digital narratives, such as web series and podcasts, often draw inspiration from literary works, creating a symbiotic relationship between traditional and new media.

While Indian English literature has adeptly engaged with popular culture, it faces challenges in balancing literary merit with mass appeal. The increasing commercialization of literature, driven by market forces, raises questions about the authenticity and depth of cultural representation.

Looking ahead, Indian English literature has the potential to further enrich the understanding of popular culture by embracing diverse voices and experimental forms. The intersection of literature with emerging technologies, such as artificial intelligence and virtual reality, offers exciting possibilities for narrative innovation.

Conclusion

In conclusion, the relationship between popular culture and Indian English literature is symbiotic, with each enriching the other. While popular culture provides a rich tapestry of themes and motifs for literary exploration, Indian English literature critically examines its impact on society. This dynamic interplay not only enriches the literary landscape but also deepens our understanding of the cultural, social, and political currents shaping contemporary India.

Indian English literature serves as a powerful medium to critique popular culture by interrogating its representations, ideologies, and impact on society. Through its exploration of identity, consumerism, media, tradition, and resistance, this body of work reveals the complexities of popular culture and its role in shaping individual and collective consciousness. By offering alternative perspectives and challenging dominant discourses, Indian English literature not only critiques the status quo but also inspires readers to envision a more inclusive and equitable cultural landscape. The interplay between popular culture and Indian English literature is a testament to the dynamic nature of cultural expression in India. By reflecting, critiquing, and shaping popular culture, Indian English literature has carved a unique space for itself in the global literary landscape. As both domains continue to evolve, their mutual engagement promises to offer fresh insights into the complexities of contemporary Indian society.

References:
Desai, Kiran. *The Inheritance of Loss*. HarperCollins, 2006.
Eagleton, Terry. *The Idea of Culture*. Blackwell Publishing, 2000.
Gokak, V.K. *Indian English Literature: Its Impact and Interactions*. Sahitya Akademi, 2009.
Jenkins, Henry. *Convergence Culture*. New York University Press, 2006.
Kellner, Douglas. *Media Culture*. Routledge, 1995.
Kumar, G.N. *Indian Popular Culture: National Identity in a Global Age*. Routledge, 2012.
Lahiri, Jhumpa. *The Namesake*. Houghton Mifflin, 2003.
Nandy, Ashis. *The Intimate Enemy: Loss and Recovery of Self Under Colonialism*. Oxford University Press, 1983.
Sangari, Kumkum, and Sudesh Vaid. *Recasting Women: Essays in Colonial History*. Kali for Women, 1990.
Williams, Raymond. *Television: Technology and Cultural Form*. Routledge, 1974.

Chapter-18
Indian Poetry Slams: A Popular Youth Revolutionary Movement

Heena Bindal

Abstract

Slam poetry in India is getting hype as a popular form of youth culture, raising youthful long silences from the ashes to the auditoriums, in the form of artistic and assertive verses. It is a cultural avant-grade of revolution, allowing virtual and physical space to the youth; to write, perform, judge and create new literature. The suppressed voices of the uncanonized budding poets are gaining momentum and are being heard at Spoken Word Poetry platforms. This nuanced popular youth culture is spreading its network in the metro cities of Urban India. Delhi Poetry Slam, Unerase Poetry, BekauffBattein, Airplane Poetry Movement, Pune Poetry Slam, are some of the examples of such Slam poetry platforms. Many a times, this form of poetry is said to be rooted in Harlem Renaissance, Beat poetry, Hip Hop culture and the Last poets. In India the blooming popularity of the slam poetry is one of the extension or a modern version of Indian performance poetry tradition of court poets, Mushaira and Kavi Darbar. This chapter brings in light the study the co-construction of this sub culture of poetic slams among the youth which is seemingly turning into a popular one in the urban India; giving rise to the new poetic communities, literature, culture and identities.

Keywords: Slam Poetry, Popular Culture, Youth Culture, New literature, Performance Poetry, Identity.

Introduction

Slam poetry is an oral poetic performance art, that is based mainly on the poem, as well as on the performance's aesthetic qualities. This is usually a competitive performance of poetry, where poet performs in front of the audience and a panel of judges. The format and regulations of such competitions may be varied from one slam to another, but it always includes poetic performance and audience participation. In this manner, Slam poetryis said to be a blend of writing, performance, competition and audience response. It is performed at poetry slams. The word "Slam" came from how the audience has the power to praise or sometimes destroy a poem. It is a form of Spoken Word Revolution.

History of Slam Poetry

This form of poetry began in 1980, with the efforts of a local poet and construction worker Marc Kelly Smith, who made an attempt to bring back poetry to the common people and let it go beyond the ideological state apparatus of academic canon. Slam Poetry gave a platform to the subalternto speak, co-exist and counter. Smith created a weekly poetry event, "The Poetry Slam" at the Get Me High Lounge in Chicago in November 1984,where anyone could participate and present his or her poem for the critical appreciation and it would be judged both by audience response and the panel of selected judges. In the same decade many other Poetic slams like Green Mill Jazz Club, National Poetry Slam, Poetry Slam, Inc. etc. came into existence. In actual slam poetry has been around, for a far longer than just the 80s. Performance Poetryhas spanned back since stories were first told. In the eighth century BC, Homer's Odyssey was orally spoken aloud to an audience, and many different civilizations have passed down oral accounts and history through verse.But,with Generation Z these poetic slams proliferated its roots.

Slam Poetry in India

By the end of 2^{0th} century, this form of poetry travelled at international stages. In India, it found popularity as a form of self-expression of the youth and started giving birth to the brave new voices.slam poetry in India, is getting a hype as a popular form of youth culture, rising youthful long silences from the ashes to the auditoriums, in the form of artistic and assertive verses. It is a cultural avant-grade of revolution, allowing virtual and physical space to the youth; to write, perform, judge and create new literature. The suppressed voices of the uncanonized budding poets are gaining momentum and are be heard at Spoken Word Poetry platforms. This nuanced popular youth culture is spreading its network in the metro cities of Urban India.

Delhi Poetry Slam, Unerase Poetry, Spill poetry, BekauffBattein, Commune India, Airplane Poetry Movement, Pune Poetry Slam, Purple Pencil Project, Bullock Cart Poetry are some of the examples of Slam poetry platforms, mostly based in metro cities of India such as Delhi, Pune, Bangalore, Mumbai and Chandigarh. Some of these are based on the original competitive spirit of the Slam poetry, whereas others are quite inclusive, liberating and non-judgmental in nature.

Slam Poetry as a Popular Culture

"Performance of popular poetry are not mere reflections of American Popular culture, they are themselves sites of cultural contestation that help articulate and generate the very culture they claim to represent", write Willett Somers and B.A. Susan. (p.52)

Spoken Word Poetry can be rooted in Harlem Renaissance of 1920s in USA, which was a revolutionary literary movement voicing out the unspaced voices of the African-Americans. The rebellious spirit of Poetry Slam can also be traced in the loud, coarse and rough notes of the Beat Poetry and Hip-Hop Culture. Slam Poetry can therefore be seen as a new popular form of culture rising from the ashes of the previous revolutionary art movements to this nuanced culture.

Popular Culture: Shades and Shadows

This form of Popular Culture can be seen as the free expression of heart and the soul on various thematic concerns and a platform for challenging the power knowledge dichotomy, suppressing the hegemonic control of ideological state apparatuses and giving oratory platform to the long silences of the subaltern. These poetry slams, usually organised at Parks, Book stores, Coffee houses, Bars, Streets and sometimes at virtual platform (which is yet another public space)initially disseminated a nuanced sub culture, which later on got popularised at mass level, hence converting it into a new popular youth culture. The Public Sphere of Slam Poetry is designed to move Poetry recitals from the elite culture to the popular audience.This form of poetry is influencing many aspects of the modern life and creating a new popular culture, affecting the prevailing political movements, art, media, literature and entertainment.

Slam Poetry as a Youth Culture

Slam poetry is being adopted and accepted as a popular form of self-expression, among many teenagers. It can be called a carnivalesque subversion of the order of power specially by youth. Youth Culture in terms of Cultural studies is a stylized form of resistance to power. Youth Sub Culture can be seen as a win space for themselves from both the parent culture and the hegemonic class culture.

In the contemporary period, the pens and mics of the budding writers and performers are a revolutionary step in the decolonization of the main stream poetry and reviving the oral tradition in India. Official website of Delhi Poetry Slam mentions about its journey when they started hosting poetry slams in small venues in Delhi. Their website mentions "These shows would be filled with young poets who were so passionate to share their lives in the form of verses with others, which motivated us to create wider spaces for the youth to express themselves. We convinced schools and colleges to let spoken word poetry be a part of their extra curriculum activities and when that finally happened it was an opportunity to break out the rigidity of old school poetry from 19th century and dive into the contemporary style of spoken word poetry which was direct, clever and relevant to the students." Most of these poetry slams attract young participants and young audience.

Young poets perform through these Poetic Slams. In fact, many uncannonised poets are adopting the poetry slams as a fulltime career option.Young Chicago Authors (YCA) and many otherworld level poetry associations provide workshops, mentoring and competition oppurtunities. "Rooted and Radical Youth Poetry Festival" formerly known as "Louder than a Bomb" was an annual youth poetry slam in Chicago every Spring. It was said to be the most popular poetic slam of the world with the participation of more than 1000 teams all around the world.

This new genre of culture is providing due self-respect, space and opportunities to the long silenced oppressed other. Most of the poems are also known to have a distinct passionate tone that Somers-Willet (2012) describe "protestive and passionate pieces are frequent at a slam, and many poets treat the slam stage as a political soapbox" (p. 52).

Slam poetry is a medium for challenging the existing values and culture. "An Open Letter to Honey Singh" is a rap video featuring Rene Sharanya, a student of St. Stephen's college, Delhi performing at Delhi Poetry Slam, which went viral on You Tube receiving over 1.5 million hits. The targeted theme of this poem is the artistic criticism of the messages, being spread by Indian Aritist YoYo Honey Singh through the lyrics of his songs.

Another such example of poetry slam is Airplane Poetry Movement, which was a project started by two college students Nandini Verma and Shantanu Anand in 2013.

In an interview Nandini Verma says "Spoken world

poetry gives you a medium to reproduce the missing voices of generation."

Slam Poetry and Indian Literature

Currently Slam poetry is one of the youngest genres of poetry, which is affecting Indian contemporary poetry. Indian poetry with its rich heritage and diversity, has always sung of its cultural linguistics and philosophical diversity. From classical Sanskrit poetry to Contemporary version of Indian poetry in English, Indian poetry encompasses a wide range of styles, themes and forms. Classical Indian poetry comprises of the religious poetry, prayers, battle songs and Epic poetry. Medieval period from 12th to 18th century brought some changes in the style, themes and forms of poetry with the bhakti poetry and Sufi poetry. After 18th century during the colonial India Western influences could be traced in the style language forms of poetry the postcolonial period poetry was more in graved in regional themes and languages. Slam poetry is another budding form of contemporary poetry which voices out the personal, socio cultural and political chaos. It can be seen as an avant-garde in the contemporary form of Indian poetry. Poetry slam is an aesthetic and cultural phenomenon, which includes the performances of the poetry and the close reading by the audience allowing them Aristotelian catharsis and Laconian jouissance.

This new form of literature has brought an acoustic turn, to put forward the ghetto realism by breaking the forth wall. The intimidated voices of the oppressed are breaking social barriers and constructing their own Self. Somewhere the blooming popularity of the slam poetry in India is one of the extension or a modern version of Indian performance poetry tradition of court poets, Mushaira and Kavi Darbar.

Slam Poetry creates New Poetic Communities and Identities

As a new poetic community these slams also provide a

shelter and homeliness to the youngsters to dwell, debate and discuss ideas, art, poetry and thoughts. One of the performers and members of Delhi poetry Slam says,"Most of my story has been said aloud with people with such big hearts and open minds. There was warmth in every heart and I learnt not just about poetry but about the beauty of strangers. I have definitely become a rich person in thoughts and experiences and I feel myself unburdened of my own chaos."

These poetic slams can be studied from the perspective of a phenomenological process of reading as Wolfgang Iser calls it, a marriage of ideas between the author and the reader. These poetry slams are situated somewhere between reading and writing the poem at the same time.

Some of these poetry slams are run by NGOs and are purely non profitable, whereas some slams charge nominal fee from the coffee houses where these are conducted, as they attract audience attention. Some of the poetry slams are commercial and the audience need to pay for procuring the passes of poetry.

Swati Pathak and et. Write, "Poetry slam serves as an outlet, a vent to release emotions or views outside the academia.Resisting the hegemony and dominance of the written word in literature is underscoredthrough this platform. In this way, Poetry Slam comes across as a pure form of democracy inart."(p- 8)

The "othered" voices are attaining new identities through these poetic slams, by reaching out to them. The new identities are formulated, heard and reconsigned as they voice out their say in such poetic slams or spoken word revolution. Hakim Bellamy asserts, "Slam as aco-constructed space where the identity of a discursive community is performed." Further he mentions, "A conventional approach to poetry analysis has focused on the study of theauthor's intent or desired meaning/message. In this approach, there is an oftenunderstated motivation to find out who the author is and how biography informs what heor she means." (p. 23)

Here is an excerpt from the poem "Witch Hunter" by A.W. from Button Poetry to establish the fact that slam poetry gives wings, spaces and voices to the silenced identities of the otherwise marganalised.

My parents are not ready for all the mystic
In my womanhood.

Don't understand this combat boot fueled
Rage and desire to shave my head

How I break daily
come out again and again
My people have been turned dirty,
Animals whose desires are unnatural,
Carnal,
degenerate

My people are carrying the burden
Of 200 years of colonial thinking

Watch how quickly the supreme court
can make an alien of you

Watch how they light your skin on fire
And call your attempts to breathe
inhumane

They easily forget that your love is an offering from the gods,
is clean water

My parents so easily assume
I must be straight

don't understand ever
Just like my ancestors
I love freely
My people are magical
they know how to fold into this skin
and hold themselves of

They know how to fit somewhere they are not welcome.
Learn how little their humanity is worth
and still love so fiercely.

This Poem is one of the examples of how slam poetry is providing a societal acceptance and acknowledgement to the new identities.

Slam Poetry as a Revolutionary Movement in Society:

This form of poetry is a rhythmic commentary about the socio-cultural condition of the society. The dramatic delivery of slam poetry is extending the canvas of literary and performing arts, while bringing into consideration various social, cultural, political and personal concerns from the hearts to the heaps.

Here is an excerpt from the poem, "A Brown Girl's Guide to Gender" by Aranya Joharprotesting against the hegemonic control over the women.

My mom telling me to wear skirts out less often.
Nirbhaya and more, left forgotten.
We don't want to be another of India's daughters, do we?
So I wear my jeans long and wear my tops high.
Don't show my cleavage
or a hint of my highs.
Risking not my virginity, but my life.
My hymen seems to be sacred,
told to keep it till I'm a wife.
If not, I'm a whore, a slut, a skank and more.
Not as pure as I was before.
15 year old Laxmi didn't like 32 year old Guddu
and Guddu dealt with it real maturely,
he made her the victim of an acid attack.
Laxmi could be your sister, your girlfriend, your cousin.
We're girls, women, human, not a burden.
I ask my male friend to drop me home
because his privilege will protect mine.
I'm sorry dad,
for I was catcalled in my uniform at the age of nine.

Popular Culture: Shades and Shadows

Many a times the theme of such poetry is personal and delivery of such content holds therapeutic value for the poet and the poem is open for the psychoanalytic criticism. Sometimes the themes of such poems are about raising voices against some mal practices prevailing in the society.

"I am in love with this World" by Megha Rao is another such poem delivered at Slam Poetry event, disseminating an aura of love, compassion and contentment in the surroundings. Here is an excerpt from the poem:

I'm in love,
With this little boy across my house...
Pushing himself into the front yard
Despite his crutches,
To teach his kid brother
How to play football.
I know he's in pain sometimes,
But he's so happy, he doesn't care.

I'm in love,
With that girl in the school,
Who learned sign language,
Because she wanted to talk to her father better.

Slam Poetry lays a foundation stone in creating a new society. The residual and the neglected culture is emerging as a new dominant one, through these poetic slams. These poetic slams discussing the issues varied from corruption, environment, male chauvinism, violence to sexuality etc. can help in a progressive societal change with the aid of poetry.

Conclusion

This Popular form of culture Slam Poetry is spreading its aura in the Urban India, where many youngsters are overtly expressing their opinions, asserting their differences, claiming for their individualities, and relocation their identities at these Open Mic events. Many a times Slam Poetry is being criticized for its lack of seriousness and originality. However, this hybrid of music, drama and poetry is providing a new public sphere to the youngsters. This Popular Culture is an embellishing garden for poetry and literature to flourish and blossom artistically, magnificently and aesthetically, while affecting the social cause and clamoring for the required change in the structures of Indian society. 'Spoken Word Revolution' aids in voicing out the racial, sexual, gendered, ecological, philosophical and many other concerns while shattering the bars of the panopticon and hegemonic and ideological apparatuses.

References:
Edward Hakim Bellamy .Identity Performance and Space in the Albuquerque Poetry Slam Scene.

Somers-Willet, S. (2012). The cultural politics of slam poetry: Race, identity, and the performance of popular verse in America. The University of Michigan Press.

Swati Pathak, Ekta Gujral, Sumedha Priyadarshini. Voicing the Word: The emerging Social Phenomenon of Poetry Slam in Delhi.

Chapter-19
Mahesh Elkunchwar's 'The Old Stone Mansion': A Critical Response through Cultural Perspective

Ayodhya Kalyan Jadhav

Abstract

Mahesh Elkunchwar is one of the leading dramatists in contemporary English Literature. His plays are widely read and brought him outstanding recognition at national and international level. The present article explores the cultural elements through Elkunchwar's most celebrated play 'Old Stone Mansion' that is included into 'The Wada Trilogy'.

Keywords: Culture, tradition, generation gap, and poverty.

Maharashtra has a rich tradition of Marathi theatre. Vishnudas Amrut Bhave's 'Sanglikar Natak Mandali' has started the theatrical activity in Maharashtra. His Marathi plays 'Raja Gopichandra' and 'Sita Swayamvar' provide a new dimension to the Indian theatre. Mahesh Elkunchwar's works depict the culture of Maharashtra and its tradition, feudal family and its ideology, natural calamities, deteriorating traditional family structure or disintegration of a joint family. His 'The Wada Trilogy' explores the conflicts between generations, decline of feudalism, dominance of men in patriarchal structure, human bond, alienation, homelessness and declining culture. The Wada Trilogy (Wada Chirebandi translated in English as Old Stone Mansion, Magna Talyakathi as The Pond and Yugant as Apocalypse)

Mahesh Elkunchwar has produced the most influential and progressive plays on the Marathi landscape. His 'The Wada Trilogy' was very successful and considered as the canonical texts in the field of Marathi Literature. His 'Wada Chire Bandi' is translated into Hindi as 'Viraasat' by Vasant

Dev. The Deshpande family of Dharangaon explores the changing socio-cultural and economic impact on the individual and society. The Deshpande family is breathing the last moment on the edge of transformation. This family talks about the sense of tradition and the Indian psyche. This play 'Old Stone Mansion' can be compared to the Russian playwright Anton Chekhov's play 'The Cherry Orchard' in terms of the collapsing culture. In the twentieth century, Elkunchwar meticulously shows India is facing many challenges through the social and cultural shifts. The play 'The Old Mansion' revolves around the dilapidated mansion and its family. The Deshpande family lives in the small village Dharangaon, somewhere in Vidarbha region of Maharashtra. The play opens with Dadi's dialogue and she says the time is passing slowly to her son (Vyenkatesh) Tatyaji. Tatyaji and Aai have three sons, elder son Bhaskar, Sudhir and younger son Chandu and the daughter Prabha. Chandu is unmarried and works for the family as a labourer. Prabha is also unmarried and wants to complete her studies. Bhaskar and Vahini have two children- one son Parag and one daughter named Ranju. Sudhir and Anjali have one son named Abhay.

    Tatyaji is died and after five days, for that Sudhir and his wife Anjali without their son Abhay come from Mumbai by bus at very late night as the telegram reached there late. They first come to Amaravati by train, then they tried to catch the last bus but could not catch. That's why, they took a taxi. It manifests the negligence, lack of affection or sometimes the hectic schedule of city life. Sudhir tells that his son Abhay has his unit tests and he is in the twelfth grade. Anjali adds that train bookings are also difficult these days and she will send Abhya for Diwali. Anjali is the representative of a particular community and she behaves like that. Vahini says: "Look, she's a Bombay girl. Born there, lived there, before marriage and after. And daughter of a Konkanastha. How could she bond with your people? Now don't say or do anything till the rites are over." (CPME138-139)

Anjali belongs to the Konkanastha (Chitpavan Brahmins) community originating from the Konkan, the coastal region in the state of Maharashtra. She is very calculated minded. She remembers everything and she reminds her husband Sudhir about his medicine. Sudhir has blood pressure and he missed a dose on the journey. Anjali behaves like a Konkanastha woman in the Warhadi Deshpande's family. Her ways and attitude are different.

People meet on the certain occasions like festivals and funerals and here Elkunchwar also very skillfully draws the attention towards it through the character of Bhaskar. When Sudhir and Anjali don't bring their son Abhay on the occasion of Tatyaji's death, Bhaskar says to Anjali: "We should try to come together at least for funerals and festivals." From the beginning, human relationships differ slightly.

Bhaskar and his wife Vahini narrated how Tatyaji died in the pooja room. Vahini says Tatyaji's death in the pooja room is an auspicious death. This is the Indian mentality and perception about death in the pooja room. The reference of the pooja room shows the belief in God and that is the culture of Indian people. In the mourning situation, no one enters in the pooja room but Bhaskar goes inside and breaks the tradition.

After Tatyaji's death, Vahini says that the family is in mourning and she has to wash the whole bedding. At the old age, Dadi gets ill treatment by the family members but only Chandu takes care of her. Even Sudhir wants to give her shawl but he does not bring on the sad occasion. Prabha expresses her views and says Dadi always wears some tattered old rug and she does not like to live till the very old age as if all that in her hands. If Sudhir will bring the shawl, it will go straight into Vahini's trunk. This shows the status of Dadi in the family, once she enjoyed the feudal system.

Popular Culture: Shades and Shadows

Now she is a symbol of stagnant lifestyle and explores the complexities of human relationships. On the other side, the rats are playing and damaging in the wada. Even Anjali came first in wada, she was surprised with its grandeur. Now it is nearly two hundred years old. There are huge cracks in the walls and some upstairs rooms are locked. Some enormous durries such as carpets, mirrors, copper vats, huge serving vessels are gone out of house. It unfolds the materialistic and worldly appearance of wada which is not maintained and here people are not able carry on the wada culture. Poverty brings hollowness in the human relationships and it becomes a battle field for everyone. Parag is an unemployed young fellow who completed his tenth grade from the school. He wants to complete his further education in Bombay but does not get a chance for it. He is not interested in farm. As a result, he becomes a victim of bad habits like chewing tobacco. He spends a lot of time out of wada. Prabha, Parag and Aai get suffocated in Wada after the death of Tatyaji. The things were changing from internal and external ways. Vahini has taken the keys of family and Aai went back in darkness. Through the dialogues of Sudhir and Vahini, it is clear that Parag admires Abhya and his clothes, his looks and the way he plays cricket. Similarly, Abhya is very fond of Parag. He talks about Parag and goes to the gym.

Parag taught him to swim in the pond. They have the beautiful memories of the village and that strengths their bond. Prabha and Chandu struggle to establish their identity but stuck in the traditional structures. Prabha wants to go out of the village for her further studies but the head of the family does not allow her as she has to live in hostel. Living in the hostel is not considered prestigious. As a woman she suffers a lot throughout the play. Similarly, Bhaskar also wants to start a diary. He expresses his feelings. Bhaskar: "Who's got that kind of land around here? Two to five acres. Twelve is the limit. Who needs a tractor for that? It's not as if I didn't try, but people should be able to afford it. Mind you, I'd already told Tatyaji that we should buy fifteen buffaloes instead of the tractor and start a dairy." (CPME143)

Bhaskar also has his passion for work but does get permission to work on his ideas because of his father Tatyaji's dislike towards such kind of business. The freedom is not given to choose the profession because of patriarchal structure. Perhaps this kind of profession does not suit to the Deshpande family. The false prestige and status are maintained by the Deshpande family as shown through the character of Vahini. She says that rich people used to have elephants in front of their house in the old days and like that the Deshpandes decided to be modern and put a tractor in front of house. The tractor is useless and become a hindrance on the way of the wada, tearing the sari of Anjali. She further adds that there is a tractor in front and the palanquin at the back. Her bridal procession came in that palanquin. The palanquin is a symbol of Indian tradition. The bridal goes to her husband's house in the palanquin. Tractor is a symbol of pseudo prestige and status. This is the beginning of modernization and globalization where society is undergoing through different paradigms. For the family, tractor is causing the hurts. Chandu gets a wound on his food by the tractor, Vahini tells him to apply some turmeric on the injured foot.

"It exposes the truth behind the stone walls of feudal mansions in the rural parts of India. The play is not just a story of one such feudal lord in the name of Deshpande, but attempts to bring into focus the changed socio-economic condition of Indian society in the post- colonial period. It locates the lasting battle in-between the ages long cultural values and harsh global realities in the present time, with fall of the former." (Online)

The relationship between servant and lord or master is not remained as the earlier relationship of feudal system.

Popular Culture: Shades and Shadows

Gaja, a cook of the Deshpande family left the job because the family was not able to give him the salary. Now he cooks in the restaurant at the bus-stand. Unfortunately, Bhaskar's son Parag chews tobacco with Gaja. Chandu has taken the place of Gaja for the family. He gives water for the cow, brings the groceries, and brings chopped firewood in the kitchen. Bansilal does not give the groceries because Bhaskar has not paid the arrears. The Deshpande family wants to perform the last rites of Tatyaji's death. Bhaskar asks for at least seven or eight hundred rupees to Sudhir but he has also not that much money. Sudhir also has high B. P. and in addition to this, he has taken loan. Somehow, they manage to live a two-room flat in Bombay. At this time Vahini tells that Bhaskar is not only responsible for everything and Tatyaji was everybody's father. They are not alone responsible for keeping up the Deshpande name. She wants to give her ornaments to the groceries. Finally, Aai, Tatyaji's wife give a few notes from the folds of a sari which is kept for an emergency. Chandu says to Aai to keep that money for her but Aai tells that Tatyaji has given her before his death. Therefore, Tatyaji's money spent on his own death. At the end of the play, the wada (mansion) is at the backside collapsing and it means the culture and tradition is also destroyed along with it. On the other hand, the transformation is taking place by developing a new cycle.

Indian culture considers that serving to mother is like serving to God. It shows the universal values through the acts of Chandu who always like to work and worship for his mother Aai. Aai is also more worried about Chandu's future. Chandu keeps a fast on Thursday. It shows his spirituality and attitude towards life.

Ranju lives in her own world and she seventeen years old. She always spends time on reading filmfare, gadding about in the village, looking in mirror, and talking about celebrities. She is failed twice in the tenth grade. Once she asks Sudhir about Amitabh, hero of film Industry. When Amitabha fell ill, she fasted five Saturdays. If anything happened to him, she could have killed herself. This is the world of Ranju. For her, Chandu kaka (uncle) is like Amitabh in the movie 'Coolie' who carries sacks like him. Her teacher whistles and calls her out of wada. When Prabha suspects about Ranju's behaviour, Vahini tells her that she should not interfere in the matter. Even Bhaskar also does not like the tuition teacher's appearance. In Indian culture, teacher has an ideal image.

Bhaskar says that the teacher wanders all over the village like some eunuch of a Hindi film hero and spends a lot of time at the bus-stand paan (beetle) shop, spewing paan juice all over the place. The teacher also put the transistor around his neck like a sacred thread. "Is this a teacher or a buggering nautch-boy?"

Bhaskar: *Your tuition stops from tomorrow. You don't go there. He doesn't come here. Why are you sniveling?*
Ranjiu: *My English is weak.*
Bhaskar: *Let it be. You're not going to have tea with the Queen of England! And get that hair out of your eyes. Look at her sari! Look at her hair! Needs to be thrashed! (CPME 158)*

The condition of Maharashtrian girl is compared with the Queen of England. It means the Queen's English is excellent and Ranju's English is very weak and after studying English, she is not going to talk with the Queen. In Indian culture, girls are not supposed to wander around the village like boys. Even Prabha never stepped out of the threshold of wada. Women have to dress up in sari neatly. However, Ranju got a chance but could not pay attention to her studies. One day she elopes with the teacher with money and traditional jewelry but somehow Sudhir helps the family to find her. She ruins the family name and fame.

Language also plays an important role in culture, Elkunchwar uses some typical words of Vidharb region of

Maharashtra such as 'Bhaitaad'. Another thing which Elunchwar brings to the attention is that the appearance of Vyenkatesh (Tatyaji) after his death. Dadi talks:

Dadi: *Veyenkatesh! Arrey Vyenkatesh. Why have you brought me so far? Why are you brought me so far? Why are you behaving like a child? Are you playing a prank on this old woman? I am so tired son! Time just won't move, the pest. How many more days must I live? Why are you laughing? I am so full of dread I can't tell you. Something is going wrong here. The Deshpande household is not doing well. How the mice trouble me all night. They run all over the house. The wretched creatures have dug through the whole wada. Nobody's filling up their holes. How much can I alone do? Daughters-in-law, grand-daughters-in-law, great-grandsons, they've all come. It's time I went. I have lived my life. Nothing remains. Why are you laughing like that? Why my son..." (CPME 188)*

Dadi states that Veyenkatesh was there but suddenly he disappears. It is only Dadi who can see him. Aai also comes more worried by seeing near tractor and asks Chandu to carry her inside the house. Aai goes in deep understanding and tells in her mind to her husband Veyenkatesh to forgive their sons if they have done anything wrong. It is supposed that if the dead person's will not be fulfilled then the soul of that person comes back. It is a kind of myth. The family could not perform all the rites of Tatyaji's death. On the occasion of 'shraddh', the family members quarrel for giving meal to the whole village. Of course, they want follow the old traditions but due to poverty they do not follow properly.

Conclusion

Mahesh Elkunchwar has shown the Indian society and its culture as a true observer in his magnum opus work 'The Old Stone Mansion'. The Deshpande family live under the pressure of tradition, false prestige and status. Poverty is the root cause for their dysfunctions of the family. Everyone wants to achieve the desires by hook or crook except Aai and Chandu. Mansion is not able to face the challenges of the new age.

Works Cited:
Arvikar, Sanjay. *Shodh Elkunchwaranchya Natyakraticha.* Pune Padmgandh, 2001. Print. Deshpande, Shashi. *Roots and Shadows.* Bombay: Orient Longman Ltd. 1983. Print.
Mahesh, Elkunchwar. *Collected Plays of Mahesh Elkunchwar.* Oxford University Press.
2009. Print.
Mahesh Elkunchwar. Translated by Kamal Sanyal. *Old Stone Mansion.* Seagull Books. 1989. Print.
https://art810943965.wordpress.com/2019/03/10/old-stone-mansion

List of Contributors

1. Dr. Anoopama Yadav
   Assistant Professor of English, Maharaja Agrasen College for Women, Jhajjar. Haryana.
2. Dr. Ashish Kumar Gupta
   Assistant Professor, Department of English, Allahabad Degree College, University of Allahabad, Prayagraj, U. P.
3. Dr. Ashwini Ashok Kadam
   Assistant Professor, Department of English Maratha Vidya Prasarak Samaj's Karmaveer Shantarambapu Kondaji Wavare Arts, Science and Commerce College, Uttam Nagar, Nashik, Maharashtra.
4. Ayodhya Kalyan Jadhav
   Head and Professor Department of English,
   Saraswati Mandir Night College of Commerce and Arts, SPPU, Pune
5. Dr. Deepshikha Parashar
   Assistant Professor- Selection Grade IIS (Deemed to be University)
6. Devika . S. Raj
   M.A English Sacred Heart college, Thevara, Kochi.
7. Dr. Dimple Dubey
   Department of English & Other European Languages, Dr. Harisingh Gour Central University, Sagar (M.P.)
8. Heena Bindal
   Assistant Professor Department of English DAV College, Bathinda
9. L G More
   Assistant Professor, Department of English, K. J. Somaiya College of Arts and Commerce, Vidyavihar, Mumbai.
10. Dr. Poonam Rani Gupta
    Professor, Dept. of English, Baikunthi Devi Kany Mahavidyalaya, Agra, UP.

11. Dr Pranali Milind Jadhav
    Asst. Professor, MVP's K.S.K.W. Arts, Science and Commerce College, CIDCO, Nashik.
13. Roshani Bhootra
    Assistant Professor, Department of English, S.B.K. Government P.G. College Jaisalmer.
14. Sangita S. Aher
    Assistant Professor, Department of English, K.S.K.W.Arts, Science and Commerce College, CIDCO, Nashik.
15. Dr. Shruti Dubey
    Aviation English Instructor, Chimes Aviation Academy, Sagar (M.P.)
16. Dr. Shruti Srivastava
    Associate Professor, Department of English, D.A.V. College, Kanpura.
17. Dr. Siddhi Tripathi
    Visiting Faculty, Department of English, Rani Awantibai Lodhi University, Sagar. (M.P.).
18. Ms. Srishti
    Research Scholar, Department of English, D.A.V. College, Kanpura.
19. Dr. Supriya Mandloi
    Head, Department of English, The Bhopal School of Social Sciences, Bhopal (M.P.)
20. Dr. Vijay Kumar Banshiwal
    Associate Professor, Department of English, Smt. Rukmani Devi Ramdev Ladha Government College Nawa City (Rajasthan.)
21. Dr. Yasir Ahmad Khanday
    Assistant Professor (English), Govt. Degree College Zainapora, Shopian Higher Education Department, Jammu & Kashmir.

www.ingramcontent.com/pod-product-compliance
Lightning Source LLC
Chambersburg PA
CBHW050246010526
44107CB00003B/198